SOCIAL WORK
Administration and Development

SOCIAL WORK
Administration and Development

P.R. Gautam
R.S. Singh

CENTRUM PRESS
NEW DELHI-110002 (INDIA)

CENTRUM PRESS
H.O.: 4360/4, Ansari Road, Daryaganj,
New Delhi-110002 (India)
Tel: 23278000, 23261597, 23255577, 23286875
B.O.: No. 1015, Ist Main Road, BSK IIIrd Stage,
IIIrd Phase, IIIrd Block, Bangalore-560085 (INDIA)
Tel: 080-41723429
Email: centrumpress@gmail.com
Visit us at: www.centrumpress.com

Social Work: Administration and Development

First Edition, 2011

ISBN 978-93-80836-02-7

PRINTED IN INDIA

Printed at Balaji Offset, Delhi.

Contents

Preface

Social Work recognizes the complexity of interactions between human beings and their environment, and the capacity of people both to be affected by and to alter the multiple influences upon them including bio-psychosocial, political and spiritual factors. The social work profession draws on theories of human development, social theory and social systems to analyse complex situations and to facilitate individual, organizational, social and cultural changes."

A hopeful development for bridging this gap is the compilation, in many practice fields, of collections of "best practices" which attempt to distil research findings and the experience of respected practitioners into effective practice techniques. Although social work has roots in the informatics revolution, an important contemporary development in the profession is overcoming suspicion of technology and taking advantage of the potential of information technology to empower users.

Administration, as a legal concept, is a procedure under the insolvency laws of a number of common law jurisdictions. It functions as a rescue mechanism for insolvent companies and allows them to carry on running their business. The process – an alternative to liquidation – is often known as *going into administration*. The profession of social work is becoming increasingly involved in empowerment for its members as employers become more invested in promoting employee satisfaction. In many other organisations a "Central Administration" department plays a key role its function. In the IT world Central Administration is key resource along with development teams. Central Administration departments are often tasked with providing IT Support to various organisations, providing key technological support. The nature of the role means the professionals have very high access to PC systems (domain Admins etc.) as they need to undertake functions that include creation and amendments of users accounts.

The book endeavours to provide all requirements of students, teachers, social workers, social work institutions to enable them to achieve success in social work and related activities.

—*Authors*

1

Introduction

Social Work is the professional activity of helping individuals, groups, or communities enhance or restore their capacity for social functioning and creating societal conditions favourable to this goal.

Social Work practice consists of the professional application of Social Work values, principles, and techniques to one or more of the following ends: helping people obtain tangible services; counselling and psychotherapy with individuals, families, and groups; helping communities or groups provide or improve processes.

The practice of Social Work requires knowledge of human development and behaviour; of social, economic, and cultural institutions; and of the interactions of all these factors.

Social Work is concerned and involved with the interactions between people and the institutions of society that affect the ability of people to accomplish life tasks, realize aspirations and values, and alleviate distress. These interactions between people and social institutions occur within the context of the larger societal good. Therefore, three major purposes of social work may be identified:

- to enhance the problem-solving, coping and developmental capacities of people;
- to promote the effective and humane operation of the systems that provide people with resources and services;
- to link people with systems that provide them with resources, services, and opportunities.

Indian Social Structure and Social Issues

India Society : Social Systems in India

Indian society is multifaceted to an extent perhaps unknown in any other of the world's great civilizations. Virtually no generalization made about Indian society is valid for all of the nation's multifarious groups. Comprehending the complexities of Indian social structure has challenged scholars and other observers over many decades.

The ethnic and linguistic diversity of Indian civilization is more like the diversity of an area as variable as Europe than like that of any other single nation-state. Living within the embrace of the Indian nation are vast numbers of different regional, social, and economic groups, each with different cultural practices. Particularly noteworthy are differences between social structures in the north and the south, especially in the realm of kinship systems. Throughout the country, religious differences can be significant, especially between the Hindu majority and the large Muslim minority; and other Indian groups—Buddhists, Christians, Jains, Jews, Parsis, Sikhs, and practitioners of tribal religions—all pride themselves on being unlike members of other faiths.

Access to wealth and power varies considerably, and vast differences in socioeconomic status are evident everywhere. The poor and the wealthy live side by side in urban and rural areas. It is common in city life to see a prosperous, well-fed man or woman chauffeured in a fine car pass gaunt street dwellers huddled beneath burlap shelters along the roadway. In many villages, solid cement houses of landowners rise not far from the flimsy thatched shacks of landless labourers. Even when not so obvious, distinctions of class are found in almost every settlement in India.

Urban-rural differences can be immense in the Indian Society. Nearly 74 percent of India's population dwells in villages, with agriculture providing support for most of these rural residents. In villages, mud-plastered walls ornamented with traditional designs, dusty lanes, herds of grazing cattle, and the songs of birds at sunset provide typical settings for the social lives of most Indians. In India's great cities, however, millions of people live amidst cacophony—roaring vehicles, surging crowds, jammed apartment buildings, busy commercial establishments, loudspeakers blaring movie tunes—while breathing the poisons of industrial and automotive pollution.

Gender distinctions are pronounced. The behaviour expected of men and women can be quite different, especially in villages, but also in urban centres. Prescribed ideal gender roles help shape the actions of both sexes as they move between family and the world outside the home.

Crosscutting and pervading all of these differences of region, language, wealth, status, religion, urbanity, and gender is the special feature of Indian society that has received most attention from observers: caste. The people of India belong to thousands of castes and castelike groups—hierarchically ordered, named groups into which members are born. Caste members are expected to marry within the group and follow caste rules pertaining to diet, avoidance of ritual pollution, and many other aspects of life.

Given the vast diversity of Indian society, any observation must be tempered with the understanding that it cannot apply to all Indians. Still, certain themes or underlying principles of life are widely accepted in India.

Caste and Class

Varna, Caste, and Other Divisions

Although many other nations are characterized by social inequality, perhaps nowhere else in the world has inequality been so elaborately constructed as in the Indian institution of caste. Caste has long existed in India, but in the modern period it has been severely criticized by both Indian and foreign observers. Although some educated Indians tell non-Indians that caste has been abolished or that "no one pays attention to caste any more," such statements do not reflect reality.

Caste has undergone significant change since independence, but it still involves hundreds of millions of people. In its preamble, India's constitution forbids negative public discrimination on the basis of caste. However, caste ranking and caste-based interaction have occurred for centuries and will continue to do so well into the foreseeable future, more in the countryside than in urban settings and more in the realms of kinship and marriage than in less personal interactions. Castes are ranked, named, endogamous (in-marrying) groups, membership in which is achieved by birth. There are thousands of castes and subcastes in India, and these large kinship-based groups are fundamental to South Asian social structure. Each caste is part of a locally based system of interdependence with other groups, involving occupational specialization, and is linked in complex ways with networks that stretch across regions and throughout the nation.

The word *caste* derives from the Portuguese *casta,* meaning breed, race, or kind. Among the Indian terms that are sometimes translated as caste are *varna, jati, jat, biradri,* and *samaj.* All of these terms refer to ranked groups of various sizes and breadth. *Varna,* or colour, actually refers to large divisions that include various castes; the other terms include castes and subdivisions of castes sometimes called subcastes.

Many castes are traditionally associated with an occupation, such as high-ranking Brahmans; middle-ranking farmer and artisan groups, such as potters, barbers, and carpenters; and very low-ranking "Untouchable" leather workers, butchers, launderers, and latrine cleaners. There is some correlation between ritual rank on the caste hierarchy and economic prosperity. Members of higher-ranking castes tend, on the whole, to be more prosperous than members of lower-ranking castes. Many lower-caste people live in conditions of great poverty and social disadvantage.

According to the Rig Veda, sacred texts that date back to oral traditions of more than 3,000 years ago, progenitors of the four ranked *varna* groups sprang from various parts of the body of the primordial man, which Brahma created from clay. Each group had a function in sustaining the life of society—the social body. Brahmans, or priests, were created from the mouth. They were to provide for the intellectual and spiritual needs of the community. Kshatriyas, warriors and rulers, were derived from the arms. Their role was to rule and to protect others. Vaishyas—landowners and merchants—sprang from the thighs, and were entrusted with the care of commerce and agriculture. Shudras—artisans and servants—came from the feet. Their task was to perform all manual labour. Later conceptualized was a fifth category, "Untouchable" menials, relegated to carrying out very menial and polluting work related to bodily decay and dirt. Since 1935 "Untouchables" have been known as Scheduled Castes, referring to their listing on government rosters, or schedules. They are also often called by Mohandas Karamchand (Mahatma) Gandhi's term Harijans, or "Children of God." Although the term *Untouchable* appears in literature produced by these low-ranking castes, in the 1990s, many politically conscious members of these groups prefer to refer to themselves as Dalit, a Hindi word meaning oppressed or downtrodden. According to the 1991 census, there were 138 million Scheduled Caste members in India, approximately 16 percent of the total population.

The first four *varnas* apparently existed in the ancient Aryan society of northern India. Some historians say that these categories were originally somewhat fluid functional groups, not castes. A greater degree of fixity gradually developed, resulting in the complex ranking systems of medieval India that essentially continue in the late twentieth century.

Although a *varna* is not a caste, when directly asked for their caste affiliation, particularly when the questioner is a Westerner, many Indians will reply with a *varna* name. Pressed further, they may respond with a much more specific name of a caste, or *jati*, which falls within that *varna*. For example, a Brahman may specify that he is a member of a named caste group, such as a Jijotiya Brahman, or a Smartha Brahman, and so on. Within such castes, people may further belong to smaller subcaste categories and to specific clans and lineages. These finer designations are particularly relevant when marriages are being arranged and often appear in newspaper matrimonial advertisements.

Members of a caste are typically spread out over a region, with representatives living in hundreds of settlements. In any small village, there may be representatives of a few or even a score or more castes.

Numerous groups usually called tribes (often referred to as Scheduled Tribes) are also integrated into the caste system to varying degrees. Some tribes live separately from others—particularly in the far northeast and in the forested centre of the country, where tribes are more like ethnic groups than castes. Some tribes are themselves divided into groups similar to subcastes.

In regions where members of tribes live in peasant villages with nontribal peoples, they are usually considered members of separate castes ranking low on the hierarchical scale.

Inequalities among castes are considered by the Hindu faithful to be part of the divinely ordained natural order and are expressed in terms of purity and pollution. Within a village, relative rank is most graphically expressed at a wedding or death feast, when all residents of the village are invited. At the home of a high-ranking caste member, food is prepared by a member of a caste from whom all can accept cooked food (usually by a Brahman). Diners are seated in lines; members of a single caste sit next to each other in a row, and members of other castes sit in perpendicular or parallel rows at some distance. Members of Dalit castes, such as Leather workers and Sweepers, may be seated far from the other diners—even out in an alley. Farther away, at the edge of the feeding area, a Sweeper may wait with a large basket to receive discarded leavings tossed in by other diners. Eating food contaminated by contact with the saliva of others not of the same family is considered far too polluting to be practiced by members of any other castes. Generally, feasts and ceremonies given by Dalits are not attended by higher-ranking castes.

Among Muslims, although status differences prevail, brotherhood may be stressed. A Muslim feast usually includes a cloth laid either on clean ground or on a table, with all Muslims, rich and poor, dining from plates placed on the same cloth. Muslims who wish to provide hospitality to observant Hindus, however, must make separate arrangements for a high-caste Hindu cook and ritually pure foods and dining area.

Castes that fall within the top four ranked *varnas* are sometimes referred to as the "clean castes," with Dalits considered "unclean." Castes of the top three ranked *varnas* are often designated "twice-born," in reference to the ritual initiation undergone by male members, in which investiture with the Hindu sacred thread constitutes a kind of ritual rebirth. Non-Hindu castelike groups generally fall outside these designations.

Each caste is believed by devout Hindus to have its own dharma, or divinely ordained code of proper conduct. Accordingly, there is often a high degree of tolerance for divergent lifestyles among different castes. Brahmans are usually expected to be nonviolent and spiritual, according with their traditional roles as vegetarian teetotaler priests. Kshatriyas are supposed to be strong, as fighters and rulers should be, with a taste for aggression, eating meat, and drinking alcohol. Vaishyas are stereotyped as adept businessmen, in accord with their traditional activities in commerce. Shudras are often described by others as tolerably pleasant but expectably somewhat base in behaviour, whereas Dalits—especially Sweepers—are often regarded by others as followers of vulgar life-styles. Conversely, lower-caste people often view people of high rank as haughty and unfeeling.

The chastity of women is strongly related to caste status. Generally, the higher ranking the caste, the more sexual control its women are expected to exhibit. Brahman brides should be virginal, faithful to one husband, and celibate in widowhood. By contrast, a Sweeper bride may or may not be a virgin, extramarital affairs may be tolerated, and, if widowed or divorced, the woman is encouraged to remarry. For the higher castes, such control of female sexuality helps ensure purity of lineage—of crucial importance to maintenance of high status. Among Muslims, too, high status is strongly correlated with female chastity.

Within castes explicit standards are maintained. Transgressions may be dealt with by a caste council, meeting periodically to adjudicate issues relevant to the caste. Such councils are usually formed of groups of elders, almost always males. Punishments such as fines and outcasting, either temporary or permanent, can be enforced. In rare cases, a person is excommunicated from the caste for gross infractions of caste rules. An example of such an infraction might be marrying or openly cohabiting with a mate of a caste lower than one's own; such behaviour would usually result in the higher-caste person dropping to the status of the lower-caste person.

Activities such as farming or trading can be carried out by anyone, but usually only members of the appropriate castes act as priests, barbers, potters, weavers, and other skilled artisans, whose occupational skills are handed down in families from one generation to another. As with other key features of Indian social structure, occupational specialization is believed to be in accord with the divinely ordained order of the universe. The existence of rigid ranking is supernaturally validated through the idea of rebirth according to a person's karma, the sum of an individual's deeds in this life and in past lives. After death, a person's life is judged by divine forces, and rebirth is assigned in a high or a low place, depending upon what is deserved. This supernatural sanction can never be neglected, because it brings a person to his or her position in the caste hierarchy, relevant to every transaction involving food or drink, speaking, or touching.

In past decades, Dalits in certain areas (especially in parts of the south) had to display extreme deference to high-status people, physically keeping their distance—lest their touch or even their shadow pollute others—wearing neither shoes nor any upper body covering (even for women) in the presence of the upper castes. The lowest-ranking had to jingle a little bell in warning of their polluting approach. In much of India, Dalits were prohibited from entering temples, using wells from which the "clean" castes drew their water, or even attending schools. In past centuries, dire punishments were prescribed for Dalits who read or even heard sacred texts.

Such degrading discrimination was made illegal under legislation passed during British rule and was protested against by pre-independence reform movements led by Mahatma Gandhi and Bhimrao Ramji (B.R.) Ambedkar, a Dalit leader. Dalits agitated for the right to enter Hindu temples and to use village wells and effectively pressed for the enactment of stronger laws opposing disabilities imposed on them. After independence, Ambedkar almost single-handedly wrote India's constitution, including key provisions barring caste-based discrimination. Nonetheless, discriminatory treatment of Dalits remains a factor in daily life, especially in villages, as the end of the twentieth century approaches.

In modern times, as in the past, it is virtually impossible for an individual to raise his own status by falsely claiming to be a member of a higher-ranked caste. Such a ruse might work for a time in a place where the person is unknown, but no one would dine with or intermarry with such a person or his offspring until the claim was validated through kinship networks. Rising on the ritual hierarchy can only be achieved by a caste as a group, over a long period of time, principally by adopting behaviour patterns of higher-ranked groups. This process, known as Sanskritization, has been described by M.N. Srinivas and others. An example of such behaviour is that of some Leather worker castes adopting a policy of not eating beef, in the hope that abstaining from the defiling practice of consuming the flesh of sacred bovines would enhance their castes' status. Increased economic prosperity for much of a caste greatly aids in the process of improving rank.

Inter Caste Relations

In a village, members of different castes are often linked in what has been called the *jajmani* system, after the word *jajman*, which in some regions means patron. Members of various service castes perform tasks for their patrons, usually members of the dominant, that is, most powerful landowning caste of the village. Households of service castes are linked through hereditary bonds to a household of patrons, with the lower-caste members providing services according to traditional occupational specializations. Thus, client families of launderers, barbers, shoemakers, carpenters, potters, tailors, and priests provide customary services to their patrons, in return for which they receive customary seasonal payments of grain, clothing, and money. Ideally, from generation to generation, clients owe their patrons political allegiance in addition to their labours, while patrons owe their clients protection and security.

The harmonious qualities of the *jajmani* system have been overidealized and variations of the system overlooked by many observers. Further, the economic interdependence of the system has weakened since the 1960s. Nevertheless, it is clear that members of different castes customarily perform a number of functions for one another in rural India that emphasize cooperation rather than competition. This cooperation is revealed in economic arrangements, in visits to farmers' threshing floors by service caste members to claim traditional payments, and in rituals emphasizing interdependence at life crises and calendrical festivals all over South Asia. For example, in rural Karnataka, in an event described by anthropologist Suzanne Hanchett, the annual procession of the village temple cart bearing images of the deities responsible for the welfare of the village cannot go forward without the combined efforts of representatives of all castes. It is believed that the sacred cart will literally not move unless all work together to move it, some pushing and some pulling.

Some observers feel that the caste system must be viewed as a system of exploitation of poor low-ranking groups by more prosperous high-ranking groups. In many parts of India, land is largely held by dominant castes—high-ranking owners of property—that economically exploit low-ranking landless labourers and poor artisans, all the while degrading them with ritual emphases on their so-called god-given inferior status. In the early 1990s, blatant subjugation of low-caste labourers in the northern state of Bihar and in eastern Uttar Pradesh was the subject of many news reports. In this region, scores of Dalits who have attempted to unite to protest low wages have been the victims of lynchings and mass killings by high-caste landowners and their hired assassins.

In 1991 the news magazine *India Today* reported that in an ostensibly prosperous village about 160 kilometers southeast of Delhi, when it became known that a rural Dalit labourer dared to have a love affair with the daughter of a high-caste landlord, the lovers and their Dalit go-between were tortured, publicly hanged, and burnt by agents of the girl's family in the presence of some 500 villagers. A similar incident occurred in 1994, when a Dalit musician who had secretly married a woman of the Kurmi cultivating caste was beaten to death by outraged Kurmis, possibly instigated by the young woman's family. The terrified bride was stripped and branded as punishment for her transgression. Dalit women also have been the victims of gang rapes by the police. Many other atrocities, as well as urban riots resulting in the deaths of Dalits, have occurred in recent years. Such extreme injustices are infrequent enough to be reported in outraged articles in the Indian press, while much more common daily discrimination and exploitation are considered virtually routine.

Changes in the Caste System

Despite many problems, the caste system has operated successfully for centuries, providing goods and services to India's many millions of citizens. The system continues to operate, but changes are occurring. India's constitution guarantees basic rights to all its citizens, including the right to equality and equal protection before the law. The practice of untouchability, as well as discrimination on the basis of caste, race, sex, or religion, has been legally abolished. All citizens have the right to vote, and political competition is lively. Voters from every stratum of society have formed interest groups, overlapping and crosscutting castes, creating an evolving new style of integrating Indian society.

Castes themselves, however, far from being abolished, have certain rights under Indian law. As described by anthropologist Owen M. Lynch and other scholars, in the expanding political arena caste groups are becoming more politicized and forced to compete with other interest groups for social and economic benefits. In the growing cities, traditional inter caste inter dependencies are negligible.

Independent India has built on earlier British efforts to remedy problems suffered by Dalits by granting them some benefits of protective discrimination. Scheduled Castes are entitled to reserved electoral offices, reserved jobs in central and state governments, and special educational benefits. The constitution mandates that one-seventh of state and national legislative seats be reserved for members of Scheduled Castes in order to guarantee their voice in government. Reserving seats has proven useful because few, if any, Scheduled Caste candidates have ever been elected in non-reserved constituencies.

Educationally, Dalit students have benefited from scholarships, and Scheduled Caste literacy increased, although not as rapidly as among the general population. Improved access to education has resulted in the emergence of a substantial group of educated Dalits able to take up white-collar occupations and fight for their rights.

There has been tremendous resistance among non-Dalits to this protective discrimination for the Scheduled Castes, who constitute some 16 percent of the total population, and efforts have been made to provide similar advantages to the so-called Backward Classes, who constitute an estimated 52 percent of the population. In August 1990, Prime Minister Vishwanath Pratap (V.P.) Singh announced his intention to enforce the recommendations of the Backward Classes Commission, issued in December 1980 and largely ignored for a decade. The report, which urged special advantages for obtaining civil service positions and admission to higher education for the Backward Classes, resulted in riots and self-immolations and contributed to the fall of the prime minister. The upper castes have been particularly adamant against these policies because unemployment is a major problem in India, and many feel that they are being unjustly excluded from posts for which they are better qualified than lower-caste applicants.

As an act of protest, many Dalits have rejected Hinduism with its rigid ranking system. Following the example of their revered leader, Dr. Ambedkar, who converted to Buddhism four years before his death in 1956, millions of Dalits have embraced the faith of the Buddha. Over the past few centuries, many Dalits have also converted to Christianity and have often by this means raised their socioeconomic status. However, Christians of Dalit origin still often suffer from discrimination by Christians—and others—of higher caste backgrounds.

Despite improvements in some aspects of Dalit status, 90 percent of them live in rural areas in the mid-1990s, where an increasing proportion—more than 50 percent—work as landless agricultural labourers. State and national governments have attempted to secure more just distribution of land by creating land ceilings and abolishing absentee landlordism, but evasive tactics by landowners have successfully prevented more than minimal redistribution of land to tenant farmers and labourers. In contemporary India, field hands face increased competition from tractors and harvesting machines. Similarly, artisans are being challenged by expanding commercial markets in mass-produced factory goods, undercutting traditional mutual obligations between patrons and clients. The spread of the Green Revolution has tended to increase the gap between the prosperous and the poor—most of whom are low-caste.

The growth of urbanization (an estimated 26 percent of the population now lives in cities) is having a far-reaching effect on caste practices, not only in cities but in villages. Among anonymous crowds in urban public spaces and on public transportation, caste affiliations are unknown, and observance of purity and pollution rules is negligible. Distinctive caste costumes have all but vanished, and low-caste names have been modified, although castes remain endogamous, and access to employment often occurs through intracaste connections. Restrictions on interactions with other castes are becoming more relaxed, and, at the same time, observance of other pollution rules is declining—especially those concerning birth, death, and menstruation. Several growing Hindu sects draw members from many castes and regions, and communication between cities and villages is expanding dramatically. Kin in town and country visit one another frequently, and television programs available to huge numbers of villagers vividly portray new lifestyles. As new occupations open up in urban areas, the correlation of caste with occupation is declining.

Caste associations have expanded their areas of concern beyond traditional elite emulation and local politics into the wider political arenas of state and national politics. Finding power in numbers within India's democratic system, caste groups are pulling together closely allied subcastes in their quest for political influence. In efforts to solidify caste bonds, some caste associations have organized marriage fairs where families can make matches for their children. Traditional hierarchical concerns are being minimized in favour of strengthening horizontal unity. Thus, while pollution observances are declining, caste consciousness is not.

Education and election to political office have advanced the status of many Dalits, but the overall picture remains one of great inequity. In recent decades, Dalit anger has been expressed in writings, demonstrations, strikes, and the activities of such groups as the Dalit Panthers, a radical political party demanding revolutionary change. A wider Dalit movement, including political parties, educational activities, self-help centres, and labour organizations, has spread to many areas of the country.

In a 1982 Dalit publication, Dilip Hiro wrote, "It is one of the great modern Indian tragedies and dangers that even well meaning Indians still find it so difficult to accept Untouchable mobility as being legitimate in fact as well as in theory...." Still, against all odds, a small intelligentsia has worked for many years toward the goal of freeing India of caste consciousness.

Classes

In village India, where nearly 74 percent of the population resides, caste and class affiliations overlap. According to anthropologist Miriam Sharma, "Large landholders who employ hired labour are overwhelmingly from the upper castes, while the agricultural workers themselves come from the ranks of the lowest—predominantly Untouchable—castes." She also points out that household-labour-using proprietors come from the ranks of the middle agricultural castes. Distribution of other resources and access to political control follow the same pattern of caste-cum-class distinctions. Although this congruence is strong, there is a tendency for class formation to occur despite the importance of caste, especially in the cities, but also in rural areas.

In an analysis of class formation in India, anthropologist Harold A. Gould points out that a three-level system of stratification is taking shape across rural India. He calls the three levels Forward Classes (higher castes), Backward Classes (middle and lower castes), and Harijans (very low castes).

Members of these groups share common concerns because they stand in approximately the same relationship to land and production—that is, they are large-scale farmers, small-scale farmers, and landless labourers. Some of these groups are drawing together within regions across caste lines in order to work for political power and access to desirable resources. For example, since the late 1960s, some of the middle-ranking cultivating castes of northern India have increasingly cooperated in the political arena in order to advance their common agrarian and market-oriented interests. Their efforts have been spurred by competition with higher-caste landed elites.

In cities other groups have vested interests that crosscut caste boundaries, suggesting the possibility of forming classes in the future. These groups include prosperous industrialists and entrepreneurs, who have made successful efforts to push the central government toward a pro-business stance; bureaucrats, who depend upon higher education rather than land to preserve their positions as civil servants; political office holders, who enjoy good salaries and perquisites of all kinds; and the military, who constitute one of the most powerful armed forces in the developing world.

Economically far below such groups are members of the menial under class, which is taking shape in both villages and urban areas. As the privileged elites move ahead, low-ranking menial workers remain economically insecure. Were they to join together to mobilize politically across lines of class and religion in recognition of their common interests, Gould observes, they might find power in their sheer numbers.

India's rapidly expanding economy has provided the basis for a fundamental change—the emergence of what eminent journalist Suman Dubey calls a "new vanguard" increasingly dictating India's political and economic direction. This group is India's new middle class—mobile, driven, consumer-oriented, and, to some extent, forward-looking. Hard to define precisely, it is not a single stratum of society, but straddles town and countryside, making its voice heard everywhere. It encompasses prosperous farmers, white-collar workers, business people, military personnel, and myriad others, all actively working toward a prosperous life. Ownership of cars, televisions, and other consumer goods, reasonable earnings, substantial savings, and educated children (often fluent in English) typify this diverse group. Many have ties to kinsmen living abroad who have done very well.

The new middle class is booming, at least partially in response to a doubling of the salaries of some 4 million central government employees in 1986, followed by similar increases for state and district officers. Unprecedented liberalization and opening up of the economy in the 1980s and 1990s have been part of the picture.

There is no single set of criteria defining the middle class, and estimates of its numbers vary widely. The mid-range of figures presented in a 1992 survey article by analyst Suman Dubey is approximately 150 to 175 million—some 20 percent of the population—although other observers suggest alternative figures. The middle class appears to be increasing rapidly. Once primarily urban and largely Hindu, the phenomenon of the consuming middle class is burgeoning among Muslims and prosperous villagers as well. According to V.A. Pai Panandikar, director of the Centre for Policy Research, New Delhi, cited by Dubey, by the end of the twentieth century 30 percent—some 300 million—of India's population will be middle class.

The middle class is bracketed on either side by the upper and lower echelons. Members of the upper class—around 1 percent of the population—are owners of large properties, members of exclusive clubs, and vacationers in foreign lands, and include industrialists, former maharajas, and top executives. Below the middle class is perhaps a third of the population—ordinary farmers, tradespeople, artisans, and workers. At the bottom of the economic scale are the poor—estimated at 320 million, some 45 percent of the population in 1988—who live in inadequate homes without adequate food, work for pittances, have under-educated and often sickly children, and are the victims of numerous social inequities.

The Fringes of Society

India's complex society includes some unique members—sadhus (holy men) and *hijras* (transvestite-eunuchs). Such people have voluntarily stepped outside the usual bonds of kinship and caste to join with others in castelike groups based upon personal—yet culturally shaped—inclinations.

In India of the 1990s, several hundred thousand Hindu and Jain sadhus and a few thousand holy women (*sadhvis*) live an ascetic life. They have chosen to wear ocher robes, or perhaps no clothing at all, to daub their skin with holy ash, to pray and meditate, and to wander from place to place, depending on the charity of others. Most have given up affiliation with their caste and kin and have undergone a funeral ceremony for themselves, followed by a ritual rebirth into their new ascetic life. They come from all walks of life, and range from illiterate villagers to well-educated professionals. In their new lives as renunciants, they are devoted to spiritual concerns, yet each is affiliated with an ascetic order or subsect demanding strict adherence to rules of dress, itinerancy, diet, worship, and ritual pollution. Within each order, hierarchical concerns are exhibited in the subservience novitiates display to revered gurus. Further, at pilgrimage sites, different orders take precedence in accordance with an accepted hierarchy. Thus, although sadhus have fores worn many of the trappings of ordinary life, they have not given up the hierarchy and interdependence so pervasive in Indian society.

The most extreme sadhus, the *aghoris,* turn normal rules of conduct completely upside down. Rajesh and Ramesh Bedi, who have studied sadhus for decades, estimate that there may be fewer than fifteen *aghoris* in contemporary India. In the quest for great spiritual attainment, the *aghori* lives alone, like Lord Shiva, at cremation grounds, supping from a human skull bowl. He eats food provided only by low-ranking Sweepers and prostitutes, and in moments of religious fervour devours his own bodily wastes and pieces of human flesh torn from burning corpses. In violating the most basic taboos of the ordinary Hindu householder, the *aghori sadhu* graphically reminds himself and others of the correct rules of social behaviour.

Hijras are males who have become "neither man nor woman," transsexual transvestites who are usually castrated and are attributed with certain ritual powers of blessing. As described by anthropologist Serena Nanda, they are distinct from ordinary male homosexuals (known as *zenana*, woman, or *anmarad*, un-man), who retain their identity as males and continue to live in ordinary society. Most *hijras* derive from a middle-or lower-status Hindu or Muslim background and have experienced male impotency or effeminacy. A few originally had ambiguous or hermaphroditic sexual organs. An estimated 50,000 *hijras* live throughout India, predominantly in cities of the north. They are united in the worship of the Hindu goddess Bahuchara Mata.

Hijras voluntarily leave their families of birth, renounce male sexuality, and assume a female identity, name, and dress. A *hijra* undergoes a surgical emasculation in which he is transformed from an impotent male into a potentially powerful new person. Like Shiva—attributed with breaking off his phallus and throwing it to earth, thereby extending his sexual power to the universe (recognized in Hindu worship of the lingam)—the emasculated *hijra* has the power to bless others with fertility. Groups of *hijras* go about together, dancing and singing at the homes of new baby boys, blessing them with virility and the ability to continue the family line. *Hijras* are also attributed with the power to bring rain in times of drought. *Hijras* receive alms and respect for their powers, yet they are also ridiculed and abused because of their unusual sexual condition and because some act as male prostitutes.

The *hijra* community functions much like a caste. They have communal households; newly formed fictive kinship bonds, marriage-like arrangements; and seven nationwide "houses," or symbolic descent groups, with regional and national leaders, and a council. There is a hierarchy of gurus and disciples, with expulsion from the community a possible punishment for failure to obey group rules. Thus, although living on the margins of society, *hijras* are empowered by their special relationship with their goddess and each other and occupy an accepted and meaningful place in India's social world.

Caste System in India

The Indian caste system describes the social stratification and social restrictions in the Indian subcontinent, in which social classes are defined by thousands of endogamous hereditary groups, often termed as *jatis* or castes. Within a jati, there exist exogamous groups known as gotras, the lineage or clan of an individual, although in a handful of sub-castes like Shakadvipi, endogamy within a gotra is permitted and alternative mechanisms of restricting endogamy are used (e.g. banning endogamy within a surname).

Although generally identified with Hinduism, the caste system was also observed among followers of other religions in the Indian subcontinent, including some groups of Muslims and Christians. The Indian Constitution has outlawed caste-based discrimination, in keeping with the socialist, secular, democratic principles that founded the nation. Caste barriers have mostly broken down in large cities, though they persist in rural areas of the country, where 72% of India's population resides. Nevertheless, the caste system, in various forms, continues to survive in modern India strengthened by a combination of social perceptions and divisive politics.

History

There is no universally accepted theory about the origin of the Indian caste system. The Indian classes are similar to the ancient Iranian classes ("*pistras*"), wherein the priests are Athravans, the warriors are Rathaestha, the merchants are Vastriya, and the artisans are Huiti.

Origin

The origin of the caste system as it is today is still obscure. A 2001 genetic study, led by Michael Bamshad of University of

Utah, found that the genetic affinity of Indians making their way to Europeans is proportionate to caste rank, the upper castes being most similar to Europeans, whereas lower castes are more like Asians. The researchers believe that the Indo-European speakers entered India from the Northwest, admixing with or displacing the proto-Dravidian speakers. Subsequently they may have established a caste system and placed themselves primarily in higher castes. The study concludes that the Indian castes "are most likely to be of proto-Asian origin with West Eurasian admixture resulting in rank-related and sex-specific differences in the genetic affinities of castes to Asians and Europeans." Because the Indian samples for this study were taken from a single geographical area, it remains to be investigated whether its findings can be safely generalized.

However the findings of this study is considered controversial since the study was limited to one state, Andhra Pradesh, in India during the regime of a Chief Minister who was reprimanded several times by the Indian courts for Anti-Hindu activities. At the end of this article, the acknowledgments state that it incorporates contributions from an anonymous reviewer and because of its financial support, it has to be classified as an *advertisement. The publication costs of this article were defrayed in part by payment of page charges. This article must therefore be hereby marked "advertisement" in accordance with 18 USC section 1734 solely to indicate this fact.* The findings of this article is also in contradiction to later Human Genetic studies conducted with larger samples.

An earlier 1995 study by Joanna L. Mountain et al. of Stanford University had concluded that there was "no clear separation into three genetically distinct groups along caste lines", although "an inferred tree revealed some clustering according to caste affiliation".

A 2002-03 study by T. Kivisild et al. concluded that the "Indian tribal and caste populations derive largely from the same genetic heritage of Pleistocene southern and western Asians and have received limited gene flow from external regions since the Holocene." A 2006 genetic study by the National Institute of Biologicals in India, testing a sample of men from 32 tribal and 45 caste groups, concluded that the Indians have acquired very few genes from Indo-European speakers.

According to a 2006 study by Ismail Thanseem et al. of Centre for Cellular and Molecular Biology (India) "the vast majority (>98%) of the Indian maternal gene pool, consisting of Indo-European and Dravidian speakers, is genetically more or less uniform", while the invasions after the late Pleistocene settlement might have been mostly male-mediated. The study concluded that the "lower caste groups might have originated with the hierarchical divisions that arose within the tribal groups with the spread of Neolithic agriculturalists, much earlier than the arrival of Aryan speakers", and "the Indo-Europeans established themselves as upper castes among this already developed caste-like class structure within the tribes."

The study indicated that the Indian caste system may have its roots much before the arrival of the Indo-Aryan immigrants; a rudimentary version of the caste system may have emerged with the shift towards cultivation and settlements, and the divisions may have become more well-defined and intensified with the arrival of Indo-Aryans. More recent studies have also debunked the British claims that so-called "Aryans" and "Dravidians" have a "racial divide". A study conducted by the Centre for Cellular and Molecular Biology in 2009 (in collaboration with Harvard Medical School, Harvard School of Public Health and the Broad Institute of Harvard and MIT) analysed half a million genetic markers across the genomes of 132 individuals from 25 ethnic groups from 13 states in India across multiple caste groups. The study establishes, based on the impossibility of identifying any genetic indicators across caste lines, that castes in South Asia grew out of traditional tribal organizations during the formation of Indian society, and was not the product of any mythical "Aryan Invasion" and "subjugation" of Dravidian people.

Hindu Scriptures

Although the Hindu scriptures contain some passages that can be interpreted to sanction the caste system, they also contain indications that the caste system is not an essential part of the Hindu religion, and both sides in the debate are able to find sections in scriptures that support their views.

In the Vedic period, there also seems to no discrimination against the Shudras (which later became an ensemble of the so-called low-castes) on the issue of hearing the sacred words of the Vedas and fully participating in all religious rights, something which became totally banned in the later times.

Later scriptures such as *Bhagavad Gita* and *Manusmriti* state that the four varnas are created by God. However, at the same time, the Gita says that one's varna is to be understood from one's personal qualities and one's *karma* (work), not one's birth. Some scholars believe that, in its initial period, the caste system was flexible and it was merit and job based. One could migrate from one caste to other caste by changing one's profession. This view is supported by records of sages who became Brahmins. For example, the sage Vishwamitra belonged to a Kshatriya caste, and only later became recognized as a great Brahmin sage, indicating that his caste was not determined by birth. Similarly, Valmiki, once a low-caste robber, became a great sage. Veda Vasa, another sage, was the son of a fisherwoman. Vasishtha was a shudra and he became sage later.

Manusmriti, dated between 200 B.C.E. and 100 A.D., contains some laws that codified the caste system. Varna is mentioned as caste equivalent in Manusmriti. Manusmriti and some other shastras mention four varnas: The Brahmins (teachers, scholars and priests), the Kshatriyas (kings and warriors), the Vaishyas (traders, landowners and some artisan groups), and Shudras (agriculturists, service providers, and some artisan groups). Another group of untouchables excluded from the main society was called Parjanya or Antyaja. A varna can be viewed as a group of castes or a social division that consists of various sub-castes called *jatis*.

The various smritis, like the Yagnaval kyasmriti and the Manusmriti strongly disapprove of marrying outside one's caste. The smritis also argue that new, despicable castes are formed out of such cases. According to these smritis, the chamars were born out of the union of a vaideha and a nishada, the chandals were born out of the sexual relations between a Brahmin and a Shudra.

Emergence of Rigid Caste Structures

Megasthenes, the Greek ambassador to Chandragupta Maurya's court in India classified people of India into seven classes: philosophers, peasants, herdsmen, craftsmen and traders, soldiers, government officials and councillors. In its later stages, the caste system is said to have become rigid, and caste began to be inherited rather than acquired by merit. In the past, members of different castes would not partake in various activities, such as dining and religious gatherings, together. In addition, the performance of religious rites and rituals were restricted to Brahmins, who were the designated priesthood. The "Pandaram" priests are an example of an order of Dravidian tamil priests, based in Nepal and South India. The Pandaram maintain the same tradition as the Brahmin priests, including the use of the Sanskrit language (traditionally reserved for the Brahmins) for the rituals. While they are not generally as well trained as the Brahmin priests, they are highly respected within their community and are addressed with reverence.

According to the Manusmriti, every caste belongs to one of the four varnas (Brahmin, Kshtriya, Vaishya, and Shudra). However, there have been many disputes about the varna of many castes, such as castes being considered Kshatriya by some scholars, while described as Shudra by others. While texts such as the Manusmriti attempted to rationalize ambiguous castes by placing them in varna-sankaras (i.e. mixed varna), the fact remains that Indian society was, and is, composed of numerous geographically diversified but endogamous groups. With many occupational groups practicing endogamy within a particular region, as well as numerous sub-divisions within the four main castes, a more complex system of subcastes and jatis is evident. The jatis have broken up into clans like Agarwal, Iyer, etc.

Mobility Across the Castes

The view of the caste system as "static and unchanging" has been disputed by many scholars. For instance, sociolgists such as Bernard Buber and Marriott McKim describe how the perception of the caste system as a static and textual stratification has given way to the perception of the caste system as a more processual, empirical and contextual stratification. Other sociologists such as Y.B Damle have applied theoretical models to explain mobility and flexibility in the caste system in India.. According to these scholars, groups of lower-caste individuals could seek to elevate the status of their caste by attempting to emulate the practices of higher castes. Some scholars believe that the relative ranking of other castes was fluid or differed from one place to another prior to the arrival of the British.

The distinctions, particularly between the Brahmans and the other castes, were in theory sharper, but in practice it now appears that social restrictions were not so rigid. Brahmans often lived off the land and founded dynasties. Most of the groups claiming Kshatriya status had only recently acquired it. The conscious reference to being Kshatriya, a characteristic among Rajputs, is a noticeable feature in post-Gupta politics. The fact that many of these dynasties were of obscure origin suggests some social mobility: a person of any caste, having once acquired political power, could also acquire a genealogy connecting him with the traditional lineages and conferring Kshatriya status. A number of new castes, such as the Kayasthas (scribes) and Khatris (traders), are mentioned in the sources of this period. According to the Brahmanic sources, they originated from inter caste marriages, but this is clearly an attempt at rationalizing their rank in the hierarchy. Many of these new castes played a major role in society. The hierarchy of castes did not have a uniform distribution throughout the country.

Flexibility in caste laws permitted very low-caste religious clerics such as Valmiki to compose the Ramayana, which became a central work of Hindu scripture. According to some psychologists, mobility across broad caste lines may have been "minimal", though sub-castes (jatis) may change their social status over the generations by fission, re-location, and adoption of new rituals..

Sociologist M. N. Srinivas has also debated the question of rigidity in Caste. In an ethnographic study of the Coorgs of Karnataka, he observed considerable flexibility and mobility in their caste hierarchies. He asserts that the caste system is far from a rigid system in which the position of each component caste is fixed for all time. Movement has always been possible, and especially in the middle regions of the hierarchy. It was always possible for groups born into a lower caste to "rise to a higher position by adopting vegetarianism and teetotalism" i.e adopt the customs of the higher castes. While theoretically "forbidden", the process was not uncommon in practice. The concept of sanskritization, or the adoption of upper-caste norms by the lower castes, addressed the actual complexity and fluidity of caste relations.

Historical examples of mobility in the Indian Caste System among Hindus have been researched. There is also precedent of certain Shudra families within the temples of the Shrivaishava sect in South India elevating their caste.

Historical Advantages of the Caste System

Historically, the caste system offered several advantages to the population of the Indian subcontinent. While Caste is nowadays seen by instances that render it anachronistic, in its original form the caste system served as an important instrument of order in a society in which mutual consent rather than compulsion ruled; where the ritual rights as well as the economic obligations of members of one caste or sub-caste were strictly circumscribed in relation to those of any other caste or sub-caste; where one was born into one's caste and retained one's station in society for life; where merit was inherited, where equality existed within the caste, but inter-caste relations were unequal and hierarchical. A well-defined system of mutual interdependence through a division of labour created security within a community.

1. Preservation of order in society through the use of institutional stratification of social groups.
2. Integration of foreigners and invading forces into Indian culture by assigning a caste to them (a process that historian Jawaharlal Nehru referred to as "Indianization"): India has faced repeated invasions from outside the region, dating back to the Macedonian invasion by Alexander the Great. Most invaders were swiftly assimilated into ancient Indian society by assigning them specific castes. Examples include the Kambojas, believed to be of Indo-Scythian descent, who were retroactively assigned a social position in the Manusmriti.
3. The Varna system, with its normative interpretation as a division of labour, had and continues to have a heavy bias towards spiritual evolution. The deep religious proclivities and the urge for spiritual uplift had induced the people

to search for simpler and effective ways to achieve the spiritual goal which led to innovations like the Bhakti movement which had a powerful impact on the socio-cultural-spiritual life of the people even at mass level without distinctions of caste or class or other social differences. It is these deeply run cultural roots which caused an abiding following for Hinduism even in the face of unrelenting assaults by other religions and had in fact continued to influence the lives of people even after their conversion to other faiths. Thus, the caste system can be said to have preserved ancient cultural values in Indian society.

4. The caste system played an influential role in shaping economic activities. The caste system functioned much like medieval European guilds, ensuring the division of labour, providing for the training of apprentices and, in some cases, allowing manufacturers to achieve narrow specialisation. For instance, in certain regions, producing each variety of cloth was the speciality of a particular sub-caste.
5. Philosophers argue that the majority of people would be comfortable in stratified endogamous groups and have been in ancient times. Membership in a particular caste, with its associated narrative, history and genealogy would instill in its members a sense of group accomplishment and cultural pride. Such sentiments are routinely expressed by the Marathas, for instance.

British Rule

The caste system was first exposed to the modern Western world during the Portuguese occupation and rule of sections of India. The word 'caste' in this context is derived from the Portuguese, 'casta'. Later, other European empires, including the British, occupied parts of the subcontinent.

The earliest use of caste as a basis for interpreting social and demographic data arose from British officials' concern to stamp out female infanticide. Later, the use of caste to classify the population formed a basis for British attempts at social engineering. According to certain British laws (such as the Criminal Tribes Act of 1871), many castes and tribes were described as habitually criminal, and adult male members of such groups forced to report weekly to the local police. The caste-based classification (moneylending, agricultural or martial) was also used for other purposes such as legislation controlling land transfers, the grant of proprietary rights, the regulation of rents, recruitment to the armed forces etc. British anthropologist Herbert Risley's *The Tribes and Castes of Bengal*, published in 1892, was one of the first works on the caste system in India written by a Western scholar.

The earliest forms of classification in the British censuses of India (1865, 1872 and 1881) were based on the varna system, with the population being divided into Brahmins, Kshatriyas, Vaishyas and Shudras. Denzil Ibbetson, in his introduction to the 1881 census of the Punjab, argued that the Indian caste system was more of a social than a religious institution, and that conversion from Hinduism to Islam had not necessarily the slightest effect upon caste. He stated that the varnas had "no present significance". The 1891 census was based primarily on castes as occupational guilds instead of the varnas.

Some scholars state that the caste system was broken up greatly during British Raj in India. However, some other historians suggest that the impact of British reforms has been greatly exaggerated.

Initially, the British strengthened the caste system. They gave the Brahmins back special privileges the Muslim rulers had taken away. During the initial days of British East India Company's rules, caste privileges and customs were encouraged in the Bengal Army. But, British law courts disagreed with the discrimination against the lower castes. Many believe that the lack of British respect for sepoys' caste traditions was one of the reasons behind the Indian Rebellion of 1857.

During British rule, the reservation of seats for the "Depressed Classes" was incorporated into the Government of India Act 1935, which went into force in 1937. The Act brought the term "Scheduled castes" into use, which was later clarified in The Government of India (Scheduled Castes) Order, 1936 which contained a list of scheduled castes.

British Census Officers determined caste hierarchy based on the principle, e.g. someone who accepts food and water from another person but the other person does not reciprocate the same way, then the other person is superior to the former. It was contested at many places (a notable example is that the Koeris of UP who said they won't accept water from Brahmins, and so should be placed higher than them). Because it was met with rampant controversies, arbitration was very common during those days. The most notable arbitration stories are:

1. Caste status of Kayastha
2. Caste status of Kurmi.

It raised more questions than it answered and subsequent census records varied radically, making it free for all, after some time.

Major Caste Groups

According to the 1891 census data, the major caste groups in India were following (listed in the order of population):

Caste-Group	*Example*	*Population %*
Cultivators	Maurya, Kurmi, Mali, Lodha, Kushwaha	20%
Village Menials	Chamar, Dosadh, Dom	13%
Military	Jat, Rajput, Nairs, Maratha	12%
Artisans	Lohar, Sunar, Julaha	12%
Pastoral	Ahir, Gaderia, Dhangar	7%
Forest tribes	Santhal, Gond, Bhil	7%
Professionals	Namboothiri, Brahmbhatt, Kayasth	6%
Services	Nai, Dhobi, Kandoi	6%
Merchants	Agrawal, Khatri, Balija, Barnwal	5%
Labourers	Musahar, Bagdi, Bawari	3%
Fishers	Kahar, Mallah	3%
Other professionals	Vaidya, Mirasi, Bhand	2%
Vagrants	Waddar, Nat, Beldar	1%

Reform Movements

There have been cases of upper caste Hindus warming to the Dalits and Hindu priests, demoted to outcaste ranks, who continued practising the religion. An example of the latter was Dnyaneshwar, who was excommunicated from society in the 13th century, but continued to compose the Dnyaneshwari, a Dharmic commentary on the Bhagavad Gita. Other excommunicated Brahmins, such as Eknath, fought for the rights of untouchables during the Bhakti period. Historical examples of Dalit priests include Chokhamela in the 14th Century, who was India's first recorded Dalit poet, Raidas, born into Dalit cobblers, and others. The 15th century saint Ramananda also accepted all castes, including untouchables, into his fold. Most of these saints subscribed to the Bhakti movements in Hinduism during the medieval period that rejected casteism. Nandanar, a low-caste Hindu cleric, also rejected casteism and accepted Dalits.

Many movements in Hinduism have welcomed Dalits into their fold, the foremost being the Bhakti movements of the medieval period. Early Dalit politics involved many Hindu reform movements which arose primarily as a reaction to the tactics of Christian Missionaries in India and their attempts to mass-convert Dalits to Christianity under the allure of escaping the caste system (unfortunately, there is Caste system among Indian Christians among large sections of Indian Christians).

In the 19th Century, the Brahmo Samaj under Raja Ram Mohan Roy, actively campaigned against untouchability. The Arya Samaj founded by Swami Dayanand also renounced discrimination against Dalits. Sri Ramakrishna Paramahamsa founded the Ramakrishna Mission that participated in the emancipation of Dalits. Upper caste Hindus, such as Mannathu Padmanabhan also participated in movements to abolish Untouchability against Dalits, opening his family temple for Dalits to worship. While there always have been places for Dalits to worship, the first "upper-caste" temple to openly welcome Dalits into their fold was the Laxminarayan Temple in Wardha in the year 1928 (the move was spearheaded by reformer Jamnalal Bajaj). Also, the Satnami movement was founded by Guru Ghasidas, a Dalit himself. Other reformers, such as Mahatma Jyotirao Phule also worked for the emancipation of Dalits. Another example of Dalit emancipation was the Temple Entry Proclamation issued by the last Maharaja of Travancore in the Indian state of Kerala in the year 1936.

The Maharaja proclaimed that "out castes should not be denied the consolations and the solace of the Hindu faith". Even today, the Sri Padmanabhaswamy temple that first welcomed Dalits in the state of Kerala is revered by the Dalit Hindu community. The 1930s saw key struggles between Mahatma Gandhi and B.R. Ambedkar, most notably over whether Dalits would have separate electorates or joint electorates with reserved seats. The Indian National Congress was the only national organisation with a large Dalit following, but Gandhi failed to gain their commitment. Ambedkar, a Dalit himself, developed a deeper analysis of Untouchability, but lacked a workable political strategy: his conversion to Buddhism in 1956, along with millions of followers, highlighted the failure of his political endeavours. India's first Prime Minister, Jawaharlal Nehru, based on his own relationship with Dalit reformer Ambedkar, also spread information about the dire need to eradicate untouchability for the benefit of the Dalit community.

In more contemporary times, India has had an elected Dalit president, K. R. Narayanan, who has stated that he was well-treated in his community of largely upper-caste Hindus (24 July 2002). Another popular Harijan includes Babaji Palwankar Baloo, who joined the Hindu Mahasabha and was both a politician and a cricketer. He was an independence fighter. In addition, other Hindu groups have reached out to the Dalit community in an effort to reconcile with them, with productive results. On August 2006, Dalit activist Namdeo Dhasal engaged in dialogue with the Rashtriya Swayamsevak Sangh in an attempt to "bury the hatchet".

Also, the "Pandaram" are an order of Dravidian Tamil Hindu priests (a task traditionally reserved for the Brahmins) based largely in Nepal and parts of South India. These Pandaram priests maintain the same tradition as the Brahmin priests, including using Sanskrit for the rituals. They perform religious ceremonies from weddings to death rituals. They are highly respected within the tamil community and are addressed reverentially. Also, Hindu temples are increasingly more receptive to Dalit priests, such as Suryavanshi Das, the Dalit priest of a notable temple in the midst of Patna, the capital of Bihar.

Discrimination against Hindu Dalits is on a slow but steady decline. The results of Bhakti Movements are clearly visible. Numerous Hindu Dalits have achieved affluence in society, although vast still remain poor irrespective of caste. In urban

India, discrimination against Dalits is largely disappeared, but rural Dalits are struggling to elevate themselves. Government organizations and NGO's work to emancipate them from discrimination, and many Hindu organizations have spoken in their favour.

Varna and Jati

According to the ancient Hindu scriptures, there are four "varnas". The Bhagavad Gita says varnas are decided based on Guna and Karma. Manusmriti and some other shastras mention four varnas: the Brahmins (teachers, scholars and priests), the Kshatriyas (kings and warriors), the Vaishyas (agriculturists and traders), and Shudras (service providers and artisans). This theoretical system postulated Varna categories as ideals and explained away the reality of thousands of endogamous Jatis actually prevailing in the country as being historical among the "pure" Varnas-*Varna Sankara*. All those, including foreigners, tribals and nomads, who did not subscribe to the norms of the Hindu society were contagious and untouchables. Another group excluded from the main society was called Parjanya or Antyaja. This group of former "untouchables" (self described as Dalits) i.e. downtrodden, was considered either the lower section of Shudras or outside the caste system altogether. Passages from scriptures such as Manusmriti indicate that the varna system was originally non-hereditary.

Several critics of Hinduism state that the caste system is rooted in the varna system mentioned in the ancient Hindu scriptures. However, many groups, such as ISKCON, consider the modern Indian caste system and the varna system as two distinct concepts. Many European scholars from the colonial era regarded the Manusmriti as the "law book" of the Hindus, and thus concluded that the caste system is a part of Hinduism, an assertion that is rejected by many Hindu scholars, who state that it is an anachronistic social practice, not a religious one.

Although many Hindu scriptures contain passages that can be interpreted to sanction the caste system, they also contain indications that the caste system is not an essential part of Hinduism. The Vedas place very little importance on the caste system, mentioning caste only once (in the Purush Sukta) out of tens of thousands of verses. B. R. Ambedkar believed that even this is a much later interpolation and gave evidence to support his conclusion. In the Vedic period, there was no prohibition against the Shudras listening to the Vedas or participating in any religious rite.

In *Early Evidence for Caste in South India,* George L. Hart stated that "the earliest Tamil texts show the existence of what seems definitely to be caste, but which antedates the Brahmins and the Hindu orthodoxy". He believes that the origins of the caste system can be seen in the "belief system that developed with the agricultural civilization", and was later profoundly influenced by "the Brahmins and the Brahmanical religion". These early Tamil texts also outline the concept of equality. Saint Valluvar has stated which means "all are equal at birth". Likewise, Saint Auvaiyaar has stated that there are only two castes in the world: those who contribute positively and those who contribute negatively. From these, it can be inferred that the caste system is more of a socioeconomic class system.

Caste and Social Status

Traditionally, although the political power lay with the Kshatriyas, historians portrayed that the Brahmins as custodians and interpreters of Dharma enjoyed much prestige and many advantages.

Fa Hien, a Buddhist pilgrim from China, visited India around 400 AD. *"Only the lot of the Chandals he found unenviable; out castes by reason of their degrading work as disposers of dead, they were universally shunned... But no other section of the population were notably disadvantaged, no other caste distinctions attracted comment from the Chinese pilgrim, and no oppressive caste 'system' drew forth his surprised censure."* In this period kings of Sudra and Brahmin origin were as common as those of Kshatriya *varna* and caste system was not wholly prohibitive and repressive.

The castes did not constitute a rigid description of the occupation or the social status of a group. Since British society was divided by class, the British attempted to equate the Indian caste system to their own social class system. They saw caste as an indicator of occupation, social standing, and intellectual ability. Intentionally or unintentionally, the caste system became more rigid during the British Raj, when the British started to enumerate castes during the ten year census and codified the system under their rule.

The Harijans, or the people outside the caste system, had the lowest social status. The Harijans, earlier referred to as "untouchables" by some, worked in what were seen as unhealthy, unpleasant or polluting jobs. In the past, the Harijans suffered from social segregation and restrictions, in addition to extreme poverty. They were not allowed temple worship with others, nor water from the same sources. Persons of higher castes would not interact with them. If somehow a member of a higher caste came into physical or social contact with an untouchable, the member of the higher caste was defiled, and had to bathe thoroughly to purge him or herself of the impurity. Social discrimination developed even among the Harijans. Sub-castes among Harijans, like *dhobi, nai* etc., would not interact with lower-order Bhangis, who were described as "outcasts even among out castes".

Sociologists have commented on the historical advantages offered by a rigid social structure, such as the caste system, and its lack of usefulness in the modern world. Historically, the caste system offered several advantages to the population of the Indian subcontinent. While Caste is nowadays seen by instances that render it anachronistic, in its original form, the caste system served as an important instrument of order in a society where mutual consent rather than compulsion ruled; where the ritual rights as well as the economic obligations of members of one caste or sub-caste were strictly circumscribed in relation to those of any other caste or sub-caste; where one was born into one's caste and retained one's station in society for life; where merit was inherited, where equality existed within the caste, but inter-caste relations were unequal and hierarchical.

A well-defined system of mutual interdependence through a division of labour created security within a community. In addition, the division of labour on the basis of ethnicity allowed immigrants and foreigners to quickly integrate into their own caste niches. The caste system played an influential role in shaping economic activities. The caste system functioned much like medieval European guilds, ensuring the division of labour, providing for the training of apprentices and, in some cases, allowing manufacturers to achieve narrow specialisation. For instance, in certain regions, producing each variety of cloth was the speciality of a particular sub-caste. Also, philosophers argue that the majority of people would be comfortable in stratified endogamous groups, and have been in ancient times.

Caste Mobility

Some scholars believe that the relative ranking of other castes was fluid or differed from one place to another prior to the arrival of the British. Sociologists such as Bernard Buber and Marriott McKim describe how the perception of the caste system as a static and textual stratification has given way to the perception of the caste system as a more processual, empirical and contextual stratification. Other sociologists such as Y.B Damle have applied theoretical models to explain mobility and flexibility in the caste system in India. According to these scholars, groups of lower-caste individuals could seek to elevate the status of their caste by attempting to emulate the practices of higher castes.

Flexibility in caste laws permitted very low-caste religious clerics such as Valmiki to compose the Ramayana, which became a central work of Hindu scripture. According to some psychologists, mobility across broad caste lines may have been "minimal", though sub-castes (jatis) may change their social status over the generations by fission, re-location, and adoption of new rituals.

Sociologist M. N. Srinivas has also debated the question of rigidity in Caste. In an ethnographic study of the Coorgs of Karnataka, he observed considerable flexibility and mobility in their caste hierarchies. He asserts that the caste system is far from a rigid system in which the position of each component caste is fixed for all time. Movement has always been possible, and especially in the middle regions of the hierarchy. It was always possible for groups born into a lower caste to "rise to a higher position by adopting vegetarianism and teetotalism" i.e adopt the customs of the higher castes. While theoretically "forbidden", the process was not uncommon in practice. The concept of sanskritization, or the adoption of upper-caste norms by the lower castes, addressed the actual complexity and fluidity of caste relations.

Historical examples of mobility in the Indian Caste System among Hindus have been researched. There is also precedent of certain Shudra families within the temples of the Sri Vaishnava sect in South India elevating their caste. The fact that many of the dynasties were of obscure origin suggests some social mobility: a person of any caste, having once acquired political power, could also acquire a genealogy connecting him with the traditional lineages and conferring Kshatriya status.

A number of new castes, such as the Kayasthas (scribes) and Khatris (traders), are mentioned in the sources of this period. According to the Brahmanic sources, they originated from inter caste marriages, but this is clearly an attempt at rationalizing their rank in the hierarchy. Many of these new castes played a major role in society. The hierarchy of castes did not have a uniform distribution throughout the country. Khatri appears to be unquestionably a Prakritised form of the Sanskrit Kshatriya.

Reforms

There have been challenges to the caste system from the time of Buddha, and from the time of Mahavira (Jaina founder) and (still earlier) of Gosala Maskarin.

Opposition to the system of varna ('caste') is regularly asserted already in the Yoga Upanishads (of early mediaeval date); and is a constant feature of Cina-acara tantrism (Chinese-derived movement in Asom, and also of mediaeval date). The Natha system (likewise mediaeval) founded by Matsya-indra Natha and by Go-rakca Natha, and spread throughout India, has likewise been in consistent opposition to the system of varna.

Many Bhakti period saints rejected the caste discriminations and accepted all castes, including untouchables, into their fold. During the British Raj, this sentiment gathered steam, and many Hindu reform movements such as Brahmo Samaj and Arya Samaj renounced caste-based discrimination. The inclusion of so-called untouchables into the mainstream was argued for by many social reformers. Mahatma Gandhi called them "Harijans" (children of God) although that term is now considered patronizing and the term Dalit ("downtrodden") is the more commonly used. Gandhi's contribution toward the emancipation of the untouchables is still debated, especially in the commentary of his contemporary Dr.

B.R. Ambedkar, an untouchable himself, who frequently saw Gandhi's activities as detrimental to the cause of upliftment of his people.

The practice of untouchability was formally outlawed by the Constitution of India in 1950, and has declined significantly since then. K. R. Narayanan, who became the President of India in 1997, and K. G. Balakrishnan (the present Chief Justice of India) have belonged to castes formerly considered untouchable.

British Rule

The fluidity of the caste system was affected by the arrival of the British. Prior to that, the relative ranking of castes differed from one place to another. The castes did not constitute a rigid description of the occupation or the social status of a group. The British attempted to equate the Indian caste system to their own class system. They saw caste as an indicator of occupation, social standing, and intellectual ability. During the initial days of the British East India Company's rule, caste privileges and customs were encouraged, but the British law courts disagreed with the discrimination against the lower castes. However, British policies of divide and rule as well as enumeration of the population into rigid categories during the 10 year census contributed towards the hardening of caste identities.

During the period of British rule, India saw the rebellions of several lower castes, mainly tribals that revolted against British rule. These were:

1. Halba rebellion (1774–79)
2. Bhopalpatnam Struggle (1795)
3. Bhil rebellion (1822–1857)
4. Paralkot rebellion (1825)
5. Tarapur rebellion (1842–54)
6. Maria rebellion (1842–63)
7. First Freedom Struggle (1856–57)
8. Bhil rebellion, begun by Tantya Tope in Banswara (1858)
9. Koi revolt (1859)
10. Gond rebellion, begun by Ramji Gond in Adilabad (1860)
11. Muria rebellion (1876)

12. Rani rebellion (1878–82)
13. Bhumkal (1910).

Modern Status of the Caste System

In some rural areas and small towns, the caste system is still very rigid. Caste is also a factor in the politics of India.

The Government of India has officially documented castes and subcastes, primarily to determine those deserving reservation (positive discrimination in education and jobs) through the census. The Indian reservation system, though limited in scope, relies entirely on quotas. The Government lists consist of Scheduled Castes, Scheduled Tribes and Other Backward Classes:

Scheduled Castes (SC): Scheduled castes generally consist of former "untouchables" (the term "Dalit" is now preferred). The present population is 16% of the total population of India (around 160 million). For example, the Delhi state has 49 castes listed as SC.

Scheduled Tribes (ST): Scheduled tribes generally consist of tribal groups. The present population is 7% of the total population of India i.e. around 70 million.

Other Backward Classes (OBC): The Mandal Commission covered more than 3000 castes under OBC Category and stated that OBCs form around 52% (which includes casts like Jat of the Indian population. However, the National Sample Survey puts the figure at 32%. There is substantial debate over the exact number of OBCs in India. It is generally estimated to be sizable, but many believe that it is lower than the figures quoted by either the Mandal Commission or the National Sample Survey.

The caste-based reservations in India have led to widespread protests, with many complaining of reverse discrimination against the forward castes (the castes that do not qualify for the reservation). The 2006 Indian anti-reservation protests are one major example. Many view negative treatment (or hatred) of forward castes as socially divisive and just as wrong.

Caste System Among Non-Hindus

In some parts of India, the Christians are stratified by sect, location, and the castes of their predecessors, usually in reference to upper class Syrian Malabar Nasranis. Christians in Kerala are divided into several communities, including Syrian Christians and the so-called "Latin" or "New Rite" Christians. Syrian Christians, especially Knanaya Christians tend to be endogamous, and tend not to intermarry with other Christian castes. Also, very rarely are there intermarriages between Syrian Christians and Latin Rite Christians (converted in the 16th and 19th centuries) in Kerala; the latter were converted mainly from lower castes where fishing was the traditional occupation. Due to active conversion by Latin Missionaries in the coastal belt of Kerala, the new Latin converts were poor and deprived. So the Government of India gave them the social benefit of OBC status (Other Backward Classes) so that the deprived members of that community can be uplifted.

It is a matter of great significance that Missionary activities were done by Western Latin rite missionaries who did not understand the significance of the caste system in India. None of the Syrian Churches ever indulged in these kinds of activities among the scheduled castes of India because they were aware of the prejudices of the caste system. Syrian Christians derive status within the caste system from the tradition that they are converted Namboodiris and Jews, who were evangelized by St. Thomas. Anthropologists have noted that the caste hierarchy among Christians in Kerala is much more polarized than the Hindu practices in the surrounding areas, due to a lack of jatis. Also, the caste status is kept even if the sect allegiance is switched (i.e. from Syrian Catholic to Syrian Orthodox).

In the Indian state of Goa, mass conversions were carried out by Portuguese Latin missionaries from the 16th century onwards. The Hindu converts retained their caste practices. The continued maintenance of the caste system among the Christians in Goa is attributed to the nature of mass conversions of entire villages, as a result of which existing social stratification was not affected. The Portuguese colonists, even during the Goan Inquisition, did not do anything to change the caste system. Thus, the original Hindu Brahmins in Goa now became Christian *Bamons* and the Kshatriya became Christian noblemen called *Chardos*. The Christian clergy became almost exclusively Bamon. Vaishyas who converted to Christianity became *Gauddos*, and Shudras became *Sudirs*. Finally, the Dalits or "Untouchables" who converted to Christianity became *Maharas* and *Chamars*.

Units of social stratification, termed as "castes" by many, have developed among Muslims in some parts of South Asia. Sources indicate that the castes among Muslims developed as the result of close contact with Hindu culture and Hindu converts to Islam. The Sachar Committee's report commissioned by the government of India and released in 2006, documents the continued stratification in Muslim society.

Among Muslims, those who are referred to as Ashrafs are presumed to have a superior status derived from their foreign Arab ancestry, while the Ajlafs are assumed to be converts from Hinduism, and have a lower status. In addition, there is also the *Arzal* caste among Muslims, who were regarded by anti-caste activists like Ambedkar as the equivalent of untouchables. In the Bengal region of India, some Muslims also stratify their society according to 'Quoms'. While many scholars have asserted that the Muslim Castes are not as acute in their discrimination as that among Hindus, some like Ambedkar argued otherwise, writing that the social evils in Muslim society were "worse than those seen in Hindu society".

The nastik Buddhists too have a caste system. In Sri Lanka, the Rodis have always been despised and they might have been out-casted by the Lankan Buddhists due to the absence of "ahimsa" (*non-violence*), which Buddhism heavily depends on. The writer Raghavan notes: "*That a form of worship in which human offerings formed the essential ritual would have been anathema to the Buddhist way of life goes without saying; and it needs no stretch of imagination that any class of people in whom the cult prevailed or survived even in an attenuated form would have been pronounced by the sangha (i.e. the Buddhist clergy) as exiles from the social order.*" Savarkar too believed that the status of the backward castes (e.g. Chamar) that performed non-violence only worsened. When Ywan Chwang travelled to South India after the period of the Chalukyan Empire, he noticed that the caste system had existed among the Buddhists and Jains.

The Jains too have castes in places such as Bihar. For example, in the village of Bundela, there are several *"jaats"* (*groups*) amongst the Jains. A person of one *"jaat"* cannot intermingle with a Jain or another *"jaat"*. They also cannot eat with the members of other *"jaats"*.

The Sikh Gurus criticized the hierarchy in the caste system. Where some castes were perceived by people as being better or higher than others (e.g. Brahmins being higher than others) they preached all sections of society were valuable and merit and hard-work were essential aspects of life. In Shiromani Gurdwara Prabandhak Committee, out of 140 seats, twenty are reserved for low caste Sikhs. However, the quota system has attracted much criticism due to the lack of meritocracy, where merit is considered the single most important component of winning a seat.

Caste-Related Violence

Independent India has witnessed considerable amount of violence and hate crimes motivated by caste. Ranvir Sena, a caste-supremacist fringe paramilitary group based in Bihar, has committed violent acts against Dalits and other members of the scheduled caste community. Phoolan Devi, who belonged to *Mallah* lower-caste, was mistreated and raped by upper-caste Thakurs at a young age. She then became a bandit and carried out violent robberies against upper-caste people. In 1981, her gang massacred twenty-two Thakurs, most of whom were not involved in her kidnapping or rape. Phoolan Devi went on to become a politician and Member of Parliament.

Over the years, various incidents of violence against Dalits, such as Kherlanji Massacre have been reported from many parts of India. At the same time, many violent protests by Dalits, such as the 2006 Dalit protests in Maharashtra, have been reported as well.

Caste Politics

B. R. Ambedkar and Jawaharlal Nehru had radically different approaches to caste especially over constitutional politics and the status of "untouchables". Until the mid-1970s, the politics of independent India was largely dominated by economic issues and questions of corruption. But since 1980s, caste has emerged as a major issue in the politics of India.

The Mandal Commission was established in 1979 to "identify the socially or educationally backward", and to consider the question of seat reservations and quotas for people to redress caste discrimination. In 1980, the commission's report affirmed the affirmative action practice under Indian law whereby members of lower castes were given exclusive access to a certain portion of government jobs and slots in public universities. When V. P. Singh Government tried to implement the recommendations of Mandal Commission in 1989, massive protests were held in the country. Many alleged that the politicians were trying to cash in on caste-based reservations for purely pragmatic electoral purposes.

Many political parties in India have openly indulged in caste-based votebank politics. Parties such as Bahujan Samaj Party (BSP), the Samajwadi Party and the Janata Dal claim that they are representing the backward castes, and rely primarily on OBC support, often in alliance with Dalit and Muslim support to win the elections. Remarkably, what is called a landmark election in the history of India's biggest state of Uttar Pradesh, the Bahujan Samaj Party was able to garner majority in the State assembly Elections with the support of the brahmin community.

Criticism

There have been many criticisms of the caste system, both within and outside India. Criticism of the Caste system in Hindu society came both from the Hindu fold and Dalit.

Historical Criticism

Gautama Buddha and Mahavira, the founders of Buddhism and Jainism respectively, were perhaps against any kind of caste structure. Further, rejection of caste may have developed before these religions within Hinduism. Many bhakti period saints such as Nanak, Kabir, Caitanya, Dnyaneshwar, Eknath, Ramanuja and Tukaram rejected all caste-based discrimination and accepted disciples from all the castes. Many Hindu reformers such as Swami Vivekananda believe that there is no place for the caste system in Hinduism. The 15th century saint Ramananda also accepted all castes, including untouchables, into his fold. Most of these saints subscribed to the Bhakti movements in Hinduism during the medieval period that rejected casteism. Nandanar, a low-caste Hindu cleric, also rejected casteism and accepted Dalits. Some other movements in Hinduism have also welcomed lower-castes into their fold, the earliest being the Bhakti movements of the medieval period. Early Dalit politics involved many Hindu reform movements which arose primarily as a reaction to the advent of Christian Missionaries in India and their attempts to convert Dalits to Christianity, who were attracted to the prospect of escaping the caste system.

In the 19th Century, the Brahmo Samaj under Raja Ram Mohan Roy, actively campaigned against untouchability and Casteism. The Arya Samaj founded by Swami Dayanand also renounced discrimination against Dalits. Sri Ramakrishna Paramahamsa and his greatest disciple Swami Vivekananda who founded the Ramakrishna Mission that participated in the emancipation of Dalits. Upper caste Hindus, such as Mannathu Padmanabhan also participated in movements to abolish Untouchability against Dalits, opening his family temple for Dalits to worship. Narayana Guru, a pious Hindu and an authority on the Vedas, also criticized casteism and campaigned for the rights of lower-caste Hindus within the context of Hinduism. The first "upper-caste" temple to openly welcome Dalits into their fold was the Laxminarayan Temple in Wardha in the year 1928.

The caste system has also been criticized by many Indian social reformers. Some reformers, such as Jyotirao Phule and Iyothee Thass argued that the lower caste people were the original inhabitants of India, and were conquered in the ancient past by "Brahmin invaders." Mahatma Gandhi coined the term "Harijan", a euphemistic word for *untouchable*, literally meaning *Sons of God*. B. R. Ambedkar, born in Hindu Dalit community, was a heavy critic of the caste system. He pioneered the Dalit Buddhist movement in India, and asked his followers to leave Hinduism, and convert to Buddhism.

India's first Prime Minister, Jawaharlal Nehru, based on his own relationship with Dalit reformer Ambedkar, also spread information about the dire need to eradicate untouchability for the benefit of the Dalit community. Another example was the Temple Entry Proclamation issued by the last Maharaja of Travancore in the Indian state of Kerala in the year 1936. The Maharaja proclaimed that "out castes should not be denied the consolations and the solace of the Hindu faith". Even today, the Sri Padmanabhaswamy temple that first welcomed Dalits in the state of Kerala is revered by the Dalit Hindu community.

Contemporary Criticism

Kancha Ilaiah, a Buddhist and professor at Osmania University is known for his polemical attacks on Hindus and the caste system and is considered an anti-Hindu by his critics. Similarly, radicals such as Udit Raj, also a Buddhist, who have attacked Hindus in polemical speeches, have achieved some popularity among evangelical Christian groups such as the Dalit Freedom Network in their criticism of Hindism. The website Dalitstan (presently taken down), once banned by the Indian government, is an example of anti-Brahmin and anti-Hindu rhetoric by Dalit extremists, allegedly supported by Christian missions.

Many Hindus point out that the caste system is related to the Indian society, and not Hinduism (as is evident by presence of caste among Indian Christians and Muslims). Hindu Nationalist organizations such as the Rashtriya Swayamsevak Sangh have actively criticized the caste system.

Some activists consider that the caste system is a form of racial discrimination. The participants of the United Nations Conference Against Racism in Durban, South Africa in March 2001, condemned discrimination due to the caste system, and tried to pass a resolution declaring that caste as a basis for the segregation and oppression of peoples in terms of their descent and occupation is a form of apartheid. However, no formal resolution was passed to that effect.

India's treatment of Dalits has been described by some authors as "India's hidden apartheid". Critics of the accusations point out the substantial improvements in the rights of Dalits (former "Untouchables") enshrined in the Constitution of India (primarily written by a Dalit, Ambedkar), which is the principal object of article 17 in the Constitution as implemented by the Protection of Civil rights Act, 1955 and the fact that India has had a Dalit, K.R. Narayanan, for a president, as well as the disappearance of the practise in urban public life.

According to William A. Haviland, however: Although India's national constitution of 1950 sought to abolish cast discrimination and the practice of untouchability, the caste svstem remains deeply entrenched in Hindu culture and is still widespread throughout southern Asia, especially in rural India. In what has been called India's "hidden apartheid", entire villages in many Indian states remain completely segregated by caste. Representing about 15 percent of India's population—or some 160 million people—the widely scatter Dalits endure near complete social isolation, humiliation, and discrimination based exclusively on their birth status. Even a Dalit's shadow is believed to pollute the upper classes. They may not cross the line dividing their part of the village from that occupied by higher castes, drink water from public wells, or visit the same temples as the higher castes. Dalit children are still often made to sit in the back of classrooms.

However, such allegations of apartheid are regarded by academic sociologists as a political epithet, since apartheid implies state sponsored discrimination, and no such thing exists in India. The Constitution of India places special emphasis on outlawing caste discrimination, especially the practice of untouchability. In addition, the Indian penal code inflicts severe punishments on those who discriminate on the basis of caste. Anti-dalit prejudice and discrimination is a social malaise that exists primarily in rural areas, where small societies can track the caste lineage of individuals and discriminate accordingly. Sociologists Kevin Reilly, Stephen Kaufman, Angela Bodino, while being critical of casteism, conclude that modern India does not practice any "apartheid" since there is no state sanctioned discrimination. They write that Casteism in India is presently "not apartheid. In fact, untouchables, as well as tribal people and members of the lowest castes in India benefit from broad affirmative action programmes and are enjoying greater political power."

Caste and Race

Allegations that caste amounts to race were addressed and rejected by B.R. Ambedkar, an advocate for Dalit rights and critic of untouchability. He wrote that "The Brahmin of Punjab is racially of the same stock as the Chamar (Dalit) of Punjab. The Caste system does not demarcate racial division. Caste system is a social division of people of the same race", Such allegations have also been rejected by many sociologists such as Andre Beteille, who writes that treating caste as a form of racism is "politically mischievous" and worse, "scientifically nonsensical" since there is no discernible difference in the racial characteristics between Brahmins and Scheduled Castes. He writes that "Every social group cannot be regarded as a race simply because we want to protect it against prejudice and discrimination".

The Indian government also rejects the claims of equivalency between Caste and Racial discrimination, pointing out that the caste issues as essentially intra-racial and intra-cultural. Indian Attorney General Soli Sorabjee insisted that "the only reason India wants caste discrimination kept off the agenda is that it will distract participants from the main topic: racism. Caste discrimination in India is undeniable but caste and race are entirely distinct". Many scholars dispute the claim that casteism is akin to racism.

The view of the caste system as "static and unchanging" has been disputed. Sociologists describe how the perception of the caste system as a static and textual stratification has given way to the perception of the caste system as a more processual, empirical and contextual stratification. Others have applied theoretical models to explain mobility and flexibility in the caste system in India. According to these scholars, groups of lower-caste individuals could seek to elevate the status of their caste by attempting to emulate the practices of higher castes.

Sociologist M. N. Srinivas has also debated the question of rigidity in Caste. For details see sanskritization. Pakistani-American sociologist Ayesha Jalal also rejects these allegations. In her book, "Democracy and Authoritarianism in South Asia", she writes that "As for Hinduism, the hierarchical principles of the Brahmanical social order have always been contested from within Hindu society, suggesting that equality has been and continues to be both valued and practiced."

In India, some observers felt that the caste system must be viewed as a system of exploitation of poor low-ranking groups by more prosperous high-ranking groups. In many parts of India, land is largely held by high-ranking property owners of the dominant castes that economically exploit low-ranking landless labourers and poor artisans, all the while degrading them with ritual emphases on their so-called god-given inferior status.

Matt Cherry, claims that karma underpins the caste system, and the caste system traditionally determines the position and role of every member of Hindu society.

Caste determines an individual's place in society, the work he or she may carry out, and who he or she may marry and meet. According to him, Hindus believe that the karma of previous life will determine the caste an individual will be (re)born into. According to Stanford University scholar Oman Jain, there is no caste system currently in place in India.

On 29 March 2007, the Supreme Court of India, as an interim measure, stayed the law providing for 27 percent reservation for Other Backward Classes in educational institutions like IITs and IIMs. This was done in response to a public interest litigation — Ashoka Kumar Thakur vs. Union of India. The Court held that the 1931 census could not be a determinative factor for identifying the OBCs for the purpose of providing reservation. The court also observed, "Reservation cannot be permanent and appear to perpetuate backwardness".

Genetic Analysis

There have been several studies examining caste members as discrete populations, examining the hypothesis that their ancestors have different origins. A 2002-03 study by T. Kivisild et al. concluded that the "Indian tribal and caste populations derive largely from the same genetic heritage of Pleistocene southern and western Asians and have received limited gene flow from external regions since the Holocene."

Studies point to the various Indian caste groups having similar genetic origins and having negligible genetic input from outside south Asia. However, a 2001 genetic study, led by Michael Bamshad of the University of Utah, found that the affinity of Indians to Europeans is proportionate to caste rank, the upper castes being most similar to Europeans. The researchers believe that the Indo-Aryans entered India from the Northwest and may have established a caste system, in which they placed themselves primarily in higher castes." Because the Indian samples for this study were taken from a single geographical area, it remains to be investigated whether its findings can be safely generalized.

An earlier 1995 study by Joanna L. Mountain et al. of Stanford University had concluded that there was "no clear separation into three genetically distinct groups along caste lines", although "an inferred tree revealed some clustering according to caste affiliation". A 2006 study by Ismail Thanseem et al. of Centre for Cellular and Molecular Biology (India) concluded that the "lower caste groups might have originated with the hierarchical divisions that arose within the tribal groups with the spread of Neolithic agriculturalists, much earlier than the arrival of Aryan speakers", and "the Indo-Europeans established themselves as upper castes among this already developed caste-like class structure within the tribes."

The study indicated that the Indian caste system may have its roots much before the arrival of the Indo-Aryans; a rudimentary version of the caste system may have emerged with the shift towards cultivation and settlements, and the divisions may have become more well-defined and intensified with the arrival of Indo-Aryans.

A 2006 genetic study by the National Institute of Biologicals in India, testing a sample of men from 32 tribal and 45 caste groups, concluded that the Indians have acquired very few genes from Indo-European speakers. More recent studies have also debunked the British claims that so-called "Aryans" and "Dravidians" have a "racial divide". A study conducted by the Centre for Cellular and Molecular Biology in 2009 (in collaboration with Harvard Medical School, Harvard School of Public Health and the Broad Institute of Harvard and MIT) analysed half a million genetic markers across the genomes of 132 individuals from 25 ethnic groups from 13 states in India across multiple caste groups. The study establishes, based on the impossibility of identifying any genetic indicators across caste lines, that castes in South Asia grew out of traditional tribal organizations during the formation of Indian society, and was not the product of any "Aryan Invasion" and "subjugation" of Dravidian people.

Classes in India

Classes in India : In village India, where nearly 74 percent of the population resides, caste and class affiliations overlap.

According to anthropologist Miriam Sharma, "Large land holders who employ hired labour are overwhelmingly from the upper castes, while the agricultural workers themselves come from the ranks of the lowest—predominantly Untouchable—castes."

She also points out that household-labour-using proprietors come from the ranks of the middle agricultural castes. Distribution of other resources and access to political control follow the same pattern of caste-cum-class distinctions. Although this congruence is strong, there is a tendency for class formation to occur despite the importance of caste, especially in the cities, but also in rural areas.

In an analysis of class formation in India, anthropologist Harold A. Gould points out that a three-level system of stratification is taking shape across rural India. He calls the three levels Forward Classes (higher castes), Backward Classes in India (middle and lower castes), and Harijans (very low castes). Members of these groups share common concerns because they stand in approximately the same relationship to land and production—that is, they are large-scale farmers, small-scale farmers, and landless labourers.

Some of these groups are drawing together within regions across caste lines in order to work for political power and access to desirable resources. For example, since the late 1960s, some of the middle-ranking cultivating castes of northern India have increasingly cooperated in the political arena in order to advance their common agrarian and market-oriented interests. Their efforts have been spurred by competition with higher-caste landed elites.

In cities other groups have vested interests that crosscut caste boundaries, suggesting the possibility of forming classes in the future.

These groups include prosperous industrialists and entrepreneurs, who have made successful efforts to push the central government toward a probusiness stance; bureaucrats, who depend upon higher education rather than land to preserve their positions as civil servants; political office holders, who enjoy good salaries and perquisites of all kinds; and the military, who constitute one of the most powerful armed forces in the developing world.

Economically far below such groups are members of the menial under class, which is taking shape in both villages and urban areas. As the privileged elites move ahead, low-ranking menial workers remain economically insecure. Were they to join together to mobilize politically across lines of class and religion in recognition of their common interests, Gould observes, they might find power in their sheer numbers.

India's rapidly expanding economy has provided the basis for a fundamental change—the emergence of what eminent journalist Suman Dubey calls a "new vanguard" increasingly dictating India's political and economic direction. This group is India's new middle class—mobile, driven, consumer-oriented, and, to some extent, forward-looking.

Hard to define precisely, it is not a single stratum of society, but straddles town and countryside, making its voice heard everywhere. It encompasses prosperous farmers, white-collar workers, business people, military personnel, and myriad others, all actively working toward a prosperous life. Ownership of cars, televisions, and other consumer goods, reasonable earnings, substantial savings, and educated children (often fluent in English) typify this diverse group. Many have ties to kinsmen living abroad who have done very well.

The new middle class is booming, at least partially in response to a doubling of the salaries of some 4 million central government employees in 1986, followed by similar increases for state and district officers. Unprecedented liberalization and opening up of the economy in the 1980s and 1990s have been part of the picture.

There is no single set of criteria defining the middle class, and estimates of its numbers vary widely. The mid-range of figures presented in a 1992 survey article by analyst Suman Dubey is approximately 150 to 175 million—some 20 percent of the population—although other observers suggest alternative figures.

The middle class appears to be increasing rapidly. Once primarily urban and largely Hindu, the phenomenon of the consuming middle class is burgeoning among Muslims and prosperous villagers as well. According to V.A. Pai Panandikar, director of the Centre for Policy Research, New Delhi, cited by Dubey, by the end of the twentieth century 30 percent—some 300 million—of India's population will be middle class.

The middle class is bracketed on either side by the upper and lower echelons. Members of the upper class—around 1 percent of the population—are owners of large properties, members of exclusive clubs, and vacationers in foreign lands, and include industrialists, former maharajas, and top executives.

Below the middle class is perhaps a third of the population—ordinary farmers, tradespeople, artisans, and workers. At the bottom of the economic scale are the poor—estimated at 320 million, some 45 percent of the population in 1988—who live in inadequate homes without adequate food, work for pittances, have under-educated and often sickly children, and are the victims of numerous social inequities.

The Fringes of Indian Society

India's complex society includes some unique members—sadhus (holy men) and *hijras* (transvestite-eunuchs). Such people have voluntarily stepped outside the usual bonds of kinship and caste to join with others in castelike groups based upon personal—yet culturally shaped—inclinations.

In India of the 1990s, several hundred thousand Hindu and Jain sadhus and a few thousand holy women (*sadhvis*) live an ascetic life. They have chosen to wear ocher robes, or perhaps no clothing at all, to daub their skin with holy ash, to pray and meditate, and to wander from place to place, depending on the charity of others.

Most have given up affiliation with their caste and kin and have undergone a funeral ceremony for themselves, followed by a ritual rebirth into their new ascetic life. They come from all walks of life, and range from illiterate villagers to well-educated professionals. In their new lives as renunciants, they are devoted to spiritual concerns, yet each is affiliated with an ascetic order or subsect demanding strict adherence to rules of dress, itinerancy, diet, worship, and ritual pollution. Within each order, hierarchical concerns are exhibited in the subservience novitiates display to revered gurus. Further, at pilgrimage sites, different orders take precedence in accordance with an accepted hierarchy. Thus, although sadhus have foresworn many of the trappings of ordinary life, they have not given up the hierarchy and interdependence so pervasive in Indian society.

The most extreme sadhus, the *aghoris*, turn normal rules of conduct completely upside down. Rajesh and Ramesh Bedi, who have studied sadhus for decades, estimate that there may be fewer than fifteen *aghoris* in contemporary India. In the quest for great spiritual attainment, the *aghori* lives alone, like Lord Shiva, at cremation grounds, supping from a human skull bowl. He eats food provided only by low-ranking Sweepers and prostitutes, and in moments of religious fervour devours his own bodily wastes and pieces of human flesh torn from burning corpses. In violating the most basic taboos of the ordinary Hindu householder, the *aghori sadhu* graphically reminds himself and others of the correct rules of social behaviour.

2

Socio-economic Issues in India

Violence

Religious Violence: Constitutionally India is a secular state, but large-scale violence have periodically occurred in India since independence. In recent decades, communal tensions and religion-based politics have become more prominent, coinciding with a rise in Islamic terrorism. Although India is generally known for religious pluralism, the Hindutva ideology propagates that India belongs to the Hindus, and the Christians and the Muslims are "aliens", and many proponents of this ideology portray violence against Muslims and Christians as a form of "self-defence" against "invaders". The Hindutva ideology is at the core of Sangh Parivar politics and its expression in violence against religious minority.

Throughout the history of post-Independence India, both Muslim and Christian communities have faced repeated attacks from Hindu activists. As the Hindutva ideology has grown more powerful over the years, many Hindutva activists have partaken in riots against minority communities. Over the last decade, religious violence in India has increasingly become what academics believe to be organized pogroms to eliminate minority communities. Some state governments in India have been accused of not effectively prosecuting those who attack religious minorities. Major religious violent incidents include Ayodhya debate, Bombay Riots, 1993 Bombay bombings, 2002 Gujarat violence.

Although related, Hinduism and Hindutva are different. Hinduism is a religion while Hindutva is a political ideology. The Hindutva movement is not supported by majority of Hindus.

Some tolerant or "secular" Hindus use the term "Hindu Taliban" to describe the supporters of the Hindutva movement. Fukuoka Asian Culture Prize-winning Indian sociologist and cultural and political critic Ashis Nandy argued "Hindutva will be the end of Hinduism."

In Jammu and Kashmir, Since March 1990, estimates of between 250,000 to 300,000 pandits have migrated outside Kashmir due to persecution by Islamic fundamentalists in the largest case of ethnic cleansing since the partition of India. The proportion of Kashmiri Pandits in the Kashmir valley has declined from about 15% in 1947 to, by some estimates, less than 0.1% since the insurgency in Kashmir took on a religious and sectarian flavour. Many Kashmiri Pandits have been killed by Islamist terrorists in incidents such as the Wandhama massacre and the 2000 Amarnath pilgrimage massacre.

In recent years, there has been a sharp increase in violent attacks on Christians in India, often perpetrated by Hindu Nationalists. The acts of violence include arson of churches, re-conversion of Christians to Hinduism, distribution of threatening literature, burning of Bibles, raping of nuns, murder of Christian priests and destruction of Christian schools, colleges, and cemeteries. The Sangh Parivar and related organisations have stated that the violence is an expression of "spontaneous anger" of "vanvasis" against "forcible conversion" activities undertaken by missionaries, a claim described as "absurd" and rejected by scholars.

Between 1964 and 1996, thirty-eight incidents of violence against Christians were reported. In 1997, twentyfour such incidents were reported. In 2007 and 2008 there was a further flare up of tensions in Orissa, the first following the Christians' putting up a Pandhal in land traditionally used by Hindus and the second after the unprovoked murder of a Hindu Guru and four of his disciples while observing Janmashtami puja. This was followed by an attack on a 150-year-old church in Madhya Pradesh, and more attacks in Karnataka.

Terrorism in India

Terrorism in India is primarily attributable to Islamic, Sikh, Christian and Naxalite radical movements. The regions with long term terrorist activities today are Jammu and Kashmir, Mumbai, Central India (Naxalism) and Seven Sister States (independence and autonomy movements). In the past, the Punjab insurgency led to militant activities in the Indian state of Punjab as well as the national capital Delhi.

As of 2006, at least 232 of the country's 608 districts were afflicted, at differing intensities, by various insurgent and terrorist movements. In August 2008, National Security Advisor M K Narayanan has said that there are as many as 800 terrorist cells operating in the country.

Chronology of Major Incidents

Western India

Maharashtra: Mumbai has been the most preferred target for most terrorist organizations, primarily the separatist forces from Pakistan. Over the past few years a series of attacks including explosions in local trains in July 2006, to the most recent and unprecedented attacks of 26 November 2008, where two of the prime hotels, a landmark train station and a Jewish Chabad house, in south Mumbai, were attacked and sieged.

Terrorist attacks in Mumbai include:

- 12 March 1993-Series of 13 bombs go off killing 257
- 6 December 2002-Bomb goes off in a bus in Ghatkopar killing 2
- 27 January 2003-Bomb goes off on a bicycle in Vile Parle killing 1
- 14 March 2003-Bomb goes off in a train in Mulund killing 10
- 28 July 2003-Bomb goes off in a bus in Ghatkopar killing 4
- 25 August 2003-Two Bombs go off in cars near the Gateway of India and Zaveri Bazaar killing 50
- 11 July 2006-Series of seven bombs go off in trains killing 209
- 26 November 2008 to 29 November 2008-Coordinated series of attacks killing at least 172.

On 13 February 2010, a bomb explosion at the German Bakery in Pune killed fourteen people, and injured at least 60 more.

Insurgency in Jammu and Kashmir

Insurgency in Kashmir has existed in various forms, both on the Indian administrated side of the disputed territory of Jammu and Kashmir and Pakistan-administered Kashmir. Kashmir has been the target of a campaign of militancy by all sides in the conflict. Thousands of lives have been lost since 1989 due to the intensified insurgency 1989, a widespread armed insurgency started in Kashmir with the disputed rigged 1987 election ;since after 1987 rigged Sate elections some of the 'states legislative assembly' 'formed militant wings' later on after the disputed rigged election and furthermore that had started a catalyst for the insurgency Casualties include civilians, Kashmiri, and Indian Armed Forces and foreign militants.

The Inter-Services Intelligence of Pakistan has been accused by India of supporting and training mujahideen to fight in Jammu and Kashmir. While, International Human Right Groups have accused Indian army of committing grave Human rights violations in Indian-administered Jammu and Kashmir.

According to official figures released in Jammu and Kashmir assembly (Indian controlled), there were 3,400 disappearance cases and the insurgency has left more than 47,000 people dead till July 2009. However, the number of insurgency-related deaths in the state have fallen sharply since the start of a slow-moving peace process between India and Pakistan.

Militancy and Military

Though there had been instances of sporadic conflict in many regions for many years, intensified attacks occurred in the late 1980s, when the 1987 state elections were rigged although disputed ; had resulted in some of the 'states legislative assembly' 'formed militant wings' later on after the election forming and creating the catalyst for the insurgency. However Indian Government believes Mujahideen fighters from Afghanistan slowly infiltrated the region, with Pakistan's help, following the end of the Soviet-Afghan War in 1989. Since then, violence has increased significantly in strength. Many separatists have carried out attacks on local Hindus, Indian civilians and Indian army installations in response to what they see as Indian army occupation.

India frequently asserts that most of the separatist militant groups are based in Pakistan and Pakistan-administered Kashmir (also known as Azad Kashmir). Some like the All Parties Hurriyat Conference and the Jammu and Kashmir Liberation Front, demand an independent Kashmir. Other militant groups such as Lashkar-e-Toiba and Jaish-e-Mohammed favour a Pakistani-Kashmir. These groups have contacts with Taliban and Bin Laden. Both the organisations no longer operate under these names after they were banned by the Indian and Pakistani government, and by other countries including the US and UK. Of the larger militant groups, the Hizbul Mujahideen, a militant organisation based in Indian administered Kashmir, unlike other groups, has only kept its name. Despite casualties, the militants are still believed to number thousands rather than hundreds. Several new separatist organizations have also emerged. According to US Intelligence, Al-Qaeda also has a main base in Pakistani Kashmir and is helping to foment terrorism in Jammu and Kashmir. However India, Pakistan and the separatist organizations call this as hoax. Inspector General Police, Kashmir range also referred this as a hoax.

It is hard to determine the total number of casualties. According to a report by the Government of India in the year 2000, 31,000 Indian civilians had lost their lives due to the insurgency. Human rights groups and local NGOs put the total figure at more than 84,000. Militancy had reached its peak in 1994 when the region saw more than 6,043 incidents and has since declined. However, Kashmir continues to remain as the most volatile region in the world with an average of 2,500 incidents every year. According to an Indian estimate in 2005 there were about 2,000 militants in the Kashmir valley alone; 1,200 of them belong to the Hizbul Mujahideen. Not all Kashmiri separatists and militant organizations share the same ideology. Some fight in the name of religion, some are openly pro-Pakistan and some favour an independent Kashmir.

Due to the presence of these numerous anti-India insurgent groups India has been compelled to deploy massive number of troops in the Indian administered *Jammu and Kashmir* for the task of counter insurgency. New Delhi has never made an official count, but military analysts estimate that anywhere from 30,000 to nearly 33,000 security personnel are most likely involved, supported by thousands of Indian paramilitary groups such as the Rashtriya rifles, and the Romeo Force(all a part of Indian army). Stimson.org notes of the Indian Armed forces in Kashmir that:

Some reports estimate that India deploys approximately 400,000 combined army and paramilitary forces in Kashmir, most of which are stationed in the interior, 80,000 of which are deployed along the LoC. Pakistani forces deployed along the LoC are reported to number in the 40,000-50,000 range.

Times Online reports that around 250,000 Indian troops are stationed in Kashmir, while Pravda. RU, a widely read Russian News source notes that 350,000-600,000 troops may be deployed in Kashmir.

In a 'Letter to American People' written by Osama bin Laden in 2002 he stated that one of the reasons he was fighting America is because of her support to India on the Kashmir issue. In 2002 U.S. Secretary of Defence Donald Rumsfeld on a trip to Delhi suggested that Al-Qaeda was active in Kashmir. An investigation in 2002 unearthed evidence that Al-Qaeda and its affiliates were prospering in Pakistan-administered Kashmir with tacit approval of Pakistan's National Intelligence agency Inter-Services Intelligence Also US Intelligence agencies believe that Al-Qaeda and Taliban are helping organize a terror campaign in Kashmir to foment conflict between India and Pakistan. A 2001 report 'Pakistan's Role in the Kashmir Insurgency' of US Think tank RAND corporation noted that 'More intrinsically, the nature of the Kashmir conflict has been transformed from what was originally a secular, locally-based struggle (conducted via the Jammu Kashmir Liberation Front-JKLF) to one that is now largely carried out by foreign militants and rationalised in pan-Islamic religious terms.' In July 2006 Al-Qaeda stated that it had established a wing in Kashmir.

Militant Groups

Over the last two years, a militant group, Lashkar-e-Toiba has split into two factions: *Al Mansurin* and *Al Nasirin*. Another new group reported to have emerged is the Save Kashmir Movement. Harkat-ul-Mujahideen (formerly known as Harkat-ul-Ansar) and Lashkar-e-Toiba are believed to be operating from Muzaffarabad,

Azad Kashmir and Muridke, Pakistan respectively. Other less well known groups are the Freedom Force and Farzandan-e-Milat. A smaller group, Al-Badr, has been active in Kashmir for many years and is still believed to be functioning. All Parties Hurriyat Conference, an organization that uses moderate means to press for the rights of the Kashmiris, is often considered as the *mediator* between New Delhi and insurgent groups.

Not much is known about collaboration between the various groups, but most say they are members of an alliance known as the United Jihad Council (UJC). The two groups which India says were behind the December 2001 attack on the Indian parliament in New Delhi – known then as Jaish-e-Mohammed and Lashkar-e-Toiba are believed to be members of the *UJC*. India says that it was Jaish-e-Mohammed that attacked the Jammu and Kashmir State Assembly in Srinagar in October 2001. It is also known that the Jaish-e-Mohammed was responsible for the hijacking of Indian Airlines Flight IC-814 to Kandahar, which forced the Government of India to release Maulana Masood Azhar, the chief of the Jaish-e-Mohammed. Recruits from various parts of the world have been sent to Pakistan-administered Kashmir for training and advice.

India and Pakistan

A 1994 report by Human Rights Watch group lends support to both Indian and Pakistani charges. In support of Indian claims, it states that " There is compelling evidence that elements of the Pakistani government have sponsored a significant flow of arms to Kashmiri militants [from arms bazaars in the North West Frontier Province], as well as an extensive training program.

While in support of Pakistani claims, its states that "*the human rights record of the Indian government in Punjab and Kashmir is appalling. Abuses in Kashmir are clearly on the rise.*" The US government has also supported the claim that anti-India terror groups exist in India. India claims that there are also other Afghan, Egyptian, Yemeni and Bangladeshi terrorists active in Jammu and Kashmir. The Council on Foreign Relations states that Pakistan's military and Inter-Services Intelligence (ISI) both include personnel who sympathize with—or even assist—Islamist militants adding that "ISI has provided covert but well-documented support to terrorist groups active in Kashmir, among other outfits." In a recent infiltration bid, a Pakistan Army officer was shot dead, with India citing that this was clear and conclusive evidence of Pakistani involvement in the insurgency. The UN Security Council has also confirmed the existence of terrorist groups based in [Pakistani] Kashmir and urged Pakistan to crack down on terrorist groups which had been operating in Kashmir and killing innocent people.

Pakistan describes the separatists as "freedom fighters" and says that it supports their effort for the cause of the Kashmiris only morally and diplomatically. Pakistan however admits that there has been 'cross border infiltration of militants' across the Line of Control. In 2008, Pakistani President Asif Ali Zardari said India has never been a threat to Pakistan, and that militants in Kashmir are terrorists. In 2002, Pakistani president Pervez Musharraf tried to clamp down on the militants operating from Pakistan. India, however, claims that Islamabad supports these groups financially and military. Sources have maintained that Pakistan's intelligence organisation, Inter Services Intelligence, is the main supplier of funds and arms to these groups; a claim that Islamabad has dismissed.

According to the Indian news site Rediff.com, British Government had stated in 2002 that there is a 'clear link' between Pakistan's Inter Services Intelligence and three major militant groups.

An article in The Guardian had uncovered evidence that Pakistani militants were openly raising funds and training new recruits and that the ISI's Kashmir Cell was instrumental in funding and controlling the militant outfits. Richard Bennett, a British military and intelligence analyst states that the ISI has armed and trained generations of Islamist extremists and has directed many of their attacks both within the Kashmir and in India's major cities.

Indian sources also allege that there are between 2,600 to 3,000 militants receiving training in camps across Pakistan and Pakistan Administered Kashmir. During a peace summit between former Pakistani President Pervez Musharraf and Indian former-Prime Minister Atal Bihari Vajpayee in January 2004, Islamabad assured India that it would do everything possible to curb the activities any training camps on its territory. However, violence has continued in Kashmir despite a 3 year long peace process between India and

Pakistan. There were as many as 166 incidents in June 2005 alone in which some 201 people have died.

According to Indian sources there are about 37 training camps in Pakistan, 49 in Azad Kashmir and 22 in Afghanistan. The FBI also has produced images of camps operating in Pakistan. India claims that every year thousands of armed insurgents infiltrate into Indian-administered Kashmir and carry out attacks against Indian Security Forces and Kashmiri civilians. In June 2005, the Indian Army had foiled at least 72 infiltration attempts along the Line of Control in Kashmir. India alleges that despite the commitments made by Pervez Musharraf, Islamabad has done little to stop the training camps on its soil. According to India, most of the militants in Kashmir come from Pakistan, Afghanistan, Egypt, Yemen and Bangladesh.

Not all Kashmiri separatists and militant organizations share the same ideology. Some fight in the name of religion, some are pro-Pakistan and some favour an independent Kashmir. While the vast majority of militants are Muslims, one report indicated a minority of fighter (40 to 50) are Hindu militants who have either taken up arms or provided safe cover for militants.

Human Rights Violations

Human Rights Violations by India

A 1996 Human Rights Watch report accuses the Indian military and Indian-government backed paramilitaries of "committing serious and widespread human rights violations in Kashmir." One such alleged massacre occurred on January 6, 1993 in the town of Sopore. *TIME Magazine* described the incident as such: "In retaliation for the killing of one soldier, paramilitary forces rampaged through Sopore's market setting buildings ablaze and shooting bystanders. The Indian government pronounced the event 'unfortunate' and claimed that an ammunition dump had been hit by gunfire, setting off fires that killed most of the victims." In addition to this, there have been claims of disappearances by the police or the army in Kashmir by several human rights organizations.

Many human rights organizations such as Amnesty International and the Human Rights Watch (HRW) have condemned human rights abuses in Kashmir by Indians such as "extra-judicial executions", "disappearances", and torture; the "Armed Forces Special Powers Act", which "provides impunity for human rights abuses and fuels cycles of violence. The Armed Forces Special Powers Act (AFSPA) grants the military wide powers of arrest, the right to shoot to kill, and to occupy or destroy property in counterinsurgency operations. Indian officials claim that troops need such powers because the army is only deployed when national security is at serious risk from armed combatants. Such circumstances, they say, call for extraordinary measures." Human rights organizations have also asked Indian government to repeal the Public Safety Act, since "a detainee may be held in administrative detention for a maximum of two years without a court order." A 2008 report by the United Nations High Commissioner for Refugees determined that Indian Administered Kashmir, was only 'partly Free'.

Human Rights Violations by Pakistan

Human rights violations have also been reported in Pakistan-administered Kashmir. A 2-day conference on Gilgit Baltistan was held on April 8–9, 2008 at the European Parliament in Brussels under the auspices of International Kashmir Alliance. Here several members of the European Parliament (MEPs) expressed concern over the human rights violation in Gilgit Baltistan and urged the government of Pakistan to establish democratic institutions and rule of law in this area of northern Kashmir. Abdul Hamid Khan, Chairman Balawaristan National Front speaking at the same conference said "no democratically elected representative (from Gilgit Baltistan) was included when Karachi Agreement was signed between Pakistan and Muslim Conference leaders in 1949."

On April 25, 2007 European Union published a report entitled 'on Kashmir: present situation and future prospects'. Section 2 of the noted the absence of democracy in Gilgit Baltistan region and in section 32 deplored the human rights violations in this region. A 2008 report by the United Nations High Commissioner for Refugees determined that Pakistan administered Kashmir, was 'Not Free'. It also criticized the Pakistani Government saying 'The appropriation of land in the Northern Areas by non-Kashmiri migrants from elsewhere in Pakistan, with the tacit encouragement of the federal government and army, has led to dwindling economic opportunities for the local population and an increase in sectarian tension between the majority Shia Muslims and a growing number of Sunnis.' The same report determined that the Indian administered Jammu and Kashmir was 'Partly Free'. Parties like Balawaristan National Front are fighting for independence of Pakistan-administered Kashmir from Pakistan.

Human Rights Violations by Militants

Militants are accused of violence against the Kashmir populace. Thousands of civilian Kashmiris (Hindus, Sikhs, Buddhists and Muslims have been killed in Kashmir over the past 10 years by militants organisations. Human rights organizations put the figure of the number of civilians killed between Jan 1, 1999 and December 31, 1999 at about 9,733. According to official figures released in 2009, Indian Health and Family Welfare Minister Ghulam Nabi Azad, a Kashmiri himself and former chief minister of Jammu and Kashmir said 14,808 Muslims lost their lives while 1,748 Hindus and 115 Sikhs were killed during the rein of militancy in the state since 1989 by militants.

Tens of thousands of Kashmiri Pandits have emigrated as a result of the violence. Estimates of the displaced varies from 170,000 to 700,000. Thousands of Pandits have to move to Jammu because of terrorism. On February 15, 2006 United States Congressman Frank Pallone introduced a resolution in United States House of Representatives condemning the violation of Human rights of Kashmiri Pandits. He stated that an ethnic cleansing campaign was being run by Islamic terrorists to convert Kashmir into a Muslim state and 400,000 Kashmiri Pandits had either been murdered or displaced from their homes. The resolution was passed by the House (with Senate concurring) and stated that (1) Congress condemns the human rights violations committed against Kashmiri Pandits in the strongest terms (2) it is the sense of Congress that the Government of the Republic of India and the State Government of Jammu and Kashmir should take immediate steps to remedy the situation of the Kashmiri Pandits and should act to ensure the physical, political, and economic security of this embattled community; and (3) Congress supports mutual discussions between the Government of India and the State

Government of Jammu and Kashmir to achieve a peaceful and equitable solution to the Kashmiri conflict that is acceptable to the Kashmiri Pandits while ensuring that they are a part of the ongoing dialogue.

Recent Developments

Violent activities in the region declined in 2004. There are two main reasons for this: warming of relations between New Delhi and Pakistan which consequently lead to a ceasefire between the two countries in 2003 and the fencing of the LOC being carried out by the Indian Army. Moreover, coming under intense international pressure, Islamabad was compelled to take actions against the militants' training camps on its territory. In 2004, the two countries also agreed upon decreasing the number of troops present in the region.

Under pressure, Kashmiri militant organisations have made an offer for talks and negotiations with New Delhi, which was accepted by India. India's Border Security Force blamed the Pakistani military for providing cover-fire for the militants whenever they infiltrated into Indian territory from Pakistan. However, ever since the ceasefire has come into action, the militants have received no back-up from Pakistani Military, which has contributed significantly to the decline in *cross-border terrorism* in the state. Even the recently elected Pakistani President, Asif Ali Zardari admitted that the militants operating in Kashmir were indeed terrorists".

Northern and Northwestern India

Bihar

Existence of certain insurgent groups like the *CPI-ML, Peoples war* and *MCC,* is a major concern as they frequently attack local policemen and politicians. Poor governance and the law and order system in Bihar have helped increase the menace caused by the militias. The State has witnessed many massacres by these groups. The main victims of the violence by these groups are helpless people (including women, old and children) who are killed in massacres. The state police is ill equipped to take on the AK-47, AK-56 of the militants with their vintage 303 rifles. The militants have used landmines to kill ambush police parties as well.

The root cause of the militant activities in the state is huge disparity among different caste groups. After Independence, land reforms were supposed to be implemented, thereby giving the low caste and the poor a share in the lands which was till then held mostly by high caste people. However, due to caste based divisive politics in the state land reforms were never implemented properly. This led to growing sense of alienation among the low caste. Communist groups like CPI-ML, MCC and People's War took advantage of this and instigated the low caste people to take up arms against establishment which was seen as a tool in the hands of rich. They started taking up lands of rich by force killing the high caste people.

The high caste people resorted to use of force by forming their own army *Ranvir Sena* to take on the naxalites. The State witnessed a bloody period in which the groups tried to prove their supremacy by mass killings. The Police remained a mute witness to these killings as it lacked the means to take any action.

However now the Ranvir Sena has significantly weakened with the arrest of its top brass. The other groups are still active. There have been arrests in various parts of the country, particularly those made by the Delhi and Mumbai police in the recent past, indicating that extremist/terrorist outfits have been spreading their networks in this State. There is a strong suspicion that Bihar is also being used as a transit point by the small-arms, fake currency and drug dealers entering from Nepal and terrorists reportedly infiltrating through Nepal and Bangladesh. However, in recent years these attacks by various caste groups have come down with better government being practised.

Punjab

During 1970s, the Indian Green Revolution brought increased economic prosperity for the Sikh community in Punjab. This propensity kindled an age old fear in the Sikh community-that of being absorbed into the Hindu fold-and led to the rise of Sikh militants. The insurgency intensified during 1980s when the movement turned violent and the name Khalistan resurfaced and sought independence from the Indian Union. Led by Jarnail Singh Bhindranwale who, though not in favour in the creation of Khalistan but also was not against it, began using militancy to stress the movement's demands. Soon things turned bloody with India alleging that neighbouring Pakistan supported these militants, who, by 1983-84, had begun to enjoy widespread support among Sikhs.

In 1984, Operation Blue Star was conducted by the Indian government to stem out the movement. It involved an assault on the Golden Temple complex, which Sant Bhindranwale had fortified in preparation of an army assault. Indira Gandhi, India's then prime minister, ordered the military to storm the temple, who eventually had to use tanks.

After a seventy-four-hour firefight, the army successfully took control of the temple. In doing so, it damaged some portions of the Akal Takht, the Sikh Reference Library and some damaged to the Golden Temple itself. According to Indian government sources, eighty-three army personnel were killed and 249 injured. Militant casualties were 493 killed and eighty-six injured.

During same year, the assassination of Indira Gandhi by two Sikh bodyguards, believed to be driven by the Golden Temple affair, resulted in widespread anti-Sikh riots, especially in New Delhi. Following Operation Black Thunder in 1988, Punjab Police, first under Julio Ribeiro and then under KPS Gill, together with the Indian Army eventually succeeded in pushing the movement underground. In 1985, Sikh terrorists bombed an Air India flight from Canada to India, killing all 329 people on board Air India Flight 182. It is the worst terrorist act in Canada's history.

The ending of Sikh militancy and the desire for a Khalistan catalysed when the then-Prime Minister of Pakistan, Benazir Bhutto handed all intelligence material concerning Punjab militancy to the Indian government, as a goodwill gesture. The Indian government used that intelligence to put an end to those who were behind attacks in India and militancy.

The ending of overt Sikh militancy in 1993 led to a period of relative calm, punctuated by militant acts (*i.e.* the assassination of Punjab CM, Beant Singh in 1995) attributed to half a dozen or so operating Sikh militant organisations. These organisations include Babbar Khalsa International, Khalistan Commando Force, Khalistan Liberation Force and Khalistan Zindabad Force. Support for

Khalistan is still widespread among Sikh communities in Canada and the United Kingdom.

New Delhi

Three explosions went off in the Indian capital of New Delhi on 29 October 2005 which killed more than 60 people and injured at least 200 others. The high number of casualties made the bombings the deadliest attack in India of 2005. It was followed by 5 bomb blasts on 13 September 2008.

Delhi Security Summit

The Delhi summit on security took place on 14 February 2007 with the foreign ministers of China, India, and Russia meeting in Hyderabad House, Delhi, India to discuss terrorism, drug trafficking, reform of the United Nations, and the security situations in Afghanistan, Iran, Iraq, and North Korea.

Attack on Indian Parliament

Terrorists on 13 December 2001 attacked the Parliament of India resulting in a 45-minute gun battle in which 9 policemen and parliament staffer were killed. All the five terrorists were also killed by the security forces and were identified as Pakistani nationals. The attack took place around 11:40 am (IST), minutes after both Houses of Parliament had adjourned for the day. The suspected terrorists dressed in commando fatigues entered Parliament in a car through the VIP gate of the building. Displaying Parliament and Home Ministry security stickers, the vehicle entered the Parliament premises.

The terrorists set off massive blasts and used AK-47 rifles, explosives and grenades for the attack. Senior Ministers and over 200 Members of Parliament were inside the Central Hall of Parliament when the attack took place. Security personnel sealed the entire premises which saved many lives.

Uttar Pradesh

Ayodhya Crisis : The long simmering Ayodhya crisis finally culminated in a terrorist attack on the site of the 16th century Babri Masjid-Demolished Ancient Masjid in Ayodhya on 5 July 2005. Following the two-hour gunfight between Lashkar-e-Toiba terrorists based in Pakistan and Indian police, in which six terrorists were killed, opposition parties called for a nationwide strike with the country's leaders condemning the attack, believed to have been masterminded by Dawood Ibrahim.

Varanasi Blasts: A series of blasts occurred across the Hindu holy city of Varanasi on 7 March 2006. Fifteen people are reported to have been killed and as many as 101 others were injured. No-one has accepted responsibility for the attacks, but it is speculated that the bombings were carried out in retaliation of the arrest of a Lashkar-e-Toiba agent in Varanasi earlier in February 2006.

On 5 April 2006 the Indian police arrested six Islamic militants, including a cleric who helped plan bomb blasts. The cleric is believed to be a commander of a banned Bangladeshi Islamic militant group, Harkatul Jihad-al Islami and is linked to the Inter-Services Intelligence, the Pakistani spy agency.

Northeastern India: Northeastern India consists 7 states (also known as *the seven sisters*): Assam, Meghalaya, Tripura, Arunachal Pradesh, Mizoram, Manipur, and Nagaland. Tensions exists between these states and the central government as well as amongst the tribal people, who are natives of these states, and migrant peoples from other parts of India. The states have accused New Delhi of ignoring the issues concerning them. It is this feeling which has led the natives of these states to seek greater participation in self-governance. There are existing territorial disputes between Manipur and Nagaland.

There is a rise of insurgent activities and regional movements in the northeast, especially in the states of Assam, Nagaland, Mizoram and Tripura. Most of these organizations demand independent state status or increased regional autonomy and sovereignty. North Eastern region tension have eased off-late with Indian and state government's concerted effort to raise the living standards of the people in these regions. However, militancy still exists in this region of India supported by external sources.

Nagaland: The first and perhaps the most significant insurgency was in Nagaland from the early 1950s until it was finally quelled in the early 1980s through a mixture of repression and co-optation. The *National Socialist Council of Nagaland-Isak-Muivah* (NSCN-IM), demands an independent Nagaland and has carried out several attacks on Indian military installations in the region. According to government officials, 599 civilians, 235 security forces and 862 terrorists have lost their lives between 1992 and 2000.

On 14 June 2001, a cease-fire agreement was signed between the Government of India and the NSCN-IM which had received widespread approval and support in Nagaland. Terrorist outfits such as the Naga National Council-Federal (NNC-F) and the National Council of Nagaland-Khaplang (NSCN-K) also welcomed the development. Certain neighbouring states, especially Manipur, raised serious concerns over the cease-fire. They feared that NSCN would continue insurgent activities in its state and demanded New Delhi scrap the ceasefire deal and renew military action. Despite the cease-fire the NSCN has continued its insurgency.

Assam: After Nagaland, Assam is the most volatile state in the region. Beginning 1979, the indigenous people of Assam demanded that the illegal immigrants who had emigrated from Bangladesh to Assam be detected and deported. The movement lead by All Assam Students Union began non-violently with satyagraha, boycotts, picketing and courting arrests.

Those protesting frequently came under police action. In 1983 an election was conducted which was opposed by the movement leaders. The election lead to widespread violence. The movement finally ended after the movement leaders signed an agreement (called Assam Accord) with the central government in 15 August 1985.

Under the provisions of this accord, anyone who entered the state illegally between January 1966 and March 1971 were allowed to remain but were disenfranchised for ten years, while those who entered after 1971 faced expulsion. A November 1985 amendment to the Indian citizenship law allows non citizens who entered Assam between 1961 and 1971 to have all the rights of citizenship except the right to vote for a period of ten years.

New Delhi also gave special administration autonomy to the Bodos in the state. However, the Bodos demanded for a separate Bodoland which led to a clash between the Bengalis, the Bodos and the Indian military resulting in hundreds of deaths.

There are several organizations which advocate the independence of Assam. The most prominent of which is the

ULFA (United Liberation Front of Assam). Formed in 1971, the ULFA has two main goals, the independence of Assam and the establishment of a socialist government.

The ULFA has carried out several terrorist attacks in the region targeting the Indian Military and non-combatants. The group assassinates political opponents, attacks police and other security forces, blasts railroad tracks, and attacks other infrastructure facilities. The ULFA is believed to have strong links with *Nationalist Socialist Council of Nagaland (NSCN),* Maoists and the Naxalites.

It is also believed that they carry out most of their operations from the Kingdom of Bhutan. Because of ULFA's increased visibility, the Indian government outlawed the group in 1986 and declared Assam a troubled area. Under pressure from New Delhi, Bhutan carried a massive operation to drive out the ULFA militants from its territory.

Backed by the Indian Army, Thimphu was successful in killing more than a thousand terrorists and extraditing many more to India while sustaining only 120 casualties. The Indian military undertook several successful operations aimed at countering future ULFA terrorist attacks, but the ULFA continues to be active in the region. In 2004, the ULFA targeted a public school in Assam killing 19 children and 5 adults.

Assam remains the only state in the northeast where terrorism is still a major issue. The Indian Military was successful in dismantling terrorist outfits in other areas, but have been criticized by human rights groups for allegedly using harsh methods when dealing with terrorists. On 18 September 2005, a soldier was killed in Jiribam, Manipur, near the Manipur-Assam border by members of the ULFA.

Tripura: Tripura witnessed a surge in terrorist activities in the 1990s. New Delhi blamed Bangladesh for providing a safe haven to the insurgents operating from its territory. The area under control of the *Tripura Tribal Areas Autonomous District Council* was increased after a tripartite agreement between New Delhi, the state government of Tripura, and the Council. The government has since been brought the movement under control though certain rebellious factions still linger.

Manipur: In Manipur, militants formed an organization known as the *People's Liberation Army.* Their main goal was to unite the Meitei tribes of Burma and establish an independent state of Manipur. However, the movement was thought to have been suppressed after a fierce clash with Indian security forces in the mid 1990s.

On 18 September 2005, six separatist rebels were killed in fighting between Zomi Revolutionary Army and Zomi Revolutionary Front in the Churachandpur District.

On 20 September 2005, 14 Indian soldiers were ambushed and killed by 20 rebels from the Kanglei Yawol Kanna Lup (KYKL) terrorist organization, armed with AK-56 rifles, in the village of Nariang, 22 miles southwest of Manipur's capital Imphal. "Unidentified rebels using automatic weapons ambushed a road patrol of the army's Gorkha Rifles killing eight on the spot," said a spokesman for the Indian government.

Mizoram: The *Mizo National Front* fought for over 2 decades with the Indian Military in an effort to gain independence. As in neighbouring states the insurgency was quelled by force.

South India

Karnataka: Karnataka is considerably less affected by terrorism in spite of having many places of historical importance and the IT hub of India, Bengaluru. However, recently Naxal activity has been increasing in the Western Ghats. Also, a few attacks have occurred, major ones including an attack on IISc on 28 December 2005 and serial blasts in Bengaluru on 26 July 2008.

Andhra Pradesh: Andhra Pradesh is one of the few southern states affected by terrorism, although of a far different kind and on a much smaller scale. The terrorism in Andhra Pradesh stems from the *People's War Group* or PWG, popularly known as Naxalites.

The 'PWG, has been operating in India for over two decades with most of its operations in the Telangana region in Andhra Pradesh. The group is also active in Orissa and Bihar. Unlike the Kashmiri insurgents and ULFA, PWG is a Maoist terrorist organisation and communism is one of its primary goals.

Having failed to capture popular support in the elections, they resorted to violence as a means to voice their opinions. The group targets Indian Police, multinational companies and other influential institutions in the name of the communism. PWG has also targeted senior government officials, including the attempted assassination of former Andhra Pradesh Chief Minister Chandrababu Naidu.

It reportedly has a strength of 800 to 1,000 well armed militiants and is believed to have close links with the Maoists in Nepal and the LTTE of Sri Lanka. According to the Indian government, on an average, more than 60 civilians, 60 naxal rebels and a dozen policemen are killed every year because of PWG led insurgency. Also one of the major terrorist attack is 25 August 2007 Hyderabad Bombing.

Tamil Nadu: Tamil Nadu had LTTE *Liberation Tigers of Tamil Eelam* militants operating in state Tamil Nadu up until the assassination of former Prime Minister Rajiv Gandhi. LTTE had given many speeches in state Tamil Nadu led by Velupillai Prabhakaran, Tamilselvan and other Eelam members. Tamil Tigers, now a banned organisation, have been receiving many donations and support from India in the past. The Tamil Nadu Liberation Army, a militant Tamil movement in India that have ties to LTTE. Tamil Nadu also faced terrorist attacks orchestrated by Muslim funadamentalists.

Air India Flight 182

Air India Flight 182 was an Air India flight operating on the Montreal-London-Delhi-Bombay route. On 23 June 1985 the Boeing 747-237B operating on the route was bombed over Irish airspace, killing all on board. Until 11 September 2001, the Air India bombing was the single deadliest terrorist attack involving aircraft. It remains to this day the largest mass murder in Canadian history. This act was taken responsibility by Babbar Khalsa known as being a hard-core terrorist group which was and still is banned in Canada, United States, United Kingdom, Germany, and India in 1985.

The incident occurred within an hour of the Narita Airport Bombing. The plane, a Boeing 747-237B named Emperor Kanishka exploded at an altitude of 31,000 feet (9500 m), crashing into the Atlantic Ocean killing all 329 people on board, of whom 280 were Canadian citizens and 22 were Indian nationals

The regions with long term terrorist activities today are Jammu and Kashmir, Central India (Naxalism) and Seven Sister States (independence and autonomy movements). In the past, the Punjab insurgency led to militant activities in the Indian state of Punjab as well as the national capital Delhi. As of 2006, at least 232 of the country's 608 districts were afflicted, at differing in tensities, by various insurgent and terrorist movements.

Terrorism in India has often been alleged to be sponsored by Pakistan. After most acts of terrorism in India, many journalists and politicians accuse Pakistan's intelligence agency, the Inter-Services Intelligence of playing a role. Recently, both the US and Afghanistan have accused Pakistan of carrying out terrorist acts in Afghanistan.

Naxalism

Naxalism is an informal name given to communist groups that were born out of the Sino-Soviet split in the Indian communist movement. Ideologically they belong to various trends of Maoism. Initially the movement had its centre in West Bengal. In recent years, they have spread into less developed areas of rural central and eastern India, such as Chhattisgarh and Andhra Pradesh through the activities of underground groups like the Communist Party of India (Maoist). The CPI (Maoist) and some other Naxal factions are considered terrorists by the Government of India and various state governments in India.

Press Freedom

According to the estimates of Reporters Without Borders, India ranks 120th worldwide in press freedom index (press freedom index for India is 39.33 for 2007). The Indian Constitution, while not mentioning the word "press", provides for *"the right to freedom of speech and expression"*. However this right is subject to restrictions under subclause (2), whereby this freedom can be restricted for reasons of "sovereignty and integrity of India, the security of the State, friendly relations with foreign States, public order, preserving decency, preserving morality, in relation to contempt of court, defamation, or incitement to an offence". Laws such as the Official Secrets Act and Prevention of Terrorism Act (PoTA) have been used to limit press freedom. Under PoTA, person could be detained for up to six months for being in contact with a terrorist or terrorist group. PoTA was repealed in 2006, but the Official Secrets Act 1923 continues.

LGBT Rights

Homosexuality is criminalised in India by interpretations of the ambiguous Section 377 of the Indian Penal Code (IPC). The punishment ranges from ten years to lifelong imprisonment. The law has been used to harass HIV/AIDS prevention efforts, as well as sex workers, men who have sex with men, and other groups at risk of the disease. Scott Long, director of Lesbian, Gay, Bisexual, and Transgender Rights Program at Human Rights Watch sent a letter to Indian Prime Minister Manmohan Singh regarding the arrests of 4 men in 2006 in Lucknow and another 4 in 2001. However, in most areas of India, this law is very rarely enforced.

The People's Union for Civil Liberties has published two reports of the rights violations faced by sexual minorities and, in particular, transsexuals (hijras and kothis) in India. Indian state of Tamil Nadu has made significant effort in integrating transgenders into the mainstream society.

Overpopulation

India suffers from the problem of overpopulation. Though India ranks second in population, it ranks 33 in terms of population density below countries such as The Netherlands, South Korea and Japan. To cure this problem, Indira Gandhi, Prime Minister of India, had implemented a forced sterilization programme in the early 1970s but failed. Officially, men with two children or more had to submit to sterilization, but many unmarried young men, political opponents and ignorant, poor men were also believed to have been sterilized.

This program is still remembered and criticized in India, and is blamed for creating a wrong public aversion to family planning, which hampered Government programmes for decades. It is believed that family planning was also hampered due to Indian people's infatuation for more and more children. Rather than having a small and happy family, people of almost all religions in India (regardless of whether they are educated or not) try to produce more and more children, and this infatuation for children puts burden on them as well as the whole nation, financially as well as otherwise.

Economic Issues

Poverty

One-third of India's population (roughly equivalent to the entire population of the United States) lives below the poverty line and India is home to one-third of the world's poor people.

Though the middle class has gained from recent positive economic developments, India suffers from substantial poverty. According to the new World Bank's estimates on poverty based on 2005 data, India has 456 million people, 41.6% of its population, living below the new international poverty line of $1.25 (PPP) per day. The World Bank further estimates that 33% of the global poor now reside in India. Moreover, India also has 828 million people, or 75.6% of the population living below $2 a day, compared to 72.2% for Sub-Saharan Africa.

Wealth distribution in India is fairly uneven, with the top 10% of income groups earning 33% of the income. Despite significant economic progress, 1/4 of the nation's population earns less than the government-specified poverty threshold of $0.40/day. Official figures estimate that 27.5% of Indians lived below the national poverty line in 2004-2005. A 2007 report by the state-run National Commission for Enterprises in the Unorganised Sector (NCEUS) found that 25% of Indians, or 236 million people, lived on less than 20 rupees per day with most working in "informal labour sector with no job or social security, living in abject poverty."

Corruption

Corruption is widespread in India. India is ranked 72 out of a 179 countries in Transparency International's Corruption Perceptions Index, although its score has improved consistently from 2.7 in 2002 to 3.5 in 2007. Corruption has taken the role of a pervasive aspect of Indian politics and bureaucracy.

In India, corruption takes the form of bribes, evasion of tax and exchange controls, embezzlement, etc. A 2005 study done by Transparency International (TI) India found that more than 50% had firsthand experience of paying bribe or peddling influence to get a job done in a public office. The chief economic consequences of corruption are the loss to the exchequer, an unhealthy climate for investment and an increase in the cost of government-subsidised services. The TI India study estimates the monetary value of petty corruption in 11 basic services provided by the government, like education, health care, judiciary, police, etc., to be around Rs.21,068 crores. India still ranks in the bottom quartile of developing nations in terms of the ease of doing business, and compared to China and other lower developed Asian nations, the average time taken to secure the clearances for a startup or to invoke bankruptcy is much greater.

Gender Inequality

Sociologically the word gender refers to the socio-cultural definition of man and woman, the way societies distinguish men and women and assign them social roles. The distinction between sex and gender was introduced to deal with the general tendency to attribute women's subordination to their anatomy. For ages it was believed that the different characteristics, roles and status accorded to women and men in society are determined by sex, that they are natural and therefore not changeable. Gender is seen closely related to the roles and behaviour assigned to women and men based on their sexual differences. As soon as a child is born families and society begin the process of gendering. The birth of the son is celebrated, the birth of a daughter filled with pain; sons are showered with love, respect, better food and proper health care. Boys are encouraged to be tough and outgoing; girls are encouraged to be home bound and shy.

All these differences are gender differences and they are created by society. Gender inequality is therefore a form of inequality which is distinct from other forms of economic and social inequalities. It dwells not only outside the household but also centrally within it. It stems not only from pre-existing differences in economic endowments between women and men but also from pre-existing gendered social norms and social perceptions. Gender inequality has adverse impact on development goals as reduces economic growth. It hampers the overall well being because blocking women from participation in social, political and economic activities can adversely affect the whole society. Many developing countries including India have displayed gender inequality in education, employment and health. It is common to find girls and women suffering from high mortality rates. There are vast differences in education level of two sexes. India has witnessed gender inequality from its early history due to its socioeconomic and religious practices that resulted in a wide gap between the position of men and women in the society.

The origin of the Indian idea of appropriate female behaviour can be traced to the rules laid down by Manu in 200 B.C.: "by a young girl, by a young woman, or even by an aged one, nothing must be done independently, even in her own house". "In childhood a female must be subject to her father, in youth to her husband, when her lord is dead to her sons; a woman must never be independent." Women's lives are shaped by customs that are centuries old. "May you be the mother of a hundred sons" is a common Hindu wedding blessing. Statistics reveal that in India males significantly outnumber females and this imbalance has increased over time.

The sex ratio according to 2001 census report stands at 933 per 1000 males. Out of the total population, 120 million are women who live in abject poverty. The maternal mortality rate in rural areas is among the world's highest. From a global perspective India accounts for 19% of all live births and 27% of all maternal deaths. The deaths of young girls in India exceed those of young boys by over 300,000 each year and every 6th infant death is specifically due to gender discrimination. Women face discrimination right from the childhood.

Gender disparities in nutrition are evident from infancy to adulthood. In fact, gender has been the most statistically significant determinant of malnutrition among young children and malnutrition is a frequent, direct or underlying, cause of death among girls below age 5. Girls are breast-fed less frequently and for a shorter duration in infancy. In childhood and adulthood, males are fed first and better. Adult women consume approximately 1,000 fewer calories per day than men according to one estimate. Nutritional deprivation has two major consequences for women: they never reach their full growth potential, and suffer from anemia, which are risk factors in pregnancy.

This condition complicates childbearing and results in women and infant deaths, and low birth weight infants. The tradition also requires that women eat last and least throughout their lives even when pregnant and lactating. Malnourished women give birth to malnourished children, perpetuating the cycle. Women receive less health care facilities than men. A primary way that parents discriminate against their girl children is through neglect during illness. As an adult they tend to be less likely to admit that they are sick and may wait until their sickness has progressed far before they seek help or help is sought for them. Many women in rural areas die in childbirth due to easily preventable complications. Women's social training to tolerate suffering and their reluctance to be examined by male personnel are additional constraints in their getting adequate health care.

The Constitution of India ensures gender equality in its preamble as a fundamental right but also empowers the state to adopt measures of positive discrimination in favour of women by ways of legislation and policies. India has also ratified various international conventions and human rights forums to secure equal rights of women, such as ratification of Convention on elimination of all forms of discrimination against women in 1993. Women have been finding place in local governance structures, overcoming gender biases. Over one million women have been elected to local panchayats as a result of 1993 amendment to the Indian Constitution requiring that 1/3rd of the elected seats to the local governing bodies be reserved for women. The passing of Pre-natal Diagnostic Tech Act in 1994 also is a step in removing gender discrimination.

This Act seeks to end sex-determination tests and female foeticide and prohibits doctors from conducting such procedures for the specific purpose of determining the sex of the fetus. The Government also announced the National policy for empowerment of women in 2001 to bring out advancement, development and empowerment of women. The Government has also drawn up a draft National policy for the empowerment of women which is a policy statement outlining the state's response to problems of gender discrimination. As persistent gender inequalities continue we need to rethink concepts and strategies for promoting women's dignity and rights. UN Secretary General Kofi Annan has stated,

"Gender equality is more than a goal in itself. It is a precondition for meeting the challenge of reducing poverty, promoting sustainable development and building good governance." There is a need for new kinds of institutions, incorporating new norms and rules that support equal and just relations between women and men. Today women are organizing themselves to meet the challenges that are hampering their development.

Child Labour in India

Millions of children in today's world undergo the worst forms of child labour which includes Child Slavery, Child prostitution, Child Trafficking, Child Soldiers. In modern era of material and technological advancement, children in almost every country are being callously exploited. The official figure of child labourers world wide is 13 million. But the actual number is much higher. Of the estimated 250 million children between the ages of 5 and 14 who are economically active, some 50 million to 60 million between the ages of 5 and 11 are engaged in intolerable forms of labour. Among the 10 to 14year-old children the working rate is 41.3 percent in Kenya, 31.4 percent in Senegal, 30.1 percent in Bangladesh, 25.8 percent in Nigeria, 24 percent in Turkey, 17.7 percent in Pakistan, 16.1 percent in Brazil, 14.4 percent in India, 11.6 percent in China.

ILO estimated that 250 million children between 5 and 14 work for a living, and over 50 million children under age twelve work in hazardous circumstances. United Nations estimate that there were 20 million bonded child labourers worldwide. Based on reliable estimates, at least 700,000 persons to 2 million, especially girls and children, are trafficked each year across international borders. Research suggests that the age of the children involved is decreasing. Most are poor children between the ages of 13 and 18, although there is evidence that very young children even babies, are also caught up in this horrific trade. They come from all parts of the world. Some one million children enter the sex trade, exploited by people or circumstances. At any one time, more than 300,000 children under 18-girls and boys-are fighting as soldiers with government armed forces and armed opposition groups in more than 30 countries worldwide. ILO estimates that domestic work is the largest employment category of girls under age 16 in the world. India has the dubious distinction of being the nation with the largest number of child labourers in the world. The child labours endure miserable and difficult lives. They earn little and struggle to make enough to feed themselves and their families. They do not go to school; more than half of them are unable to learn the barest skills of literacy. Poverty is one of the main reasons behind this phenomenon. The unrelenting poverty forces the parents to push their young children in all forms of hazardous occupations. Child labour is a source of income for poor families. They provide help in household enterprises or of household chores in order to free adult household members for economic activity elsewhere. In some cases, the study found that a child's income accounted for between 34 and 37 percent of the total household income.

In India the emergence of child labour is also because of unsustainable systems of landholding in agricultural areas and caste system in the rural areas. Bonded labour refers to the phenomenon of children working in conditions of servitude in order to pay their debts. The debt that binds them to their employer is incurred not by the children themselves but by their parent. The creditors cum employers offer these loans to destitute parents in an effort to secure the labour of these children. The arrangements between the parents and contracting agents are usually informal and unwritten. The number of years required to pay off such a loan is indeterminate. The lower castes such as dalits and tribal make them vulnerable groups for exploitation.

The environmental degradation and lack of employment avenues in the rural areas also cause people to migrate to big cities. On arrival in overcrowded cities the disintegration of family units takes place through alcoholism, unemployment or disillusionment of better life etc. This in turn leads to emergence of street children and child workers who are forced by their circumstances to work from the early age. The girls are forced to work as sex-workers or beggars. A large number of girls end up working as domestic workers on low wages and unhealthy living conditions.

Some times children are abandoned by their parents or sold to factory owners. The last two decades have seen tremendous growth of export based industries and mass production factories utilizing low technologies. They try to maintain competitive positions through low wages and low labour standards. The child labourers exactly suit their requirements. They use all means to lure the parents into giving their children on pretext of providing education and good life. In India majority of children work in industries, such as cracker making, diamond polishing, glass, brass-ware, carpet weaving, bangle making, lock making and mica cutting to name a few. 15% of the 100,000 children work in the carpet industry of Uttar Pradesh. 70-80% of the 8,000 to 50,000 children work in the glass industry in Ferozabad. In the unorganized sector child labour is paid by piece-by-piece rates that result in even longer hours for very low pay.

Inadequate schools, a lack of schools, or even the expense of schooling leaves some children with little else to do but work. The attitudes of parents also contribute to child labour; some parents feel that children should work in order to develop skills useful in the job market, instead of taking advantage of a formal education. From the time of its independence, India has committed itself to be against child labour. Article 24 of the Indian constitution clearly states that "No child below the age of fourteen years shall be employed to work in any factory or mine or employed in any hazardous employment" The Bonded Labour System Act of 1976 fulfills the Indian Constitution's directive of ending forced labour A Plethora of additional protective legislation has been put in place. There are distinct laws governing child labour in factories in commercial establishments, on plantations and in apprenticeships.

There are laws governing the use of migrant labour and contract labour. A recent law The Child Labour (Prohibition and Regulation law) of 1986 designates a child as a person who has not completed their 14th year of age. It purports to regulate the hours and the conditions of child workers and to prohibit child workers in certain enumerated hazardous industries. However there is neither blanket prohibition on the use of child labour, nor any universal minimum age set for child workers. All of the policies that the Indian government has in place are in accordance with the Constitution of India, and all support the eradication of Child Labour. The problem of child labour still remains even though all of these policies are existent. Enforcement is the key aspect that is lacking in the government's efforts.

Child labour is a global problem. If child labour is to be eradicated, the governments and agencies and those responsible for enforcement need to start doing their jobs. The most important thing is to increase awareness and keep discussing ways and means to check this problem. We have to decide whether we are going to take up the problem head-on and fight it any way we can or leave it to the adults who might not be there when things go out of hand.

Literacy in India

Literacy is an effective instrument for social and economic development and national integration. It is defined in Census operations, as the ability to read and write with understanding in any language. Any formal education or minimum educational standard is not necessary to be considered literate. The latest census report (2001) reveal that at the beginning of new millennium literacy rate in India stands at 65.38% with male literacy level at 75.85% and female literacy level at 54.16%. There has been only marginal increase in literacy level from the last census in 1991 (literacy level was 52.2%).

The pace of progress in literacy rates, as revealed by decennial censuses, is very slow in India. Between 1961 and 1991, a span of thirty years, literacy rate has gone up by a mere 23.9 percentage points, from 28.3 in 1961 to 52.2 in 1991. From 1991 to 2001 there is 13.36% increase. However the literacy scenario in India is characterized by wide inequalities among different sections of the population. The female literacy rate is still low in comparison to male population. Country's half of the female population is still illiterate even after so many years of independence. No less disturbing is the rural-urban disparity in literacy rates that again differ by ever a wider margin the disparity has persisted over the years.

The scheduled castes and scheduled tribes form two other specially disadvantaged population groups in India and disparity in their case too is equally wide and persisting. Finally, there again exists a wide disparity among the various regions/states in India vis-a-vis their literacy rates. At the top of the hierarchy, lies the state of Kerala that has an exceptionally high literacy rate of 90.92 %. This is basically because of strong social movements in this state even during the pre-independence period. For Bihar (the least literate state) the rate is merely 47.53 %.In Bihar, Kishanganj district has the lowest literacy rate (31% for males and 18.49% for females).

When illiteracy begins to impinge upon livelihoods issues it becomes critical. Illiteracy often results in missed opportunities. Women usually receive lower wages than men. In Kishanganj district of Bihar women and girls work in the tea gardens and brickklins but as they are illiterate they often get exploited and do not get proper wages. Both men and women often earn less than the minimum wage but they are often unaware of the Minimum Wages Act. Illiteracy and lack of information can adversely affect human rights. In an era when technology has shrunk the world into a global village and when information has been brought to the fingertips of a small section of society, it would be unfortunate if the masses were denied access to basic information due to the inability to read and write.

During the first Five Year Plan, the program of Social Education, inclusive of literacy, was introduced as part of the Community Development Program 1952.

The National Policy on Education in 1968 not only endorsed the recommendations of the Education Commission but also reiterated the significance of universal literacy and developing adult and continuing education as matters of priority. While the formal elementary education program was supplemented by a Non-formal Education system, it was also decided to undertake Adult Literacy programs culminating in the Total Literacy mission approach.

(a) A multi-pronged approach of universalization of elementary education and universal adult literacy has been adopted for achieving total literacy.

(b) A systematic program of non-formal education in the educationally backward states.

(c) The National Literacy Mission that aims at making 100 million adults literate.

The major thrust of these programs is on promotion of literacy among women, Scheduled Castes and Scheduled Tribes particularly in the rural areas. The Adult Education Program consists of three components: basic literacy (including numeracy), functionality and civic awareness. The third component is obviously literacy. The National Adult Education Program (NAEP) was inaugurated on October 2, 1978. Then came the National Literacy Mission (NLM). In 1989, the district-based Total Literacy Campaigns (TLC) emerged as a program strategy for the National Literacy Mission against this background. In the budget of 1999-2000, the total allocation of resources (both Plan and non-plan) for the four programs of Elementary Education, Operation Black board, Non-formal education and Adult Education was 3037, 400, 350 and 113.4 crores respectively. The Total Literacy campaign districts had been set the optimistic goal of achieving 80% literacy amongst the target age-group of 15-35 years. Now Sarva Shikha Abiyan is doing rounds in all the districts in most of the states for which there is huge fund allocation under 9th and 10th Five year plans.

In spite of the enormous expansion of adult education, nonformal and elementary education in India, the problem of illiteracy has been lingering on. It is both colossal and complex given the size of the country, its huge population, wide regional and gender disparities, economic and other cultural factors such as poverty, communalism, casteism etc. It needs action from people, communities Government agencies, NGOs and international organizations such as UN bodies to totally eradicate illiteracy from India.

Drug Abuse in India

June 26 is celebrated as International Day against Drug Abuse and Illicit Trafficking every year. It is an exercise undertaken by the world community to sensitize the people in general and the youth in particular, to the menace of drugs. The picture is grim if the world statistics on the drugs scenario is taken into account. With a turnover of around $500 billions, it is the third largest business in the world, next to petroleum and arms trade. About 190 million people all over the world consume one drug or the other. Drug addiction causes immense human distress and the illegal production and distribution of drugs have spawned crime and violence worldwide. Today, there is no part of the world that is free from the curse of drug trafficking and drug addiction. Millions of drug addicts, all over the world, are leading miserable lives, between life and death.

India too is caught in this vicious circle of drug abuse, and the numbers of drug addicts are increasing day by day. According to a UN report, One million heroin addicts are registered in India, and unofficially there are as many as five million. What started off as casual use among a minuscule population of high-income group youth in the metro has permeated to all sections of society. Inhalation of heroin alone has given way to intravenous drug use, that too in combination with other sedatives and painkillers. This has increased the intensity of the effect, hastened the process of addiction and complicated the process of recovery.

Cannabis, heroin, and Indian-produced pharmaceutical drugs are the most frequently abused drugs in India. Cannabis products, often called charas, bhang, or ganja, are abused throughout the country because it has attained some amount of religious sanctity because of its association with some Hindu deities. The International Narcotics Control Board in its 2002 report released in Vienna pointed out that in India persons addicted to opiates are shifting their drug of choice from opium to heroin. The pharmaceutical products containing narcotic drugs are also increasingly being abused. The intravenous injections of analgesics like dextropropoxphene etc. are also reported from many states, as it is easily available at 1/10th the cost of heroin. The codeine-based cough syrups continue to be diverted from the domestic market for abuse.

Drug abuse is a complex phenomenon, which has various social, cultural, biological, geographical, historical and economic aspects. The disintegration of the old joint family system, absence of parental love and care in modern families where both parents are working, decline of old religious and moral values etc. lead to a rise in the number of drug addicts who take drugs to escape hard realities of life. Drug use, misuse or abuse is also primarily due to the nature of the drug abused, the personality of the individual and the addict's immediate environment. The processes of industrialization, urbanization and migration have led to loosening of the traditional methods of social control rendering an individual vulnerable to the stresses and strains of modern life. The fast changing social milieu, among other factors, is mainly contributing to the proliferation of drug abuse, both of traditional and of new psychoactive substances. The introduction of synthetic drugs and intravenous drug use leading to HIV/AIDS has added a new dimension to the problem, especially in the Northeast states of the country.

Drug abuse has led to a detrimental impact on the society. It has led to increase in the crime rate. Addicts resort to crime to pay for their drugs. Drugs remove inhibition and impair judgment egging one on to commit offences. Incidence of eve-teasing, group clashes, assault and impulsive murders increase with drug abuse. Apart from affecting the financial stability, addiction increases conflicts and causes untold emotional pain for every member of the family. With most drug users being in the productive age group of 18-35 years, the loss in terms of human potential is incalculable. The damage to the physical, psychological, moral and intellectual growth of the youth is very high. Adolescent drug abuse is one of the major areas of concern in adolescent and young people's behaviour. It is estimated that, in India, by the time most boys reach the ninth grade, about 50 percent of them have tried at least one of the gateway drugs. However, there is a wide regional variation across states in term of the incidence of the substance abuse.

For example, a larger proportion of teens in West Bengal and Andhra Pradesh use gateway drugs (about 60 percent in both the states) than Uttar Pradesh or Haryana (around 35 percent). Increase in incidences of HIV, hepatitis B and C and tuberculosis due to addiction adds the reservoir of infection in the community burdening the health care system further. Women in India face greater problems from drug abuse. The consequences include domestic violence and infection with HIV, as well as the financial burden. Eighty seven percent of addicts being treated in a de-addiction centre run by the Delhi police acknowledged being violent with family members. Most of the domestic violence is directed against women and occurs in the context of demands for money to buy drugs. At the national level, drug abuse is intrinsically linked with racketeering, conspiracy, corruption, illegal money transfers, terrorism and violence threatening the very stability of governments.

India has braced itself to face the menace of drug trafficking both at the national and international levels. Several measures involving innovative changes in enforcement, legal and judicial systems have been brought into effect. The introduction of death penalty for drug-related offences has been a major deterrent. The Narcotic Drugs and Psychotropic Substances Act, 1985, were enacted with stringent provisions to curb this menace. The Act envisages a minimum term of 10 years imprisonment extendable to 20 years and fine of Rs. 1 lakh extendable up to Rs. 2 lakhs for the offenders. The Act has been further amended by making provisions for the forfeiture of properties derived from illicit drugs trafficking.

Comprehensive strategy involving specific programmes to bring about an overall reduction in use of drugs has been evolved by the various government agencies and NGOs and is further supplemented by measures like education, counselling, treatment and rehabilitation programmes. India has bilateral agreements on drug trafficking with 13 countries, including Pakistan and Burma. Prior to 1999, extradition between India and the United States occurred under the auspices of a 1931 treaty signed by the United States and the United Kingdom, which was made applicable to India in 1942. However, a new extradition treaty between India and the United States entered into force in July 1999. A Mutual Legal Assistance Treaty was signed by India and the United States in October 2001. India also is signatory to the following treaties and conventions:

- 1961 U.N. Convention on Narcotic Drugs
- 1971 U.N. Convention on Psychotropic Substances
- 1988 U.N. Convention Against Illicit Traffic in Narcotic Drugs and Psychotropic Substances
- 2000 Transnational Crime Convention.

The spread and entrenchment of drug abuse needs to be prevented, as the cost to the people, environment and economy will be colossal. The unseemly spectacle of unkempt drug abusers dotting lanes and by lanes, cinema halls and other public places should be enough to goad the authorities to act fast to remove the scourge of this social evil. Moreover, the spread of such reprehensible habits among the relatively young segment of society ought to be arrested at all cost. There is a need for the government enforcement agencies, the non-governmental philanthropic agencies, and others to collaborate and supplement each other's efforts for a solution to the problem of drug addiction through education and legal actions.

Corruption in Education System in India – A UNESCO Report

India's education system is mired in corruption and a high rate of teacher absenteeism in the country was a key factor for it according to the new global study. The UNESCO's International Institute of Educational Planning study on corruption in education released recently says that 25% teacher absenteeism in India is among the highest in the world, second only after Uganda that has a higher rate. The global average of teacher absenteeism is about 20%.

Teacher absenteeism does not just affect quality of education; it is also a huge drain on resources resulting in the wastage of 22.5% of education funds in India the study said. Politics in teacher appointments and transfers is a major reason for teacher absenteeism according to a professor at National University for Education Planning and Administration.

The study identifies the absence of well established criteria for teacher recruitment a uniform policy on promotion, remuneration and deployment as some of the main reasons identified for teacher absenteeism. However the report found married teachers to be more regular at job than unmarried teachers.

In Bihar two of every five teachers were reported absent the figure in UP was reported to be one-third of the total teachers. However in states like Gujarat and Kerala the figure was lower than 15% the report based on several small studies.

Teachers also believe highly in private tutoring a practice identified by UNESCO as unethical. It does not complement learning at school and leads to corruption the report said. The practice of ghost teachers and involvement of teachers in mismanagement of schools were other gray areas identified in the Indian education system.

Another indictment of the sorry state of Indian education was the view held by students that cheating in examinations is their traditional right. In India universities cheating is now well-established. The fees for manipulating entrance tests ranges between $ 80 to $ 20,000 for popular programmes such as computer science, medicine and engineering the report said.

Plight of Women in India-Witch Branding

Even after so many years of independence, women in India continue to suffer socially as well as economically at different levels and in different forms. One of the most horrific violence against women is branding them as witch. Scores of women are regularly killed on charges of witchcraft across the county. This largely happens in states like Assam, Bihar, Jharkhand and West Bengal annually. Women mostly widows are beaten, often paraded in the village and sometimes forced to eat excrete.

According to a recent report by NGO-Association for Social and Human Activities, between 2001 and 2008,452 women were killed in Jharkhand. Jharkhand's economic backwardness and a low literacy rate of 53.6% and 38.9% for women have led to prevalence of superstition, illiteracy and violence against women. Even the death of an animal becomes a source for condemning some poor woman as a witch or dayan. Often it is an excuse to grab property or settle scores with someone.

Though Jharkhand has witchcraft prevention Act under which the maximum punishment is a one year imprisonment, its implementation is still awaited. Lack of access to justice is cited as one of the main reasons for not availing it.The other reasons being distance and attitude of people.

Health care in India

Health care in India is the responsibility of constituent states and territories of India. The Constitution charges every state with "raising of the level of nutrition and the standard of living of its people and the improvement of public health as among its primary duties". The National Health Policy was endorsed by the Parliament of India in 1983 and updated in 2002.

The art of Health Care in India can be traced back nearly 3500 years. From the early days of Indian history the Aryurvedic tradition of medicine has been practiced. During the rule of Emperor Ashoka Maurya (third century B.C.E.), schools of learning in the healing arts were created. Many valuable herbs and medicinal combinations were created. Even today many of these continue to be used. During his rein there is evidence that Emperor Ashoka was the first leader in world history to attempt to give health care to all of his citizens, thus it was the India of antiquity which was the first state to give it's citizens national health care.

In recent times India has eradicated mass famines, half of children in India are underweight, one of the highest rates in the world and nearly the same rate of Sub-Saharan Africa. Water supply and sanitation in India continue to be a challenged, only one of three Indians has access to improved sanitation facilities such as toilet. India's HIV/AIDS epidemic is a growing threat. Cholera epidemics are not unknown. The maternal mortality in India is the second highest in the world.

Providing health care and disease prevention to India's growing population of more than a billion people becomes challenging in the face of increased competition for resources. 2.47 million people in India are estimated to be HIV positive. India is one of the four countries worldwide where polio has not as yet been successfully eradicated and one third of the world's tuberculosis cases are in India. Three out of four children who died from measles in 2008 were in India.

According to the World Health Organization 900,000 Indians die each year from drinking contaminated water and breathing in polluted air. As India grapples with these basic issues, new challenges are emerging for example there is a rise in chronic adult diseases such as cardiovascular illnesses and diabetes as a consequence of changing lifestyles.

There are vast disparities in people's health even among the different states across the country largely attributed to the resource allocation by the state governments where some states have been more successful than others. Critics say better efforts are needed by the local governments to ensure that the health services provided are actually reaching the poor in worst-affected areas.

However, at the same time, India's health care system also includes entities which are world class. India is a magnet for medical tourists, who are able to get medical treatments and surgeries at a fraction of the cost of these procedures in developed countries. The Apollo set of hospitals, for example, thrives on this business. Each hospital, however, must also set aside a number of beds for the poor. However, as the BBC reported, access to these services by the poor is plagued with corruption. While many foreign medical experts criticize medical tourism, many private hospitals are able to demonstrate that their level of care is comparable, if not better, than that received in developed countries.

Medical Professionals

In a 2005 World Bank study, World Bank reported that "a detailed survey of the knowledge of medical practitioners for treating five common conditions in Delhi found that the average doctor in a public primary health centre has around a 50-50 chance of recommending a harmful treatment".

Random visits by government inspectors showed that 40% of public sector medical workers were not found at the work place.

Diseases

Malaria is Endemic in India

On going government of India education about HIV has led to decreases in the spread of HIV in recent years. The number of people living with AIDS in India is estimated to be between 2 and 3 million. However in terms of the total population this is a small number. The country has had a sharp decrease in the estimated number of HIV infections; 2005 reports had claimed that there were 5.2 million to 5.7 million people afflicted with the virus.

Issues

Malnutrition: Half of children in India are underweight, one of the highest rates in the world and nearly same as Sub-Saharan Africa. India contributes to about 5.6 million child deaths every year, more than half the world's total.

Women: Most Indian women are malnourished. The average female life expectancy today in India is low compared to many countries, but it has shown gradual improvement over the years.

In many families, especially rural ones, the girls and women face nutritional discrimination within the family, and are anemic and malnourished.

The maternal mortality in India is the second highest in the world. Only 42% of births in the country are supervised by health professionals. Most women deliver with help from women in the family who often lack the skills and resources to save the mother's life if it is in danger. According to UNDP Human Development Report (1997), 88% of pregnant women (age 15-49) were found to be suffering from anemia.

Water and Sanitation

Water supply and sanitation in India continue to be abysmal, despite long standing efforts by the various levels of government and communities at improving coverage. The situation is particularly inadequate for sanitation, since only one of three Indians has access to improved sanitation facilities (including improved latrines). While the share of those with access to an improved water source is much higher than for sanitation (86%), the quality of service is poor and most users that are counted as having access receive water of dubious quality and only on an intermittent basis. As of 2003, it was estimated that only 30% of India's wastewater was being treated, with the remainder flowing into rivers or ground water. The lack of toilet facilities in many areas also presents a major health risk; open defecation is widespread even in urban areas of India, and it was estimated in 2002 by the World Health Organisation that around 700,000 Indians die each year from diarrhoea. No city in India has full-day water supply. Most cities supply water only a few hours a day. In towns and rural areas the situation is even worse.

Health Care Infrastructure

The Indian health care industry is seen to be growing at a rapid pace and is expected to become a US$280 billion industry by 2022. The Indian health care market was estimated at US$35 billion in 2007 and is expected to reach over US$70 billion by 2012 and US$145 billion by 2017. According to the Investment Commission of India the health care sector has experienced phenomenal growth of 12 percent per annum in the last 4 years.

Rising income levels and a growing elderly population are all factors that are driving this growth. In addition, changing demographics, disease profiles and the shift from chronic to lifestyle diseases in the country has led to increased spending on health care delivery.

Even so, the vast majority of the country suffers from a poor standard of health care infrastructure which has not kept up with the growing economy. Despite having centres of excellence in health care delivery, these facilities are limited and are inadequate in meeting the current health care demands. Most public health facilities lack efficiency, are understaffed and have poorly maintained or outdated medical equipment.

Approximately one million people, mostly women and children, die in India each year due to inadequate health care. 700 million people have no access to specialist care and 80% of specialists live in urban areas. In addition to poor infrastructure India faces a shortage of trained medical personal especially in rural areas where access to care is altogether limited.

In order to meet manpower shortages and reach world standards India would require investments of up to $20 billion over the next 5 years. Forty percent of the primary health centres in India are understaffed. According to WHO statistics there are over 250 medical colleges in the modern system of medicine and over 400 in the Indian system of medicine and homeopathy (ISM&H). India produces over 250,000 doctors annually in the modern system of medicine and a similar number of ISM&H practitioners, nurses and para professionals. Better policy regulations and the establishment of public private partnerships are possible solutions to the problem of manpower shortage.

India faces a huge need gap in terms of availability of number of hospital beds per 1000 population. With a world average of 3.96 hospital beds per 1000 population India stands just a little over 0.7 hospital beds per 1000 population. Moreover, India faces a shortage of doctors, nurses and paramedics that are needed to propel the growing health care industry. India is now looking at establishing academic medical centres (AMCs) for the delivery of higher quality care with leading examples of The Manipal Group & All India Institute of Medical Sciences (AIIMS) already in place.

As incomes rise and the number of available financing options in terms of health insurance policies increase, consumers become more and more engaged in making informed decisions about their health and are well aware of the costs associated with those decisions. In order to remain competitive, health care providers are now not only looking at improving operational efficiency but are also looking at ways of enhancing patient experience overall.

Central Government Role

Critics say that the national policy lacks specific measures to achieve broad stated goals. Particular problems include the failure to integrate health services with wider economic and social development, the lack of nutritional support and sanitation, and the poor participatory involvement at the local level.

Central government efforts at influencing public health have focused on the five-year plans, on coordinated planning with the states, and on sponsoring major health programs. Government expenditures are jointly shared by the central and state governments.

Goals and strategies are set through central-state government consultations of the Central Council of Health and Family Welfare. Central government efforts are administered by the Ministry of Health and Family Welfare, which provides both administrative and technical services and manages medical education. States provide public services and health education.

The 1983 National Health Policy is committed to providing health services to all by 2000. In 1983 health care expenditures varied greatly among the states and union territories, from Rs 13 per capita in Bihar to Rs 60 per capita in Himachal Pradesh, and Indian per capita expenditure was low when compared with other Asian countries outside of South Asia.

Although government health care spending progressively grew throughout the 1980s, such spending as a percentage of the gross national product (GNP) remained fairly constant. In the meantime, health care spending as a share of total government spending decreased. During the same period, private-sector spending on health care was about 1.5 times as much as government spending.

Expenditure

In the mid-1990s, health spending amounted to 6% of GDP, one of the highest levels among developing nations. The established per capita spending is around Rs 320 per year with the major input from private households (75%). State governments contribute 15.2%, the central government 5.2%, third-party insurance and employers 3.3%, and municipal government and foreign donors about 1.3, according to a 1995 World Bank study. Of these proportions, 58.7% goes toward primary health care (curative, preventive, and promotive) and 38.8% is spent on secondary and tertiary inpatient care. The rest goes for nonservice costs.

The fifth and sixth five-year plans (FY 1974-78 and FY 1980-84, respectively) included programs to assist delivery of preventive medicine and improve the health status of the rural population. Supplemental nutrition programs and increasing the supply of safe drinking water were high priorities. The sixth plan aimed at training more community health workers and increasing efforts to control communicable diseases. There were also efforts to improve regional imbalances in the distribution of health care resources.

The Seventh Five-Year Plan (FY 1985-89) budgeted Rs 33.9 billion for health, an amount roughly double the outlay of the sixth plan. Health spending as a portion of total plan outlays, however, had declined over the years since the first plan in 1951, from a high of 3.3% of the total plan spending in FY 1951-55 to 1.9% of the total for the seventh plan. Mid-way through the Eighth Five-Year Plan (FY 1992-96), however, health and family welfare was budgeted at Rs 20 billion, or 4.3% of the total plan spending for FY 1994, with an additional Rs 3.6 billion in the nonplan budget.

Primary Srvices

Health care facilities and personnel increased substantially between the early 1950s and early 1980s, but because of fast population growth, the number of licensed medical practitioners per 10,000 individuals had fallen by the late 1980s to three per 10,000 from the 1981 level of four per 10,000. In 1991 there were approximately ten hospital beds per 10,000 individuals. However for comparison, the in China for comparison there are 1.4 doctors per 1000 people.

Primary health centres are the cornerstone of the rural health care system. By 1991, India had about 22,400 primary health centres, 11,200 hospitals, and 27,400 clinics. These facilities are part of a tiered health care system that funnels more difficult cases into urban hospitals while attempting to provide routine medical care to the vast majority in the countryside. Primary health centres and subcentres rely on trained paramedics to meet most of their needs. The main problems affecting the success of primary health centres are the predominance of clinical and curative concerns over the intended emphasis on preventive work and the reluctance of staff to work in rural areas. In addition, the integration of health services with family planning programs often causes the local population to perceive the primary health centres as hostile to their traditional preference for large families. Therefore, primary health centres often play an adversarial role in local efforts to implement national health policies.

According to data provided in 1989 by the Ministry of Health and Family Welfare, the total number of civilian hospitals for all states and union territories combined was 10,157. In 1991 there was a total of 811,000 hospital and health care facilities beds. The geographical distribution of hospitals varied according to local socioeconomic conditions. In India's most populous state, Uttar Pradesh, with a 1991 population of more than 139 million, there were 735 hospitals as of 1990. In Kerala, with a 1991 population of 29 million occupying an area only one-seventh the size of Uttar Pradesh, there were 2,053 hospitals.

Although central government has set a goal of health care for all by 2000, hospitals are distributed unevenly. Private studies of India's total number of hospitals in the early 1990s were more conservative than official Indian data, estimating that in 1992 there were 7,300 hospitals. Of this total, nearly 4,000 were owned and managed by central, state, or local governments. Another 2,000, owned and managed by charitable trusts, received partial support from the government, and the remaining 1,300 hospitals, many of which were relatively small facilities, were owned and managed by the private sector.

The use of state-of-the-art medical equipment, often imported from Western countries, was primarily limited to urban centres in the early 1990s. A network of regional cancer diagnostic and treatment facilities was being established in the early 1990s in major hospitals that were part of government medical colleges. By 1992 twenty-two such centres were in operation. Most of the 1,300 private hospitals lacked sophisticated medical facilities, although in 1992 approximately 12% possessed state-of-the-art equipment for diagnosis and treatment of all major diseases, including cancer. The fast pace of development of the private medical sector and the burgeoning middle class in the 1990s have led to the emergence of the new concept in India of establishing hospitals and health care facilities on a for-profit basis.

By the late 1980s, there were approximately 128 medical colleges-roughly three times more than in 1950. These medical colleges in 1987 accepted a combined annual class of 14,166 students. Data for 1987 show that there were 320,000 registered medical practitioners and 219,300 registered nurses. Various studies have shown that in both urban and rural areas people preferred to pay and seek the more sophisticated services provided by private physicians rather than use free treatment at public health centres.

Indigenous or traditional medical practitioners continue to practice throughout the country. The two main forms of traditional medicine practised are the ayurvedic system, which deals with mental and spiritual as well as physical well-being, and the unani (or Galenic) herbal medical practice. A *vaidya* is a practitioner of the ayurvedic tradition, and a *hakim* is a practitioner of the unani or Greek tradition. These professions are frequently hereditary. A variety of institutions offer training in indigenous medical practice. Only in the late 1970s did official health policy refer to any form of integration between European-trained medical personnel and indigenous medical practitioners. In the early 1990s, there were ninety-eight ayurvedic colleges and seventeen unani colleges operating in both the governmental and non-governmental sectors.

Health Insurance

The majority of the Indian population is unable to access high quality health care provided by private players as a result of high costs. Many are now looking towards insurance companies for providing alternative financing options so that they too may seek better quality health care.

The opportunity remains huge for insurance providers entering into the Indian health care market since75% of expenditure on health care in India is still being met by 'out-of-pocket' consumers. Even though only 10% of the Indian population today has health insurance coverage, this industry is expected to face tremendous growth over the next few years as a result of several private players that have entered into the market.

Health insurance coverage among urban, middle-and upper-class Indians, however, is significantly higher and stands at approximately 50%.

The Insurance Regulatory and Development Authority (IRDA) is the governing body responsible for promoting insurance business and introducing insurance regulations in India.

The share of public sector companies in health insurance premiums was 76% and that of private sector companies was 24% for the period 2005-06. Health insurance premiums collected over 2005-06 registered a growth of 35% over the previous year. In 2001 the IRDA introduced provisions for Third Party Administrators (TPAs) to support the administration and management of health insurance products offered by insurance companies. TPAs are facilitators in the coordination process between the health insurance provider and the hospital. Currently there are 27 TPAs registered under the IRDA.

Health insurance has a way of increasing accessibility to quality health care delivery especially for private health care providers for whom high cost remains a barrier. In order to encourage foreign health insurers to enter the Indian market the government has recently proposed to raise the foreign direct investment (FDI) limit in insurance from 26% to 49%. Increasing health insurance penetration and ensuring affordable premium rates are necessary to drive the health insurance market in India.

Rate of Gowth

India has approximately 600,000 allopathic doctors registered to practice medicine. This number however, is higher than the actual number practicing because it includes doctors who have emigrated to other countries as well as doctors who have died. India licenses 18,000 new doctors a year.

Public Health System: Issues

Public health system in India suffers from many problems which includes insufficient funding, shortage of facilities leading to overcrowding and severe shortage of trained health personnel. There is also lack of accountability in the public health delivery mechanisms.

These are some of the reasons which have placed India at the lowest rank in the Human Development Index.

India however holds top position in migration of physicians to developed countries like UK and the US. According to Planning Commission the country has a shortfall of six lakh doctors, 10 lakh nurses and two lakh dental surgeons. This has led to a dismal patient-doctor ratio in the country. For every 10,000 Indians, there is just one doctor.

The much publicized National Urban Health Mission is yet to see the light of day. The scheme plans to monitor and improve the health of 22 crore people living in urban slums in 429 cities and towns.

It was to be launched mid 2008 but the mission is yet to become functional. NURM is aimed at providing accessible, affordable, effective and reliable primary health care facilities especially to urban poor. Even for NHRM there is limited progress due to lack of standardization of medical facilities.

India has banned tobacco consumption in public places but only 12 states have started implementing the ban.

More than 10 lakh people at present die in India every year due to tobacco consumption. At present more than 57% male and 10.9% female consume tobacco while 15% children consume tobacco.

Female feticide continues to tarnish India's image. The child sex ratio (0-6 years) was 945 (1991 census) and this declined to 927 girls per thousand boys (in 2001 census). The figures are alarming in prosperous states like Punjab(798), Haryana (819),

Chandigarh (845), Delhi (868), Gujarat (883) and Himachal Pradesh (896).

Number of PHCs, CHC and SCs

Year	*CHC*	*PHC*	*SC*
2007	4,045	22,370	1, 45,272

Infant Mortality Rate

Year	Rural	Urban	Total
2007	61	37	55

Number of Health Care Workers

Year	*Doctors at PHCs*	*Specialists at PHC*	*Health workers Male*	*Health workers Female*
2007	22,608	5,117	62,881	1, 47,439

3

Social Change and Development

Social Change

Social Change and Sociology

Social change as a sociological term is defined as, alterations in basic structures of a social group or society. Social change is an ever present phenomenon in social life, but has become especially intense in the modern era. The origins of modern sociology can be traced to attempts to understand the dramatic changes shattering the modern world and promoting new forms of social order. An example of this is globalization.

For examples throughout human history the vast majority of people produced their own food and shelter and lived in tiny groups or small villages. Even at the height of the most developed civilizations-such as ancient Rome or China-fewer than 10% of the population lived in urban areas. In present day United States only 2%-3% of people work in agriculture and 90% of people now live in urban areas. Urbanization in the rest of the world is also changing at a rapid pace due to economic activity. By 2030, about 60% of the world population is expected to live in urban areas and in more developed regions as high as 81% of people are expected to be urbanized.

Other examples of social change include:

- Technology influx in recent years such as email, cell phone, online social networks. In the past communicating with other was held to certain constraints such as mail or face to face interact

- Increased voting rights in the United States for women and people of other ethnicity
- Everyone is required to go to school for a certain amount of years, as opposed to being able to withdraw at young ages.

According to sociologist, Ann Swidler, culture is like a "tool kit" from which people select different under standings and behaviours. Because people participate in so many different, and often conflicting, cultures this "tool kit" can be quite large and the contents vary. Social changes come about when individuals or groups choose to go against social norms. Social change in this manner does not necessarily mean, however, that a change in morals or values has occurred.

- A change in social structure: the nature, the social institutions, the social behaviour or the social relations of a society, community of people and so on.
- When behaviour patterns change in large numbers, and this change is visible and sustained: once there is deviance from culturally-inherited values, rebellion against the established system may result, resulting in a change in the social order.
- Any event or action that affects a group of individuals who have shared values or characteristics.
- Acts of advocacy for the cause of changing society in a way subjectively perceived as normatively desirable.

One of the most popular and succinct definitions of social change is supplied by Charles L. Harper in his *Exploring social change* (1993), where it is characterised as the "significant alteration of social structure and cultural patterns through time." He goes on to explain that this social structure is made up of "a persistent network of social relationships" in which interaction between people or groups has become repetitive. The resultant changes can effect everything from population to the economy, which, as it so happens, alongside such others as industrialisation and shifting cultural norms and values, are also established agents of social change. The term is used in the study of history, sociology, economies and politics, and includes such topics as the success or failure of different political systems, globalisation, democratisation, development and economic growth. The term can encompass concepts as broad as revolution and paradigm shift, right down to narrow changes such as a particular cause within small-town government.

The concept of social change implies measurement of some of the characteristics of a group of individuals. While the term is usually applied to changes that are beneficial to society, it may also result in negative side-effects and consequences that undermine or eliminate existing ways of life that are considered positive.

Social change is a topic in sociology and social work, but also involves political science, economics, history, anthropology and many other social sciences. Among the many means of creating social change are direct action, protest, advocacy, community organisation, community practice, revolution, and political activism. According to Anthony Giddens, Sociology was born of the transformations that wrenched the industrializing social order of the West away from the ways of life characteristic of preceding societies.

The world that was created by these changes is the primary object of concern of sociological analysis. The pace of social change has continued to accelerate, and it is possible that we stand on the threshold of transitions as significant as those that occurred in the late eighteenth and nineteenth centuries.

Modelled of People

Generally there are two sources or dimensions of changed (Shackman, Liu, Wang, 2002). One source is non-systematic change, such as climate change, some kind of technological innovation from the outside, or changes forced by foreign countries.

The other source is a systems change: Eisenstadt (1973) argued that modernization required a basic level of free resources and the development of standardised and predictable institutions, such as a stable but flexible market system and political process. An additional requirement was that governing institutions be flexible enough to adapt to the changes that come up. Most of the time, changes to society come about through some combination of both systematic and non-systematic processes.

- Hegelian: The classic Hegelian dialectic model of change is based on the interaction of opposing forces. Starting from a point of momentary stasis, Thesis countered by Antithesis first yields conflict Lebron James is greatt subsequently results in a new Synthesis.
- Kuhnian: Thomas Kuhn in *The Structure of Scientific Revolutions* argued with respect to the Copernican Revolution that people are unlikey to jettison an unworkable paradigm, despite many indications that the paradigm is not functioning properly, until a better paradigm can be presented.
- Heraclitan: The Greek philosopher Heraclitus used the metaphor of a river to speak of change thus, "On those stepping into rivers staying the same other and other waters flow" (DK22B12). What Heraclitus seems to be suggesting here, later interpretations notwithstanding, is that, in order for the river to remain the river, change must constantly be taking place. Thus one may think of the Heraclitan model as parallel to that of a living organism, which, in order to remain alive, must constantly be changing.
- Daoist: The Chinese philosophical work Dao De Jing, I.8 and II.78 uses the metaphor of water as the ideal agent of change. Water, although soft and yielding, will eventually wear away stone. Change in this model is to be natural, harmonious and steady, albeit imperceptible.

The Functionalist Perspective

Functionalists perceive society to be a system comprising various functions that operate collectively to maintain order and stability. According to Talcott Parsons, one of the leaders of this school, change stems from other social systems (through, for instance, cultural influence, as in the case of English education in the former colonies of the British Empire) and tensions and strains within the system itself, especially those related to economic activities. Functionalism, writes Michael Haralambos, holds that the economy is solely responsible for resolving societal problems, with industrialism playing an especially crucial role. He explains how, through production and various other economic activities, social change is accelerated such that society has to adapt as a whole: a change in one part effects all the others.

These activities include improvements in technology, whereby new innovations come to the fore, and trade with other countries. Social change in the functionalist view can also occur at different levels, be it on a micro scale (involving the groups and people within one's immediate environment) or at a macro level (economic, political and educational systems, for instance). Functionalists also believe that cultural norms and values unite society, which is largely resistant to change, and thus ensure that change in social structure is likely to be slow if it conflicts with entrenched cultural, religious or political principles. The time frame of change also plays a significant role, and the distinction between long-term and short-term change is important. According to Harper, short-term changes, as in family developmental stages, may be obvious and easy to comprehend, but they may not actually constitute changes at all in the long run.

Shortcomings

There are two main criticisms of the functionalist perspective to which most sociologists subscribe:

1. The theory places too much emphasis on external sources of social change, being based largely on the premise that society operates in a state of equilibrium, and that the various changes that take place can be accounted for uniformly by the various political, religious and especially the economic activities that are dominant at the time.
2. Society does not meet the needs of all its members. Emphasis is laid in this regard on the fact that ethnic and gender segregation that occurs politically and economically is created by these structures.

Social Development

Social development is a process which results in the transformation of social structures in a manner which improves the capacity of the society to fulfil its aspirations. Society develops by consciousness and social consciousness develops by organization. The process that is subconscious in the society emerges as conscious knowledge in pioneering individuals.

Development is a process, not a programme. Its power issues more from its subtle aspects than from material objects.

Not all social change constitutes development. It consists of four well-marked stages – survival, growth, development and evolution, each of which contains the other three within it. The quantitative expansion of existing activities generates growth or horizontal expansion. Development implies a qualitative change in the way the society carries out its activities, such as through more progressive attitudes and behaviour by the population, the adoption of more effective social organizations or more advanced technology which may have been developed elsewhere. The term evolution refers to the original formulation and adoption of qualitative and structural advances in the form of new social attitudes, values, behaviours, or organizations.

While the term is usually applied to changes that are beneficial to society, it may result in negative side-effects or consequences that undermine or eliminate existing ways of life that are considered positive.

Social change is important to study because a full understanding of many topics, such as the success or failure of different political systems, globalization, democratization, development and economic growth, are all rooted in this basic idea of social change.

For example, successful economic growth depends on a number of factors, such as technology and natural and social resources. However, only some countries can take advantage of technology and their resources. Thus, a more basic question is: why is it that only some countries are so well poised. In general, successful utilization of resources depends on having a stable and fairly flexible economic and political system, and a social system compatible with growth, for example, having values and customs which are favourable toward capital development and accumulation.

Thus, at the next deeper level, the question is why have only some countries developed these kinds of political, economic and social conditions (e.g., stable and flexible systems, values favouring capitalism). That is, the root question is how to explain the historical development of those societies.

Similarly, globalization and democratization eventually lead to the same questions. For example, whether a country is able to participate in the globalization process depends on... Again, whether a country's political system was able to develop into a democracy depends on.

What this Review Covers

The root question is how and why social, economic and political systems developed and how they are now changing. Overall, change is a highly complex process, involving many factors, such as demography, technology, availability of resources, politics, economics, and the interaction of these factors. We briefly review, in Section II, some of the major theories of change, what factors have been studied, and how these factors relate to change. Also, some aspects of change are seen as systematic and predictable, and others as random or coincidental. We review these two approaches to change. Section III describes one particular approach about the process of social change. Finally, there are a number of major areas of study of the current world situation: e.g., development, globalization, democratization, demographic changes, and the shift toward the knowledge based society. In Section IV, we give a brief overview of these topics, and then discuss data that can be used to study these topics.

Approach to Change

The process of social, political and economic change is very complex. Change may involve many different factors, and multiple processes operating concurrently. First, many coincidental, unique or random factors influence the change process. For example, geography can have an impact on whether a civilization developes one great centre versus many smaller independent centres. Similarly, the presence or absence of specific people may be one major determinant of the path a society takes. Consequently, the specific forms that a society takes, and the particular paths, for example of development, taken by different societies will not be the same among different societies. On the other hand, there are systematic or common processes which affect all societies. For example, successful development generally requires a basic degree of social mobilization, structural differentiation, development of free resources, specialization and diversity of social organization, and a stable and flexible governmental system. Social, political and economic change can best be understood by combining systematic with more unique, andom or coincidental factors.

General Theories of Change

This review is organized into two parts. First, we discuss non systematic factors, such as geography, technology, human factors (e.g., human will) and how they interact. Second, we describe some systems theories of change.

Non Systematic Factors

Geography is often seen as a coincidental factor. For example, Hibbs and Olsson (2004) indicate that geography played a key role in earliest economic development (i.e. the transition from huter-gatherers to agriculture) because it provided the natural resources that made possible building institutions to support further development.

Later, the emergence of capitalism in the west was also described as depending on geography (Chirot and Merton, 1986; Weber, in Collins, 1986). In North West Europe, geography led to the development of independent cities, the possibility of capital accumulation, and a semi-independent bourgeoisie (Chirot and Merton, 1986), which in turn resulted in more or less independent bureaucratic states based on universal citizenship, an egalitarian legal system, and a religion emphasizing the economic ethic (Weber, in Collins, 1986). All of these factors led to the development of systems of rights and responsibilities, legal regulations for fiscal and economic exchange, and standard rules for transactions (Chirot and Merton, 1986), which were positive preconditions for the development of capitalism. In contrast, the geography of China led to dependence on large scale irrigation, which required strong centralized authority, and cities developed as dependents of monarchial authorities, rather then as more independent entities. Consequently, rule was by patrimony, rather than by a egalitarian legal system, and this kind of legal system was not suitable for entrepreneurial organization of capital.

Another example is described in Nevins and Commager (1986). In North America, since the Atlantic coast had many small bays and inlets, many small colonies could be established, rather than having one or a few large colonies. Thus, independence led to a federation of colonies or states, rather than any other form of government. Later, when the central plains were populated, the flatness and navigable rivers made communication and transportation comparatively easy. Thus, this land was settled by people from all of the eastern seaboard, and all of Europe, interacting on equal terms, leading to a new democracy and a new American sentiment.

Chirot also indicates that environment can also be a cause of failure to change. For example, the earliest civilizations developed in constricted river valleys. These centres had high population densities and centralized authority. The problem was that these centres of civilization were subject to great catastrophes. There could be extreme droughts, or invasions by nomadic raiders who lived in surrounding dry regions. When the droughts or invasions occurred, the civilizations fell, and it could take centuries to recover. The necessary complex irrigation systems, the animal stock and the human population all took long times to recover from the great disasters. Thus, because of constrictions places by geographic conditions, very long term continuous growth could not occur, since the civilizations had to spend centuries repeatedly recovering from recurring disasters.

In contrast, western Europe could continuously accumulate capital and raise productivity over a very long time period, because it did not have to deal with continuous disasters. Western Europe had rainfall throughout the year, and thus rarely had periods of extreme drought or flooding, and did not need centralized authority required to maintain complex irrigation systems. Western Europe also did not have adjacent dry zones with nomads, hence far fewer major invasions and disruptions than the earlier civilizations. Western Europe, unlike earlier centres of civilizations, also was composed of many small river valleys, and thus difficult to unify, which meant more possibility of internal competition, and less bureaucratic roadblocks to innovation.

External events are another coincidental factor. The development of capitalism also depended on the discovery of the new world, which consequently allowed for an increase in overseas commerce, which in turn led to the growth of new manufacturing and industrial centres independently of the older forms of social organization, that is, of the feudal system.

Technology can be a coincidental factor or part of a systematic process. For example, technological innovation, in the form of the invention of the heavy plow and improved harnessing of horses was one of the main factors which allowed northwestern Europe to develop between the ninth and thirteenth centuries (Chirot, 1994, 2000). The plow and harness made it possible to efficiently turn the heavy soil of northwestern Europe, which allowed for a faster population growth. More recently, the railroad was an engine of change, as it lowered transportation costs, more effectively connected remote regions with more advanced areas, and "brought modernization everywhere it went". These innovations were not neccessarily inevitable, that is, not part of some logically flowing system dynamic of capitalist development. Thus, some societies did develop innovations which allowed them to prosper and grow, while others did not develop innovations, and failed, and it is not always clear why some did and some did not. More recently, many see technology or scientific innovations as a driving force of modern growth. In this case, it seems likely that technological innovation is part of the systematic process of capitalism.

Human factors such as decision making are also important non systematic sources of change. Bendix (1984) mentions that it is "the clash of wills which is necessary for the emergence of the present". This clash of wills is related to the political structures of states, and, recently, how they enter the modern industrial age. For example, Bendix (1964) indicates how important political management was in "reconciling tradition and modernity" in Japan's transition. Much of the source of Japanese development was from foreign technology and ideas, and these modern factors had to be managed to some degree, and integrated into the more traditional ways. Individual and collective decisions about political management thus had some influence in how successful Japan was in maintaining economic success, along with how well she integrated past and present culture. Similarly, the clash of wills relates to success in other states. Nevins and Commager (1986) describe the American Revolution by saying that it was led by people who were well organized, while their opposition, the loyalists, were not, and it was the organization of the revolutionaries which helped them to succeed. Again, during the revolutionary war, Nevins and Commager (1986) indicate that there were several occasions when the British army *could* have defeated the revolutionaries, but failed to do so because of decisions by their commanders. In this clash of wills, the British failed, and delivered success to the emerging American state.

Historical situation and context are also critical factors. Change is not a single path or pattern, but depends on many factors, such as how a society is organized, it's relations with neighbours, or its previous level of development. For example, in discussing modernization, Eisenstadt (1973) makes reference to a set of variables which seem to, at least partly, explain the different forms modernization takes. First, the material and social position of a people at the initial stages of modernization is an important influence. People who are socially organized in tribal groups will modernize differently than people in caste systems. Likewise, the process will differ according to the level of economic development. More backwards economies may undergo more stress and discontinuity. Secondly, the temporal sequence of the process will lead to varying patterns of modernization. The western modernization was led by the economic and cultural spheres.

On the other hand, more recently, in Latin American, Asian and African countries, political modernization occurs first. Finally, Eisenstadt (1973), like Bendix (1984) also refers to individual will, in this case, to the actions of the "modernizing elite". That is, those who lead the modernization process will influence the form and content of the modernization process. Different elite groups may choose different policies of social or economic development. For example, Eisenstadt (1973) writes "the processes of modernization are... borne or 'pushed' by the charismatic groups or personality". In some cases, an absence of an elite group may also delay or prevent the modernization process. These three factors, the previous level of a society's development, the temporal sequence, and the actions of the modernizing elite, combine in a variety of ways and produce a variety of forms and processes of modernization.

Conclusion: The development path does not necessarily follow a single pattern. The specific forms of institutions which emerge, and the relations between socio-demographic characteristics and modernization, will not be the same for different societies. For example, in the western societies, as mentioned, modernization was accompanied by expansion of components of social mobilization (e.g., higher literacy, education, urbanization) and growth of specialized and separate spheres (political, economic, cultural). However, in the modernization process of more recent cases, including Latin American or Asian countries, beyond a certain point, there was a negative correlation between some socio-demographic factors (e.g., literacy and urbanization) and institutional capacity for sustained growth. Also, the kind of structural differentiation and separate and specialized development of institutionalized spheres which occurred in the west was not duplicated in other modernizing countries. For example, Russia developed a more centralized and merged system which included both the political and economic systems. Also, other differences may occur. For example, Japan incorporated much more of it's traditional sphere into it's modern framework than did western nations, and also developed orientations toward particularistic units (e.g., schools, companies), rather than an emphasis on universalistic and achievement criteria in all institutional spheres, as occurred in the west.

Systems Explanations

The capitalist system, however, has a structural tendency which eventually leads to declining rates of profit (Giddens, 1971). In the search for profit, technological improvement and increasing mechanization are the major means used by each individual capitalist to compete with other capitalists. More mechanization and technology can help each entrepreneur to produce at cheaper rates and to increase his share of profits. However, each entrepreneur will similarly use more technology, so that all will eventually have higher ratios of capital expenditure on constant capital (e.g., technology, etc.), and less workers to expropriate surplus value from, so the average rates of profits for all will decline.

There are mitigating factors (Giddens, 1971). For example, spending more on constant capital may increase productivity of labour, so the proportion of ratio expended on constant capital can be steady or decline, and so profit can stay steady or increase. Countervailing forces also include the "intensified exploitation of labour" (Giddens, 1971), which is expanding the work day or decreasing wages below their true value.

The capitalist system also experiences periodic "crises" of over production, which are manifestations of the structural contradictions of the system, and are also a regulating mechanism, which allow the system to work through the periodic fluctuations, restore an equilibrium and grow further.

Finally, Marx indicates that "capitalism is an inherently unstable system, built upon antagonism that can only be resolved through changes which eventually undermine it" (Giddens, 1971).

Eisenstadt also provides a systematic explanation for part of change. He uses a comparative approach in attempting to lay out conditions of social growth and development, for example, for laying out laws or patterns of development of political systems of empires (1993), in specifying those conditions under which successful modernization occurs (1983), when revolution and revolutionary transformation occurs (1978), or under what circumstances axial age civilizations arose (1986). He is interested in specifying dynamics of social growth, or explaining why something occurred where and when it did.

In Tradition, Change and Modernity (1983) Eisenstadt describes the dynamics of modernization. He first points out that modernization requires the development of a base level of certain factors, including social mobilization, structural differentiation, the development of free resources, specialization and diversity of social organization, and the development of regulative and allocative mechanisms in the economic, political and other institutional spheres. Examples of these regulative and allocative mechanisms include the market system and political parties, in the economic and political spheres, respectively. Eisenstadt (1983) goes on to indicate that achieving a certain level on these factors is necessary for the development of modernity, but is not sufficient alone to guarantee continuation of modernization.

In order for a society to continue to modernize, it needs to develop an institutional framework capable of continuous absorption of change. That is, as the society modernizes, new demands arise, new constituencies come to power, and the political, economic, social, and other spheres need to adapt to these changes, and also need to maintain some kind of continuity. So for example, the political system must be able to deal with suffrage or national independence movements and still be able to maintain continuity. Thus, beyond a certain minimal level of social mobilization and structural differentiation required for modernization, in addition there is a need for an institutional framework that can successfully cope with the changes and problems associated with modernization, and that can also maintain a continuous existence for itself.

Eisenstadt (1983) sees modernization as partially systematic, and, as mentioned above, partially indeterminate. Thus, while there are certain factors required for modernization, there is also a great variety in the specific forms society may take and how the modernization process occurs, and the differences in the modernization process may be partially explained by the previous level of a society's development, the temporal sequence, and the actions of the modernizing elite.

North, and Institutions

North (1996b) is concerned with the dynamics of political, social, and economic change. In particular, he writes about institutions as the carrier of the process of economic change (North, 1996b).

Institutions are a society's "formal rules (constitutions, statute and common law, regulations, etc.), informal constraints (norms of behaviour, conventions, and internally imposed codes of conduct), and the enforcement characteristics of each". Institutions are created to reduce uncertainty in pursuit of goals in economic, political and social exchanges. and to provide the underlying structure to exchange and human organization.

The broad process of economic change is that organizations-economic, political and social-are the actors, and will "introduce new institutions or technology when they perceive that they can improve their competitive position by such innovation.". For example, when there are secure monopolies, there is little incentive to innovate. On the other hand, when there are competitive markets, there are more incentives to innovate.

However, organizations are a product of their society's institutions. The form, structure and even competitive behaviour of organizations depends on the institutions of society. Thus, competition is the immediate determinant whether organizations innovate, but the institutions determine how and what kinds of innovations occur. For example, under certain conditions, it may happen that innovation involves improving productivity, but innovation can also involve creating monopolies or blocking further competition. The form that innovation takes, as mentioned, depends on the existing institutions.

Further, only some kinds of institutions support sustained economic growth, basically those institutions which reduce costs of transactions. "Sometimes they (institutions) are created to facilitate exchange, encourage technological change, and induce human capital formation and in consequence reduce transaction and/or transformation costs; at other times they are created to support monopoly, prevent technological change, thwart human capital development, and generally raise the costs of transacting and/or transformation". Thus, for example, institutions may lead to social investment in education, dissemination of knowledge and encouraging applied and pure research, or on the other hand may lead to 'investment' in support skills for more redis tributive activities, such as piracy.

North gives some examples. Some belief systems in Africa and somewhat in Latin America, following their historical economic experience, did not lead to the creation of political and economic institutions which permitted impersonal exchange. As these economies became exposed to the larger world economy, rather, they developed organizations which favoured redis tributive activities. That is, the state basically became a theft machine.

On the other hand, some economies, for example England and the Netherlands, developed economic organizations which favoured productive activities. This modern economic growth of Europe "had as its source the growth in the stock of knowledge that is associated with the scientific revolution of the sixteenth and seventeenth centuries." In turn, the institutional developments of the scientific revolution — political, economic, and social – were the result of the development of a belief system "that had its origins in the way religious beliefs (and reaction to those beliefs) evolved in medieval-early modern Europe and the way those beliefs in turn were heavily influenced by the unique experiences that characterized that part of the world.". North also indicates that the key to the success of England and the Netherlands was "the dynamic consequences of the competition among fragmented political bodies that resulted in an especially creative environment. Europe was politically fragmented; but it was integrated in having both an overall belief structure, derived from Christendom, and information and transportation connections that resulted in scientific, technological, and artistic developments in one part spreading rapidly throughout the others."

Process of Change

Murdock (1961) does not present a theory of change, but rather describes the process of cultural change. According to Murdock, culture is a system of collective habits. The collective habits may be habits of actions, ie, customs, or habits of thoughts, ie, collective ideas. These habits are learned, collectively.

Some of the habits, for example language, may be shared throughout the society, while others may be limited to certain classes or groups. Habits are shared because some people are in similar situations, so would learn similar habits. More importantly, each generation is socialized to adopt the habits that previous generations found to be adaptive and satisfying. Further, social pressure is exerted in order to ensure that people conform to the habits which the social group consider to be right and appropriate. Adoption of the appropriate habits equips the individuals to deal with the various social situations, and to develop reliable expectations of how others may respond.

Since each society develops under different geographic and social conditions, the collective habits of each society differs for each society. Consequently, changes in social behaviour, or culture, generally has its origin in "some significant alteration in the life condition of a society". If the situation of the society changes, old behaviour patterns may be discouraged and new patterns are encouraged. Typical events that result in change may include changes in the population, in the geographical environment, movement to a different environment, contact with people of different culture, natural or social disasters, wars, discoveries, even particular leaders.

Murdock also indicates that any event which produces change is historical. It occurs at a certain time and place, and the consequent changes will depend on the context. However, it is possible that similar events could have similar effects on other cultures.

Murdock outlines a general process of cultural change. First, there may be an *innovation*, which is "the formation of a new habit by a single individual which is subsequently accepted or learned by other members of the society". Innovations may be variations, that is slight changes of already existing habits. Variations may be small at any given time, but the accumulation over time may be very large. Innovations may also be inventions, which is transferring behaviours from one context to another, or is combining old behaviours in new ways. Murdock indicates that most of the technological innovations have been inventions. In addition, inventions can occur simultaneously within the same or similar cultures. A third type of innovation happens when, basically, entirely new habits are developed. These happen through trial and error, and may occur because old habits prove ineffective and people in the situations are strongly motivated to find new solutions.

Crises, for example, economic crises, famines or epidemics are particularly conducive to this third type of innovation. The final type of innovation is cultural borrowing, or diffusion. This type is the most common and important. Murdock writes that almost every culture owes at least 90 percent of it's culture to borrowing. He gives as an example, the U.S. culture, with it's language borrowed from England, it's alphabet from the Phoenicians, paper and printing from China, family and property system from medieval Europe, banking and finance system from Babylonia along with modern elabourations from Italy and England, and so on. Most often, societies borrow mostly from immediate neighbours, and trade, missionary activities, political conquest and inter-marriage are the usual means of enabling borrowing. Borrowing only occurs when there is need, when a society does not already have a trait or habit that fills its need. Borrowing is not necessarily exact, but commonly includes modification, for example, to fit the current cultural situation and needs.

The second process in change is social acceptance. That is, in order for an innovation to become part of the culture, it has to be accepted by more than the innovator. Thus, the innovation has to be socially shared. Whether the innovation is adopted by others largely depends on the prestige of the innovator and of the initial adopting group.

The third process is selective elimination. Those innovations which are more rewarding than their alternatives are more likely to be picked up, while, consequently, those which are less adaptive are likely to be dropped, and disappear. Murdock mentions through that many innovations, even when they become less effective or adaptive, are retained, but with a change in function. For example candles were replaced by electric lights, but were retained for ceremonial or other purposes.

The final process of change is integration. The shared habits that are accepted become adapted with other shared habits, such that they all form, more or less, an integrated whole. The adopted habit both is modified as it is adapted, and modifies the social situation, or culture, to which it is adapting.

Murdock concludes. "The net effect of the various processes of cultural change is to adapt the collective habits of human societies progressively over time to the changing conditions of existence".

Benedict (1961) in the same book, reminds us that the change process is complex, and cannot be reconstructed logically and by deduction. The habits of any particular culture are deeply ingrained and are not always easily changed. There may be times when some simple and obvious thing or idea may not be invented or adopted, even when there is a great need for it, and very complex things or ideas may be developed in simple societies. She gives the example of the metric system, something very useful and logical, which was none the less not adopted in the United States.

Thus, Murdock gives an overview of what the change process may look like, while Benedict reminds us how complex and illogical the process may be.

Current World Change

Many organizations list a variety of issues that are important in todays world. For example, the United Nations University (UNU, 2000) lists human development, security, governance and environment. The United Nations Association in Canada (Spencer, 2001) lists conflict, crime, development, disarmament, economic issues, environment, extra state actors, globalization, health, human rights, knowledge revolution, population trends, including movements and other issues, and scientific development. Similarly, the Canadian International Development Agency (2003) lists basic education, capacity development, desertification, child protection, gender equality, health and nutrition, HIV/AIDS, humanitarian crises, information and communication technologies, human rights, democratization and good governance, peace building, poverty reduction, and private sector development. The Global Education program sponsored by the Australian Agency for International Development (2006) lists a variety of topics, lists a wide variety of issues, such as children's rights, desertification, food security, infrastructure, rice, urbanization, water and others.

We review main points for a number of these topics, focusing on social, economic and political issues, such as globalization, democratization, economic and demographic changes, technology, health and human development, human rights, social change, environment, and the interaction among these above areas. The last section will describe data that can be used to study these changes.

Globalization

Guillen (2001) provides an excellent overview of current research on globalization. Globalization, or "the rapid increase in cross-border economic, social, technological and cultural exchange" is becoming increasingly discussed in social science literature. In his review, Guillen starts by indicating that globalization is "far from a uniform, irreversible, and inexorable trend. Rather, globalization is a fragmented, incomplete, discontinuous, contingent, and in many ways contradictory and puzzling process" Some indicators seem to be clear evidence of globalization. For example, "Foreign direct (excluding portfolio) investment as a percentage of GDP is 2.5 times greater today than twenty years ago". Similarly, international tourism has more than doubled and international calling has nearly doubled. On the other hand, stock of international migrants has been nearly stable. There has also been an increase in the number of independent nation states and there are currently many ethnic groups who are aiming toward national independence.

That is, national individualization is still a strong process. In addition, foreign investment and trade are concentrated in Western Europe, North America and Japan. Further, while inward direct foreign investment has increased, it is still only 14% of total world GDP. Finally, regarding whether there is convergence among states and organizations, Guillen writes "globalization does not seem to compel governments, firms, and individuals to converge in their patterns of behaviour". For example, "firms pursue different modes of economic action and adopt different organizational forms depending on the institutional and social structures of their home countries even as globalization increases. Similarly, government policy making and interactions with other economies remains diversified among states, rather than becoming more convergent. Guillen writes that research, overall, seems to argue that globalization is occurring, and he refers to social and political writers who present pursuasive cases, although he doesn't describe the cases and the references seem to describe mainly internet and phone use. Guillen also points out several issues such as the world AIDS epidemic and global warming, that show how important it is, at least in some areas, to use global perspectives in addressing problems.

Giddens (1999) also discusses globalization. He believes that the world is really undergoing great changes, related to globalization, and outlines a few of the fundamental changes in the global economy. For example, Held et al (1999) point out that the level of world trade in commodities is much higher than it ever has been. In addition, Giddens argues, trade in services is more intense, and financial and currency trade is the most intense. The economy has especially become more global in the trade in information, about commodities and finance, for example. Further, globalization is not just an economic phenomena, but also a social, political and cultural phenomena. Globalization has effects on local culture, and influences our identities and relationship with other people.

The result of globalization is that tradition and customs have less of an impact on us, that we have to live a more reflexive life toward an open future. We have more options in creating our identity, rather than accepting what is given in our traditional culture. Politically, the nation state is still a vital power in the globalized world and in some respects more important. The nation state is the near universal form of governance in the current world. Further, nation states, or at least the larger ones, are still more powerful than corporations. Nation states are territories, have control over military power, and nations are responsible for establishing rules of law in which corporations operate. Giddens argues that the development of electronic world communication systems (e.g., the satellite) was a main feature of globalization, through the ability of instant electronic communication among all parts of the world. The new form of communication called for new forms of political and social systems.

Held et al (1999) also summarize globalization. In terms of defence and military power, the current world has a greater degree than ever before of diplomatic links, "multilateral arrangements or multilateral fora for military or security matters", and "organization of defence production in the direction of more extensive and intensive transnationalization through licensing, co-production agreements, joint ventures, corporate alliances, sub-contracting, etc." In terms of economics, international trade is greater than ever before, leading to greater interrelationships among economies, and "Social protection and the welfare state play an important role in ameliorating the impact of structural change arising from trade".

As does Guillen, Held et al also point out the importance of environmental issues. "the pollution and degradation of the global commons (such as the oceans and the atmosphere); the overspill of the effects of environmental degradation from one state to another (environmental refugees); transboundary pollution and risks (nuclear power, acid rain); the transportation and diffusion of wastes and polluting products across the globe (toxic waste trade, global relocation of dirty industries); and, finally, the formation of global institutions, regimes, networks and treaties that seek to regulate all these forms of environmental degradation". Held et al also describe the political implications of globalization. Because of the many interconnections, in military, environment and economy, there is a political shift from government to multilevel governance, e.g., "coordination and collaboration across shifting transnational and international networks" (conclusions). Held et al conclude that "Far from globalization leading to 'the end of the state', it is stimulating a range of government and governance strategies and, in some fundamental respects, a more activist state" (conclusions).

Democratization and Political Change

Giddens (2000) defines democracy as "a system involving effective competition between political parties for positions of power. In a democracy, there are regular and fair elections, in which all members of the population may take part. These rights of democratic participation go along with civil liberties-freedom of expression and discussion, together with the freedom to form and join political groups or associations." Giddens (2000) goes on to write that the past few decades has seen a good deal of growth of democracy.

Other democratization researchers include Gurr, Jaggers and Moore (1990), Jaggers and Gurr (1995), Freedom House (2000), and O'Loughlin, Ward, Lofdohl, Cohen, Brown, Reilly, Gleditsch and Shin (1997). For example, Jaggers and Gurr (1995) describe global and regional trends in democracy and show that states in the Middle East and Africa are much behind states in other regions in the transition to democracy, and that, as autocratic elites attempt to resist pressures to liberalize, the results are unconsolidated, or 'incoherent', polities. O'Loughlin et al (1997) use Polity data to describe temporal and spatial aspects of diffusion of democracy. They point out that there are geographic and temporal clustering of autocracy and democracy and that democratization is subject to reversal. They also indicate that there is not necessarily a single form of diffusion of democracy, and that external conditions are important. For example, some situations such as economic crises may affect a group of related countries all at the same time.

Gurr, Marshall and Khosla (2000) describe trends in armed conflicts, self determination movements and democracy. They report three main findings (all in the report highlights). First, there has been a large increase in societal wars (e.g., internal wars) from the 1950's to the early 1990's, but "The number and magnitude of armed conflicts within and among states have lessened since the early 1990s by nearly half." Second, "Conflicts over self-determination are being settled with ever greater frequency, usually when ethnic groups gain greater autonomy and power-sharing within existing states." Finally, "Democratic governments now outnumber autocratic governments two to one and continue to be more successful than autocracies in resolving violent societal conflicts." However, the high proportion of democratic states to autocratic states is a very recent phenomena.

Gurr et al show trends in the numbers of democratic, autocratic and transitional regimes from 1946-1999. The number of democratic regimes had increased slowly but steadily up to almost 1990. During this time period, the number of autocratic states grew faster and outnumbered democratic states. With the collapse of western communism in 1989, the number of democratic states increased rapidly. However, Gurr, Marshall and Kholsa (2000) go on to warn that these three positive trends are limited and can potentially be reversed by three problems (in highlights). First, "Virulent armed conflicts persist in parts of Eurasia and Africa and have the potential for metathesis into neighbouring states." Second, "New and transitional democracies everywhere are at risk for reverting to autocracy." Finally, "Lack of economic development undermines democratic institutions and breeds violent conflict." In research related to democratization, The Freedom House (2000) described changes in political freedom over time, based on political rights and civil liberties. Many countries in their data show fair stability over time. A few, such as Bolivia, Romania and Uruguay show large improvements. On the other hand, some, such as Bhutan, Antigua & Barbuda, and The Gambia show changes toward less freedom.

Demographic Changes

A main feature of society is it's demographic make up, including, for example, population size, age and race/ethnic breakdown, and urbanization. We review here some of the major trends in these characteristics.

One of the major features of the 20th century has been a population growth larger than at any other time in history. Although the population growth is expected to continue into the next several decades, the pace of growth has decelerated since 1970. The majority of the high growth has been occuring in developing countries. A consequence of the higher growth rate among less developed countries is that population in the less developed countries is becoming an increasingly large proportion of world total population, growing from 70% in 1960 to 81% in 2001. In addition, there have also been increases in life expectancy, declines in childbirth, and shifts in population distributions. The causes of population increase are highly complex, and involve many different biological, cultural, economic, geographic, political, and social factors, such as cultural traditions that encourage girls to marry at a young age. Decreases in fertility, on the other hand, is associated with, for example, increasing age of marriage and higher education.

Relatedly, the aging of the population is another major trend. The population age 65 and older is increasing at an unprecedented rate, both in developed and developing countries, and expected to continue to increase well into the 21st century. The increase is occurring more in developing countries, though. Related trends are that public pension take a large part of GDPs, that disability rates are more likely to be a problem in developing states than in developed states, and that in most countries, there are more elderly women than elderly men. Another major change taking place, specifically in the developing countries, involves increasing urbanization, especially in concentrations of populations in the largest cities. While some cities may manage the growth process well, some of the concerns are about the threat of increasing morbidity and mortality, depletion of non-renewable natural resources, and increasing urban poverty and inequality, with "consequent weakening of the state, civil unrest, urban-based revolutions, and radical religious fundamentalism".

Economic Changes

Growth trends are described by various writers. For example, Maddison (2001) shows long term economic growth, including growth over the past century. Total output showed a many fold increase in the 1900's for the world and most regions, with most of the growth concentrated in the 1950-1973 period, except Asia (excluding Japan) experiencing its main growth in the more recent decades. In another exception, the former Soviet Union had a decline in output in the most recent two decades. World and regional output per capita followed similar patterns, except of course for the former Soviet Union, which again experienced a large decline in output per capita in the most recent decades.

In many theories of growth, economists such as Abramovitz (1989, 1990), Kendrick (1989), Kuznets (1989), Maddison (1989), Romer (1990) and Robelo (1991) emphasize technology or growth in knowledge as sources of growth, along with social and institutional conditions that allow knowledge to be applied. For example, Kuznets (1989) writes that a source of growth is "a high rate of accumulation of useful knowledge and of technological innovations derived from it". This knowledge and technology, though, can only be used along with the appropriate conditions, such as financial and legal systems which allow mobilization of savings and investment, and with a stable government, which can deal with social or economic disruptions which may occur during periods of change. Thus, the rapid growth of Europe and Japan in the 1950's was due to the relative peace and stability following WW II, which allowed those countries to restructure their organizational systems, so to take advantage of newer technology, to rebuild, and so forth, in other words, to achieve high growth rates. Once they "caught up", or organized around the newest technology, their rates of growth would naturally slow down. The recent slow down in Europe and Japan is simply the result of those countries catching up to their technological potential (Abramovitz, 1990), rather than to problems in policy, technology and so on.

Boettke points out that culture is one of the important social conditions allowing for growth. For example, protection of private property rights, freedom of contract, and rule of law are all important in fostering growth, but it is not just a simple matter of introducing these constructs into a society, because the society has to have the cultural values and history which allow these factors to fit in and be accepted.

There has also been considerable research about growth and development. One set of papers examines how different variables affect economic growth. Koropecky (no date given) presents an overview of these papers. Some of the main points are that, for example, "moderate income inequality sustains economic growth while immoderate income inequality chokes it off", and that "developing countries that have achieved the most rapid gains in income per capita are also those that have recorded the fastest growth in manufactured exports... all of the successful developing-country exporters of manufactures established an export platform... which, esentially, is an enclave that is at least partially free of the conditions that hold back the rest of the economy (poor trade policies, weak infrastructure, inconsistent rule of law), so that firms there can become more competitive and more fully integrated into the global economy." This set of papers also examines how growth affects various variables, including climate and population.

Research in development also points to the importance of investment in infrastructure, physical capital and education, including investment in information technology (Pohjola, no date given). Infrastructure may include the number of telephones, the number of telephone main lines, kilo-watts of electricity-generating capacity, kilometers of total roads, kilometers of paved roads, and kilometers of railway lines (Canning, 1998), of which there may be an optimal mix.

Easterly, Kremer, Pritchett and Summers (1993) write that a country's growth rate varies quite a lot over time while other country characteristics such as educational level or political stability, tend to remain stable. They concluded that either shocks or worldwide technological change are important in determining long run growth, and that country characteristics may determine relative income levels. They also showed that, for a set of 28 countries, over the very long term, country rank order of GDP per capita stays the same. That is, countries with relatively lower GDP per capita tended to remain at the lower levels, comparatively, of GDP per capita.

Gwartney and Lawson (2000) show how country's levels of economic freedom have changed over time. Many countries do increase their freedom, but some also decline. Gwartney and

Lawson (2000) also show that economic freedom is related to factors such as per capita income and life expectancy.

Poverty and Inequality

There is considerable debate around global trends in poverty and inequality (Ravallion, 2003). For example, there is disagreement about the amount of decline, and a few argue that poverty has increased (IFG, undated) or that the data are insufficient to determine whether poverty levels have changed (Reddy and Pogge, 2003). One World Bank report shows that, for developing countries as a whole, there has been a slight decline in poverty rates (percent below $1 a day per capita) between 1990 and 1999. Not all regions improved though. There was an increase in poverty rates in Europe and Central Asia (the transition economies) and a slight increase in Sub Saharan Africa and in the Middle East and North Africa. The remainder of the regions experienced a decline in poverty rates. In addition, for developing countries as a whole, there was a slight decrease in the number of people in poverty. Most of this decline was in China. Excluding China showed an increase in the number of people in extreme poverty. The increases were especially marked in Europe and Central Asia and in Sub Saharan Africa.

On the other hand, Bhalla (2002) argues that there were large declines in poverty rates, from 37% in 1985 to 13% in 2000. Bhalla's estimate of poverty in 2000 is much lower than the World Bank estimate, of 23% in 1999. One report from the International Forum on Globalization (IFG, undated) argues the opposite though, that a consequence of globalization has been increased poverty. A summary of their book is described on the IFG web site. The book, unfortunately, is not freely available, so that details of their methods and results are not available on the web.

Several researchers discuss the apparent contradictions in counting world poverty and inequality numbers, rates and trends. For example, Ravallion (2003) argues that the differences are due to measurement issues, e.g., how poverty is defined, use of absolute versus relative poverty, what levels are used to define poverty, and so forth. According to Ravallion (2003), defining poverty in absolute terms (e.g., the same purchasing power in all countries), results in finding larger declines in world poverty. Similalrly, defining inequality in absolute terms (absolute differences in levels of living, compared to relative differences) results in finding larger increases in inequality. Ravallion (2003) also points out that poverty and inequality data are generally questionnaire based, and there are a number of problems in using surveys. For example, questionnaires from different countries may use different definitions (e.g., using income versus consumption to measure well-being) or may ask about different time periods (e.g., last year, last month, etc.). All of these variations may result in finding different levels of poverty.

Reddy and Pogge (2003) also criticize the World Bank estimates, and argue for a better measure. According to Reddy and Pogge (2003), the main problems with the World Bank estimates are, "The Bank uses an arbitrary international poverty line unrelated to any clear conception of poverty. It employs a misleading and inaccurate measure of purchasing power "equivalence" that creates serious and irreparable difficulties for international and inter-temporal comparisons of income poverty. It extrapolates incorrectly from limited data and thereby creates an appearance of precision that masks the high probable error of its estimates. The systematic distortion introduced by these three flaws may have led to an understatement of the extent of global income poverty and to an incorrect inference that it has declined".

In sum, a decline in poverty would be consistent with other changes among less developed countries, such as improved literacy rates, declines in infant mortality rates, increased political freedom, increased newspapers, televisions and radios per capita, and increase in per capita GDP. However, there are still a number of problems with data and methods, and conclusions are therefore our 'best guess', though reasonable.

Health and Human Development

The 2002 UN Human Development Report (UNDP, 2003) indicates that life expectancy is a good indicator of a country's health, and that in the last several decades, life expectancy has increased in most regions of the world, except Sub-Saharan Africa (due to AIDS and conflicts), Eastern Europe and the Commonwealth of Independent States (former Russian Federation states). Also, though, life expectancy in high income OECD countries were still higher than life expectancy in other countries.

Similarly, there has dramatic decreases in infant mortality rates throughout the world. For the world, and for both less developed countries and more developed countries, Infant Mortality Rate (IMR) declined significantly between 1960 and 2001. For example, IMR among less developed countries declined from 141 infant deaths per 1000 births in 1960 to 63 in 2001. However, infant mortality rate was and still is very high for some countries. In 2001, the IMR among less developed countries, on average, was about 10 times as large as it was among more developed countries, and infant mortality rate for several west and north Africa countries was still above 150.

Social Changes

There appears to be little multinational research about changes in society that is available over the web. One study, described below, examines change in social values over a short time interval (Ehrlich, Franzese and Inglehart, 1999). One other study (Smith and Jarkko, 1998) examines national pride among 23 countries, and part of the study examined change in national pride over time. They found that "National pride is greatest in stable, established, developed democracies. Pride is lowest in ex-Socialist states, countries riven by ethnic conflict, and nations with war guilt." (summary section). In addition, rankings of national pride are very stable over time.

Interrelationships Among Social, Economic and Political Areas

A number of studies discuss the integration of social, political and economic change, or some aspects of these interrelationships. Ehrlich et al and Welzel et al use World Value Survey data to look at the interrelationship among changes in political, economic and social systems. Tilly examines the relationship between the state and the economy. Farr, Lord and Wolfenbarger look at how political freedom, economic freedom and economic growth are related.

Ehrlich, Franzese and Inglehart (1999) researched specifically the relationships among social values, economic growth and level of democracy. They examined how values, democracy and growth at one time period were related to values, democracy and growth at periods about 6-9 years later. Social values was an indicator of where a society was located on a survival-self expression continuum, varying from mainly focusing on survival issues to having their survival secure enough that they could focus on self expression.

They found that all three variables had a significant positive impact on each other. For example, "Higher levels of democracy in the past tend to produce more democracy, higher GNP, and more self expressive values in the present". The results are similar relating past GNP and self expressive values to present GNP, self expressive values and democracy, although the relationship of past self expressive values to present democracy is indirect.

They conclude that "Economic development and movements toward democracy and self expressive citizen-values tend to reinforce the others, supporting a theory that posits these three processes as the main elements of a larger syndrome, namely the modernization process". They also note that, for policy makers, the implication is that progress make on any one of these three dimensions will have positive results on the other two dimensions.

Welzel, Inglehart and Klingemann (2000) also discuss the relationships among expressive value change, economic modernization, and democratization. They note first that, while there is a great deal of research about the relationship between any two of these concepts, there is very little on the relationship among all three. Without an underlying theory of the interrelationships, it is very difficult to understand causal relationships between modernization, value changes and democratization.

Welzel, Inglehart and Klingemann argue that growth of human choice in society, or Human Development (HD) is the underlying concept that unifies these three major trends. Human Development "can be understood as the development of human beings' capabilities and opportunities to base their lives on free choice". Thus, "modernization, or economic HD, reduces constraints on the level of objective means by enlarging peoples' physical and cognitive resources. Value change, or ethical HD, reduces constraints on the level of subjective aspirations by intensifying human strive for self-expression. And democratization, or institutional HD, reduces constraints on the level of formal rules by granting citizens with 'negative' and 'positive' freedom rights". In sum, "economic resources, expressive values and freedom rights improve the societal opportunity structure in favour of human choice".

At the level of the individual person, these three concepts are tied together though aspiration adjustment. That is, people adjust their aspirations to their objective means. That is, "Human motivation is led in general by the strive for self-expression or growing choice.... people with higher education and higher incomes (i.e., greater physical and cognitive resources) put stronger emphasis on self-expression. These people have greater means to unfold their potential which makes it perfectly rational that they put stronger emphasis on self-expression. This is the micrological origin of the relation between resource mobilization and expressive values. In addition, there is a micrological origin of the relation between expressive values and democratic institutions. When people gain an increasingly self-expressive orientation it becomes perfectly rational that they support democracy, since democracy is the regime that enlarges their formal opportunities for self-expression. Exactly for this reason we will see that people tend to be the more supportive of democracy the stronger they emphasize expressive values".

Tilly (1997) describes the relationship between the state and economies in several different ways. First, the state influences the economy through political activities (i.e., war), creating administrative structures, infrastructural investment, and regulating, to varying degrees, exchanges, commitments and other relations among economic actors. Most historians have claimed that the relationship between the state and the economy is that autocratic empires typically coincide with landlord-dominated but peasant-based agrarian economies, and urbanized trading economies typically support thinner oligarchic states. Tilly examines Europe over the last 1000 years, using a comparison of organized capital versus organized coercion.

In this comparison, states range from "regions of sparse capital and abundant coercive means" at one end, to "regions featuring extensive concentrations of capital along with great fragmentation of coercive means" at the other end. States in different parts of the range practiced policies that had much different effects on their economies. Thus, coercion-intensive states, such as landlord dominated Russia, taxed those who were politically vulnerable rather than those who had wealth or income, and used its army to seize conspicuous unprotected wealth. On the other hand, capital-intensive states, such as merchant-dominated Venice, obtained money from excise taxes and customs, and purchased its armed forces national or international markets, activities which led to further commercialization of their economies. England and France, Tilly indicates, were in the middle of this range throughout most of this time period.

Tilly also describes the relationship between the state and the economy in a second way. The state, aside from it's other functions, serves as an instrument of exploitation, that is, as a support of owners of production, so that they can extract more from workers than the value workers put into the product. The state supports exploitation through regulations of the production of goods in ways that favour the owners of the means of production. Democratic governments mitigate exploitation by producing public goods and by increasing within its state of the numbers of beneficiaries of its system of exploitation.

However, there is as yet no general agreement on the relationship among democracy, capitalism, and economic growth. For example, some view democracy as an outgrowth of capitalism, while others describe countries experiencing rapid economic growth without moving toward capitalism. Since there are different views of the past and current relationships, there are consequently different expectations of the future. Thus, there are different views on how well development of currently mature capitalist economies represent probable paths for newly emerging economies,, how much pre-existing social and cultural organization constrains developing economies, and how much specific historical circumstances constrain development. As Tilly writes, "The debate continues."

A good deal of research also looks at the relationship among political and economic freedom, and economic growth. Farr, Lord and Wolfenbarger (1998), for example, looked at the time series relationship among economic and political freedom, and economic well being (real per capita GDP). They showed that "past economic freedom is significantly related to the current level of real per capita GDP" (Empirical results section). Also, past economic well being predicts current economic freedom. Thus, they argue, economic well being and economic freedom are bilateral, each contributing to the other. Their results also showed that past economic well being causes current political freedom. However, past political freedom did not predict current level of either economic well-being or economic freedom. Farr et all mention that "results in this paper provide no support for previous studies that suggest that political freedom significantly affects the level of economic well-being" (conclusion section). But they also mention that perhaps political freedom takes a longer time to have an effect on economic well being than was covered in their data set.

Data

Just as there is research on a wide range of social, political and economic change areas, there is a great deal of data. All of the following is available for free over the web.

Population data is often quite varied in timeliness, and data from different sources may have different time frames available. For example, the US Census Bureau (International Data Base, 2000) has recent estimates for total populations of most countries. However, for other variables, such as Urban Population as a Percent of Total Population, there are data for many countries from the 1970's, and in some cases even earlier. Similarly, data for age and sex is often from the 1980's and in some cases, earlier. On the other hand, the United Nations Economic and Social Commission for Asia and the Pacific has more recent data on some variables. For example, their sources for data on percent urban are from 1990's data sources, and the appear to be estimating percent urban for recent years.

Human development data has been released every year since 1990, by the UN has released Human Development Program (UNDP, no date). In particular, they publish the Human Development Indicator (HDI), a composite measure using life expectancy, adult literacy and schooling, and purchasing power.

Economic data includes GDP, Purchasing Power, and a variety of other measures. Gwartney and Lawson (2000) describe ratings of countries in terms of economic freedom. Several data sets describe GDP. "The Penn World Table displays a set of national accounts economic time series covering many countries. Its expenditure entries are denominated in a common set of prices in a common currency so that real quantity comparisons can be made, both between countries and over time." GPD data is also available from the Groningen Growth and Development Centre (GGDC, date). One of their data sets contains real gross domestic product in constant US dollars, and population, for 65 countries. Maddison's (1989, 1991) economic data covers OECD states, including annual data on GDP, the consumer price index and exports; periodic data for employment patterns, productivity and investment; and some similar data for a number of Asian and Latin American countries. Maddison's (1991) data, for the western states, often begins at 1870.

4

Administration of Social Welfare

Social work is a profession and a social science committed to the pursuit of social justice, to quality of life, and to the development of the full potential of each individual, group and community in a society. Social workers draw on the social sciences to solve social problems. They may work in research, practice, or both. Practitioners will usually possess a degree or registered license in the discipline, dependent on national law. Social work research is often focused in areas such as individual and family therapy, social policy, public administration and development. Social workers are organized into local, national, continental and international Professional bodies to further the aims of the profession.

History

Contemporary Professional Development

International Federation of Social Workers states, of social work today, "social work bases its methodology on a systematic body of evidence-based knowledge derived from research and practice evaluation, including local and indigenous knowledge specific to its context. It recognizes the complexity of interactions between human beings and their environment, and the capacity of people both to be affected by and to alter the multiple influences upon them including bio-psychosocial factors. The social work profession draws on theories of human development, social theory and social systems to analyse complex situations and to facilitate individual, organizational, social and cultural changes."

A hopeful development for bridging this gap is the compilation, in many practice fields, of collections of "best practices" which attempt to distill research findings and the experience of respected practitioners into effective practice techniques. Although social work has roots in the informatics revolution, an important contemporary development in the profession is overcoming suspicion of technology and taking advantage of the potential of information technology to empower users.

Qualifications

Professional social workers are generally considered those who hold a masters (MSW) in Social Work. Often these practitioners must also obtain a license or be professionally registered.

In some areas of the world, social workers start with a Bachelor of Social Work (BA, BSc or BSW and some university conduct Diploma in Social Work Programme) degree. Some countries offer post-Graduate degrees like the master's degree (MA, MSc or MSW and Post Graduate Diploma in Social work) or the doctoral degree (Ph.D or DSW).

In a number of countries and jurisdictions, registration or licensure of people working as social workers is required and there are mandated qualifications. In other places, a professional association sets academic and experiential requirements for admission to membership. The success of these professional bodies' efforts is demonstrated in the fact that these same requirements are recognized by employers as necessary for employment.

Professional Associations

There are a number of professional associations for social workers. The purpose of these associations is to provide ethical guidance, and other forms of support for their members and social workers in general. The International Federation of Social Workers (IFSW) and the International Association of Schools of Social Work (IASSW) are among the professional associations that exist to enhance the profession of social work. *Network of Professional Social Workers* is a fast growing professional network of Social Workers across the globe. Network of Professional Social Workers aims to connect social workers beyond their local and national associations across the globe. Network of Professional Social Workers effectively uses Social networking media such as Linkedin, Face Book etc. to network with Social Workers across many countries and initiate discussions on various issues affecting Social Work Profession. Network of Professional Social Workers Group list serve, NPSW. A large, national group in the United States is the National Association of Social Workers (NASW). In addition to providing ethical guidance and support, it also provides accreditation opportunities and a current listing of employment opportunities.

Role of the Professional

The main tasks of professional social workers can include a variety of services such as case management (linking clients with agencies and programs that will meet their psychosocial needs), counselling (psychotherapy), human services management, social welfare policy analysis, policy and practice development, community organizing, international, social and community development, advocacy, teaching (in schools of social work), and social science research.

Types of Professional Intervention

There are three general categories or levels of intervention. The first is "Macro" social work which involves society or communities as a whole. This type of social work practice would include policy forming and advocacy on a national or international scale.

The second level of intervention is described as "Mezzo" social work practice. This level would involve work with agencies, small organizations, and other small groups. This practice would include policy making within a social work agency or developing programs for a particular neighbourhood.

The final level is the "Micro" level that involves service to individuals and families. Currently, there is a great deal of concern among some in the profession that it has left behind its historical roots and is focused overwhelmingly on the practice of micro, primarily psychological, interventions.

There are a wide variety of activities that can be considered social work and professional social workers are employed in many different types of environments. The following list details some of the main fields of social work.

Social Work Perspectives

Perspectives are ways of viewing and thinking about practice. They are used as a framework to assist clients in therapy or other social work settings.

In US, there are four main perspectives social workers employ: Ecosystemic/Ecological System, Feminist, Generalist, and Strengths Perspectives.

Ecosystemic/Ecological System-This perspective honours the mutual relationship between individuals and their environment. It looks at the goodness of fit between the individual's capacities and the environment's resources and capacities.

Feminist-This perspective examines the impact of societal beliefs, stereotypes and practices as the related to gender and sex roles. It values the feminine attributes of clients and attempts to address societal patriarchy, androcentrism and sexist practices which seek to oppress and exploit women.

Generalist-An approach to practice that involves a holistic understanding of the client on multiple levels-individual, family, community, organizational. This approach integrates various models and theories to help understand the client's situation and uses an eclectic mix of interventions and techniques. Inherent in this perspective is a collaborative process in which the client and the worker have mutual responsibility.

Strengths-This perspective focuses on what the client is already doing that is successful. The goal of all interactions is to identify and augment the client's strengths and resources. There is an expectation that strengths exist both in the client and in their larger environment and that the clients know best how to utilize these resources. It also assumes that nobody knows the upper limits of an individual's capacity to grow.

Social Welfare System

The social welfare system refers to "the whole set of modern social programs offering income maintenance in cases of unemployment, industrial accident, illness, forced retirement, loss of a family breadwinner, or extreme deprivation, as well as various sorts of educational, preventive, and regulatory programs". President Franklin D. Roosevelt's New Deal policies, especially the Social Security Act of 1935, are regarded as the inauguration of the modern social welfare system in the United States. Social scientists and historians tend to have a much more expansive view of welfare than that put forth in the popular media, which associates welfare with certain types of aid to the poor. From the 1950s to the 2000s, scholars have been concerned with explaining both the origins of social welfare systems and the substantial variation in its form among advanced industrial countries.

The Emergence of Welfare States

An early and influential approach to understanding the origins of welfare states argued they emerged as part of the "logic of industrialism." That is, scholars such as Harold Wilensky and Clark Kerr, among others, stressed that complex societies require a modern social welfare system in order to ensure a healthy, well-trained workforce and care for retired workers. Scholars criticized this view on a number of grounds. For example, in *Protecting Soldiers and Mothers* (1992) Theda Skocpol noted that in some places welfare provisions predated industrialization. In addition, Skocpol and other scholars such as Gosta Esping-Anderson noted that the logic of industrialism approach failed to explain the variation among welfare state systems.

Another group of scholars emphasized the humanitarian or idealistic motives for the expansion of welfare programs in the 1960s. This perspective argued that President Lyndon B. Johnson and other proponents of the Great Society programs implemented these policies and programs in response to the needs of the poor and oppressed. In *Regulating the Poor* (1971) Frances Fox Piven and Richard Cloward criticized this view, emphasizing that political and economic elites were primarily concerned with controlling the poor, not helping them out of poverty. Through an historical discussion of early reform efforts in England and the New Deal era in the United States, Piven and Cloward noted that welfare relief expanded during times of crisis so as to quell social unrest and then was retracted after the crisis was averted.

Three Worlds of Welfare Capitalism

Whether or not and to what extent elites could roll back welfare provisions depended, according to Esping-Anderson, on the strength of political class coalitions. In his *Three Worlds of Welfare Capitalism* (1990), Esping-Anderson argued modern welfare state systems emerged in response to the political class coalitions of workers and farmers in the late nineteenth and early twentieth centuries. Then welfare states expanded or contracted depending on the strength of the coalition of the working and middle classes. These political class coalitions sought state policies that enabled individuals to live outside the demands of the market, what Esping-Anderson termed *decom-modification*. For example, workers have historically organized to demand unemployment compensation, pensions, health care, and other programs. These provisions enable individuals to exist without having to work. This improves the quality of life for workers and enables them to demand better work conditions from their employers.

Furthermore, welfare states in advanced capitalist countries display significant variation in the levels of decom-modification each system provides for its citizens. In fact, Esping-Anderson argued they can be grouped together into what he called three worlds of welfare capitalism: the conservative (e.g., Germany), the liberal (e.g., United States), and the social democratic (e.g., Sweden).

For example, in liberal welfare regimes, such as the United States, working class movements and parties have been historically weak. In these countries workers were unable to forge durable coalitions with farmers and later with the new middle classes. As a result, the welfare system in liberal regimes is relatively small and dualistic. That is, instead of a universal system where everyone benefits from welfare policies and programs, it creates two segments in society: one group receives benefits based on their tax contributions while a second group receives benefits regardless of whether or not they pay into the system. In the United States, social security and unemployment insurance are considered contributory entitlements.

For most workers, a portion of each pay check goes toward funding these programs. The second group of welfare recipients is comprised of those who receive aid without making a contribution. This type of aid is means-tested; that is, recipients have to demonstrate they qualify for relief and have to submit to government surveillance, else forfeiting the aid. In addition, in this dualistic system recipients of entitlements (e.g., Social Security) are not stigmatized while those who receive non-contributory aid (e.g., Aid to Families with Dependent Children [AFDC]) are heavily stigmatized. This stigma is supposed to provide a disincentive to receiving aid. For Esping-Anderson decom-modification in liberal welfare regimes is low.

In conservative welfare regimes, such as Germany, working class movements are stronger and successfully forge coalitions first with farmers and later with the middle class. However, all social policy is cast in the light of Catholic ideals of tradition and stability. Emphasis is placed on maintaining the traditional family, with a male breadwinner and female homemaker. Thus decom-modification is higher than in liberal regimes; yet feminists have pointed out that conservative regimes maintain a subordinate role for women.

In social democratic welfare regimes, such as Sweden, working class movements are strong and successfully forge alliances with farmers and the middle class. Thus for Esping-Anderson decom-modification is the highest in social democratic welfare regimes. In these countries, taxes are relatively high, and instead of a dualistic system, benefits are granted on a universal basis, thus preventing the negative consequences of dualism and assuring continued support from the middle classes.

Modern Interpretations

Feminists such as Skocpol have criticized class-based explanations of welfare state systems for failing to take seriously the role of state managers in the production of social policy. Skocpol argued that class-based scholars have emphasized the role of working class (male) movements in provoking the rise of welfare states. As such, they have offered an explanation of the so-called paternal welfare state. Skocpol argued that in the United States a maternalist welfare state predated the paternalist one.

Skocpol found that the earliest efforts at social provision focused on taking care of Northern Civil War veterans in the late 1800s. This was an early and important form of old age pension. In addition, she traced the efforts of early feminists who played key roles in gaining pensions for women and policies that helped children in the early twentieth century. These feminists successfully influenced the creation of a welfare state that sought to protect soldiers and mothers.

Linda Gordon studied many of the same early feminists as Skocpol and offered important insights into maternalist welfare states and the origins of welfare in the United States. In *Pitied but Not Entitled* (1994) Gordon argued that feminists played key roles in agitating for and making governmental policy, noting that early welfare policies sought to reinforce traditional under standings of femininity, especially those that emphasized homemaking and care giving. Thus the maternalist policies aimed at "protecting soldiers and mothers" were also paternalist, premised on the idea that men should work and women should be subordinate to them, taking care of the housework and the children.

Moreover, Gordon demonstrated how welfare policies of the early twentieth century emphasized care for white women who were married with children. Single mothers and women of colour were excluded from policies that were designed to complement the "family wage" earned by male husbands/workers. As such, the role of welfare aid was to help maintain the integrity of the traditional white family without usurping the role of male breadwinner. However, a substantial number of male workers had a very hard time earning enough money to support their families, a situation even more pronounced for single mothers.

In addition, Gordon maintained that New Deal welfare policies did more to help the nonpoor than the poor. Policy makers restricted the kinds of jobs that could contribute to Social Security and unemployment insurance. Due to the kinds of jobs they had, such as in agriculture or as domestic help, most women and blacks, for example, were not eligible for these benefits.

This gendered and racialized nature of early welfare policies in part reflected the power of southern elites who influenced social policy so as to maintain a loose agricultural labour market in the South. As a result of concerted political behaviour of southern elites, the New Deal welfare policies were enacted unevenly in the South, if they were enacted at all. In the South, welfare provisions were meager, while in the industrialized North they were more generous.

This point is expanded upon by Jill Quadagno, who studied welfare policies from the New Deal through President Johnson's Great Society programs of the 1960s. In *The Colour of Welfare* (1994), Quadagno showed how the Great Society programs sought to incorporate blacks and other minorities into the welfare state for the first time. However, such efforts resulted in a conservative backlash that pushed for a retrenchment of welfare to deny blacks an equal footing in society. This retrenchment, inaugurated by President Jimmy Carter, became a key platform of President Ronald Reagan, and was capped off by the signing of President Bill Clinton's "End Welfare as We Know It" bill in 1996, which ended the U.S. government's commitment to providing a safety net for the poor.

The 1996 welfare reform bill transformed the pivotal AFDC program into TANF (Temporary Assistance to Needy Families), premised on the belief that instead of aid the government should provide inducements to work. Under these so-called workfare programs, there is a lifetime limit of five years of support, recipients must find work within two years or perform free community service, unmarried mothers must identify fathers to receive aid, and immigrants as well as unmarried teen parents are denied access to welfare programs.

Social Welfare

So what is "Social Welfare"?

Here is a simple definition: Social welfare is about how people, communities and institutions in a society take action to provide certain minimum standards and certain opportunities. It is generally about helping people facing contingencies.

What Contingencies?

- unemployment
- illness, disease, violence
- injured or disabled
- working poor
- homeless
- divorce or separation
- raising children
- elderly requiring care.

Categories of Contingencies

- interruptions of earning capacity
- occasions requiring special expenditure
- greater continuous budgetary needs than the family income.

Three Directions of Social Welfare

- provision of minimum income (example: social assistance, Old Age Security)
- provision of income for certain contingencies (example: Employment Insurance)
- provisions of social services (example: child services).

What are Social Services?

Personal or community services provided by the state and non-profit organizations for members of the community, such as day-care, housing, health, crisis intervention, support groups for abused women, and probation.

Social Reform and Social Action

There is another part to social work and welfare and that is the doing part, the active part.

Social work originated in part, in the 19th century revulsion to the effects of the industrial system which included :

- the destruction of family life
- the poverty
- the numbers of homeless adults and children.

It was and remains an action oriented subject in which individual and social change is a key part. So social work and social welfare is about understanding and about acting on that understanding to try to change the world that is observed.

5

Economic Planning and Development

Economy of India

The economy of India is the twelfth largest economy in the world by nominal value and the fourth largest by purchasing power parity (PPP). In the 1990s, following economic reform from the socialist-inspired economy of post-independence India, the country began to experience rapid economic growth, as markets opened for international competition and investment. In the 21st century, India is an emerging economic power with vast human and natural resources, and a huge knowledge base. Economists predict that by 2020, India will be among the leading economies of the world.

India was under social democratic-based policies from 1947 to 1991. The economy was characterised by extensive regulation, protectionism, and public ownership, leading to pervasive corruption and slow growth. Since 1991, continuing economic liberalisation has moved the economy towards a market-based system. A revival of economic reforms and better economic policy in 2000s accelerated India's economic growth rate. By 2008, India had established itself as the world's second-fastest growing major economy. However, the year 2009 saw a significant slow down in India's official GDP growth rate to 6.1% as well as the return of a large projected fiscal deficit of 10.3% of GDP which would be among the highest in the world. India's large service industry accounts for 62.6% of the country's GDP while the industrial and agricultural sector contribute 20% and 17.5% respectively. Agriculture is the predominant occupation in India, accounting for about 52% of employment. The service sector makes up a further 34%, and industrial sector around 14%. The labour force totals half a billion workers. Major agricultural products include rice, wheat, oilseed, cotton, jute, tea, sugarcane, potatoes, cattle, water buffalo, sheep, goats, poultry and fish. Major industries include telecommunications, textiles, chemicals, food processing, steel, transportation equipment, cement, mining, petroleum, machinery, information technology enabled services and software.

India's per capita income (nominal) is $1032, ranked 139th in the world, while its per capita (PPP) of US$ 2,932 is ranked 128th. Previously a closed economy, India's trade has grown fast. India currently accounts for 1.5% of World trade as of 2007 according to the WTO. According to the World Trade Statistics of the WTO in 2006, India's total merchandise trade (counting exports and imports) was valued at $294 billion in 2006 and India's services trade inclusive of export and import was $143 billion. Thus, India's global economic engagement in 2006 covering both merchandise and services trade was of the order of $437 billion, up by a record 72% from a level of $253 billion in 2004. India's trade has reached a still relatively moderate share 24% of GDP in 2006, up from 6% in 1985.

Despite robust economic growth, India continues to face many major problems. The recent economic development has widened the economic inequality across the country. Despite sustained high economic growth rate, approximately 80% of its population lives on less than $2 a day (PPP). Even though the arrival of Green Revolution brought end to famines in India, 40% of children under the age of three are underweight and a third of all men and women suffer from chronic energy deficiency.

History

India's economic history can be broadly divided into three eras, beginning with the pre-colonial period lasting up to the 18th century. The advent of British colonisation started the colonial period in the early 19th century, which ended with independence in 1947. The third period stretches from independence in 1947 until now.

Pre-Colonial

The citizens of the Indus Valley civilisation, a permanent settlement that flourished between 2800 BC and 1800 BC, practiced agriculture, domesticated animals, used uniform weights and measures, made tools and weapons, and traded with other cities. Evidence of well planned streets, a drainage system and water supply reveals their knowledge of urban planning, which included the world's first urban sanitation systems and the existence of a form of municipal government.

The 1872 census revealed that 99.3% of the population of the region constituting present-day India resided in villages, whose economies were largely isolated and self-sustaining, with agriculture the predominant occupation. This satisfied the food requirements of the village and provided raw materials for hand-based industries, such as textiles, food processing and crafts. Although many kingdoms and rulers issued coins, barter was prevalent. Villages paid a portion of their agricultural produce as revenue to the rulers, while its craftsmen received a part of the crops at harvest time for their services.

Religion, especially Hinduism, and the caste and the joint family systems, played an influential role in shaping economic activities. The caste system functioned much like medieval European guilds, ensuring the division of labour, providing for the training of apprentices and, in some cases, allowing manufacturers to achieve narrow specialization. For instance, in certain regions, producing each variety of cloth was the specialty of a particular sub-caste.

Assessment of India's pre-colonial economy is mostly qualitative, owing to the lack of quantitative information. One estimate puts the revenue of Akbar's Mughal Empire in 1600 at £17.5 million, in contrast with the total revenue of Great Britain in 1800, which totalled £16 million. India, by the time of the arrival of the British, was a largely traditional agrarian economy with a dominant subsistence sector dependent on primitive technology. It existed alongside a competitively developed network of commerce, manufacturing and credit. After the decline of the Mughals, western, central and parts of south and north India were integrated and administered by the Maratha Empire. The Maratha

Empire's budget in 1740s, at its peak, was Rs. 100 million. After the loss at Panipat, the Maratha Empire disintegrated into confederate states of Gwalior, Baroda, Indore, Jhansi, Nagpur, Pune and Kolhapur. Gwalior state had a budget of Rs. 30M. However, at this time, British East India company entered the Indian political theatre. Until 1857, when India was firmly under the British crown, the country remained in a state of political instability due to internecine wars and conflicts.

Colonial

Company rule in India brought a major change in the taxation environment from revenue taxes to property taxes, resulting in mass impoverishment and destitution of majority of farmers and led to numerous famines. The economic policies of the British Raj effectively bankrupted India's large handicrafts industry and caused a massive drain of India's resources. Indian Nationalists employed the successful Swadeshi movement, as strategy to diminish British economic superiority by boycotting British products and the reviving the market for domestic-made products and production techniques. India had become a strong market for superior finished European goods. This was because of vast gains made by the Industrial revolution in Europe, the effects of which was deprived to Colonial India.

The Nationalists had hoped to revive the domestic industries that were badly effected by polices implemented by British Raj which had made them uncompetitive to British made goods.

An estimate by Cambridge University historian Angus Maddison reveals that "India's share of the world income fell from 22.6% in 1700, comparable to Europe's share of 23.3%, to a low of 3.8% in 1952". It also created an institutional environment that, on paper, guaranteed property rights among the colonisers, encouraged free trade, and created a single currency with fixed exchange rates, standardized weights and measures, capital markets. It also established a well developed system of railways and telegraphs, a civil service that aimed to be free from political interference, a common-law and an adversarial legal system. India's colonisation by the British coincided with major changes in the world economy—industrialisation, and significant growth in production and trade. However, at the end of colonial rule, India inherited an economy that was one of the poorest in the developing world, with industrial development stalled, agriculture unable to feed a rapidly growing population, India had one of the world's lowest life expectancies, and low rates for literacy.

The impact of the British rule on India's economy is a controversial topic. Leaders of the Indian independence movement, and left-nationalist economic historians have blamed colonial rule for the dismal state of India's economy in its aftermath and that financial strength required for Industrial development in Europe was derived from the wealth taken from Colonies in Asia and Africa. At the same time right-wing historians have countered that India's low economic performance was due to various sectors being in a state of growth and decline due to changes brought in by colonialism and a world that was moving towards industrialization and economic integration.

Independence to 1991

Indian economic policy after independence was influenced by the colonial experience (which was seen by Indian leaders as exploitative in nature) and by those leaders' exposure to Fabian socialism. Policy tended towards protectionism, with a strong emphasis on import substitution, industrialization, state intervention in labour and financial markets, a large public sector, business regulation, and central planning. Five-Year Plans of India resembled central planning in the Soviet Union. Steel, mining, machine tools, water, telecommunications, insurance, and electrical plants, among other industries, were effectively nationalized in the mid-1950s. Elaborate licences, regulations and the accompanying red tape, commonly referred to as Licence Raj, were required to set up business in India between 1947 and 1990.

Jawaharlal Nehru, the first prime minister, along with the statistician Prasanta Chandra Mahalanobis, carried on by Indira Gandhi formulated and oversaw economic policy. They expected favourable outcomes from this strategy, because it involved both public and private sectors and was based on direct and indirect state intervention, rather than the more extreme Soviet-style central command system. The policy of concentrating simultaneously on capital-and technology-intensive heavy industry and subsidizing manual, low-skill cottage industries was criticized by economist

Milton Friedman, who thought it would waste capital and labour, and retard the development of small manufacturers. The rate from 1947–80 was derisively referred to as the Hindu rate of growth, because of the unfavourable comparison with growth rates in other Asian countries, especially the "East Asian Tigers".

The Rockefeller Foundation's research in high-yielding varieties of seeds, their introduction after 1965 and the increased use of fertilizers and irrigation are known collectively as the Green Revolution in India, which provided the increase in production needed to make India self-sufficient in food grains, thus improving agriculture in India. Famine in India, once accepted as inevitable, has not returned since the end of colonial.

Since 1991

In the late 80s, the government led by Rajiv Gandhi eased restrictions on capacity expansion for incumbents, removed price controls and reduced corporate taxes. While this increased the rate of growth, it also led to high fiscal deficits and a worsening current account. The collapse of the Soviet Union, which was India's major trading partner, and the first Gulf War, which caused a spike in oil prices, caused a major balance-of-payments crisis for India, which found itself facing the prospect of defaulting on its loans. India asked for a $1.8 billion bailout loan from IMF, which in return demanded reforms.

In response, Prime Minister Narasimha Rao along with his finance minister Manmohan Singh initiated the economic liberalisation of 1991. The reforms did away with the Licence Raj (investment, industrial and import licensing) and ended many public monopolies, allowing automatic approval of foreign direct investment in many sectors. Since then, the overall direction of liberalisation has remained the same, irrespective of the ruling party, although no party has tried to take on powerful lobbies such as the trade unions and farmers, or contentious issues such as reforming labour laws and reducing agricultural subsidies. Since 1990 India has emerged as one of the fastest-growing economies in the developing world; during this period, the economy has grown constantly, but with a few major setbacks. This has been accompanied by increases in life expectancy, literacy rates and food security.

While the credit rating of India was hit by its nuclear tests in 1998, it has been raised to investment level in 2007 by S&P and Moody's. In 2003, Goldman Sachs predicted that India's GDP in current prices will overtake France and Italy by 2020, Germany, UK and Russia by 2025 and Japan by 2035. By 2035, it was projected to be the third largest economy of the world, behind US and China. In 2009 India purchased 200 Tons of Gold for $6.7 Billion from IMF as a total role reversal from 1991.

Sectors

Agriculture

India ranks second worldwide in farm output. Agriculture and allied sectors like forestry, logging and fishing accounted for 16.6% of the GDP in 2007, employed 60% of the total workforce and despite a steady decline of its share in the GDP, is still the largest economic sector and plays a significant role in the overall socioeconomic development of India. Yields per unit area of all crops have grown since 1950, due to the special emphasis placed on agriculture in the five-year plans and steady improvements in irrigation, technology, application of modern agricultural practices and provision of agricultural credit and subsidies since Green revolution in India. However, international comparisons reveal the average yield in India is generally 30% to 50% of the highest average yield in the world.

India is the largest producer in the world of milk, cashew nuts, coconuts, tea, ginger, turmeric and black pepper. It also has the world's largest cattle population: 193 million. It is the second largest producer of wheat, rice, sugar, cotton, silk, peanuts and inland fish. It is the third largest producer of tobacco. India is the largest fruit producer, accounting for 10% of the world fruit production. It is the leading producer of bananas, sapotas and mangoes.

India is the second largest producer and the largest consumer of silk in the world, with the majority of the 77 million kg (2005) production taking place in Karnataka State, particularly in Mysore and the North Bangalore regions of Muddenahalli, Kanivenarayanapura, and Doddaballapura, the upcoming sites of a INR 700 million "Silk City".

Industry and Services

Industry accounts for 54.6% of the GDP and employ 17% of the total workforce. However, about one-third of the industrial labour force is engaged in simple household manufacturing only. In absolute terms, India is 16th in the world in terms of nominal factory output. India's small industry makes up 5% of carbon dioxide emissions in the world.

Economic reforms brought foreign competition, led to privatisation of certain public sector industries, opened up sectors hitherto reserved for the public sector and led to an expansion in the production of fast-moving consumer goods. Post-liberalisation, the Indian private sector, which was usually run by oligopolies of old family firms and required political connections to prosper was faced with foreign competition, including the threat of cheaper Chinese imports. It has since handled the change by squeezing costs, revamping management, focusing on designing new products and relying on low labour costs and technology.

Textile manufacturing is the second largest source for employment after agriculture and accounts for 26% of manufacturing output. Tirupur has gained universal recognition as the leading source of hosiery, knitted garments, casual wear and sportswear. Dharavi slum in Mumbai has gained fame for leather products. Tata Motors' Nano attempts to be the world's cheapest car. India is fifteenth in services output. It provides employment to 23% of work force, and it is growing fast, growth rate 7.5% in 1991–2000 up from 4.5% in 1951–80. It has the largest share in the GDP, accounting for 55% in 2007 up from 15% in 1950.

Business services (information technology, information technology enabled services, business process out sourcing) are among the fastest growing sectors contributing to one third of the total output of services in 2000. The growth in the IT sector is attributed to increased specialization, and an availability of a large pool of low cost, but highly skilled, educated and fluent English-speaking workers, on the supply side, matched on the demand side by an increased demand from foreign consumers interested in India's service exports, or those looking to out source their operations. The share of India's IT industry to the country's GDP increased from 4.8 % in 2005-06 to 7% in 2008. In 2009, seven

Indian firms were listed among the top 15 technology out sourcing companies in the world. In March 2009, annual revenues from out sourcing operations in India amounted to US$60 billion and this is expected to increase to US$225 billion by 2020.

Organized retail such supermarkets accounts for 24% of the market as of 2008. Regulations prevent most foreign investment in retailing. Moreover, over thirty regulations such as "signboard licences" and "anti-hoarding measures" may have to be complied before a store can open doors. There are taxes for moving goods to states, from states, and even within states. Tourism in India is relatively undeveloped, but growing at double digits. Some hospitals woo medical tourism.

Banking and Finance

The Indian money market is classified into: the organised sector (comprising private, public and foreign owned commercial banks and cooperative banks, together known as *scheduled banks*); and the unorganised sector (comprising individual or family owned indigenous bankers or money lenders and non-banking financial companies (NBFCs)). The unorganised sector and micro-credit are still preferred over traditional banks in rural and sub-urban areas, especially for non-productive purposes, like ceremonies and short duration loans.

Prime Minister Indira Gandhi nationalised 14 banks in 1969, followed by six others in 1980, and made it mandatory for banks to provide 40% of their net credit to priority sectors like agriculture, small-scale industry, retail trade, small businesses, etc. to ensure that the banks fulfil their social and developmental goals. Since then, the number of bank branches has increased from 10,120 in 1969 to 98,910 in 2003 and the population covered by a branch decreased from 63,800 to 15,000 during the same period. The total deposits increased 32.6 times between 1971 to 1991 compared to 7 times between 1951 to 1971. Despite an increase of rural branches, from 1,860 or 22% of the total number of branches in 1969 to 32,270 or 48%, only 32,270 out of 5 lakh (500,000) villages are covered by a scheduled bank.

The public sector banks hold over 75% of total assets of the banking industry, with the private and foreign banks holding 18.2% and 6.5% respectively. Since liberalisation, the government has approved significant banking reforms. While some of these relate to nationalised banks (like encouraging mergers, reducing government interference and increasing profitability and competitiveness), other reforms have opened up the banking and insurance sectors to private and foreign players. More than half of personal savings are invested in physical assets such as land, houses, cattle, and gold.

Natural Resources

India's total cultivable area is 1,269,219 km^2 (56.78% of total land area), which is decreasing due to constant pressure from an ever growing population and increased urbanisation. India has a total water surface area of 314,400 km^2 and receives an average annual rainfall of 1,100 mm. Irrigation accounts for 92% of the water utilisation, and comprised 380 km^2 in 1974, and is expected to rise to 1,050 km^2 by 2025, with the balance accounted for by industrial and domestic consumers. India's inland water resources comprising rivers, canals, ponds and lakes and marine resources comprising the east and west coasts of the Indian ocean and other gulfs and bays provide employment to nearly 6 million people in the fisheries sector. In 2008, India had the world's third largest fishing industry.

India's major mineral resources include coal, iron, manganese, mica, bauxite, titanium, chromite, limestone and thorium. India meets most of its domestic energy demand through its 92 billion tonnes of coal reserves (about 10% of world's coal reserves).

India's huge thorium reserves — about 25% of world's reserves — is expected to fuel the country's ambitious nuclear energy program in the long-run. India's dwindling uranium reserves stagnated the growth of nuclear energy in the country for many years. However, the Indo-US nuclear deal has paved the way for India to import uranium from other countries. India is also believed to be rich in certain renewable sources of energy with significant future potential such as solar, wind and biofuels (jatropha, sugarcane).

Petroleum and Natural Gas

India's oil reserves, found in Bombay High, parts of Gujarat, Rajasthan and eastern Assam, meet 25% of the country's domestic oil demand. India's total proven oil reserves stand at 11 billion barrels, of which Bombay High is believed to hold 6.1 billion barrels and Mangala Area in Rajasthan an additional 3.6 billion barrels.

In 2009, India imported 2.56 million barrels of oil per day, making it one of largest buyers of crude oil in the world. The petroleum industry in India mostly consists of public sector companies such as Oil and Natural Gas Corporation (ONGC), Hindustan Petroleum Corporation Limited (HPCL) and Indian Petrochemicals Corporation Limited (IPCL). There are some major private Indian companies in oil sector such as Reliance Industries Limited (RIL) which operates the world's largest oil refining complex.

Pharmaceuticals

India has a self reliant Pharmaceuticals industry. The majority of its medical consumables are produced domestically. Pharmaceutical Industry in India is dotted with companies like Ranbaxy Labouratories, Dr. Reddy's Labouratories, Cipla which have created a niche for themselves at world level.

Today, India is an exporter of countries like United States and Russia. In terms of the global market, India currently holds a modest 1-2% share, but it has been growing at approximately 10% per year. Indian Pharmaceutical Industry is often compared to Pharmaceutical Industry in the USA.

External Trade and Investment

Global Trade Relations

India's economy is mostly dependent on its large internal market with external trade accounting for just 20% of the country's GDP. In 2008, India accounted for 1.45% of global merchandise trade and 2.8% of global commercial services export. Until the liberalization of 1991, India was largely and intentionally isolated from the world markets, to protect its economy and to achieve self-reliance. Foreign trade was subject to import tariffs, export taxes and quantitative restrictions, while foreign direct investment (FDI) was restricted by upper-limit equity participation, restrictions on technology transfer, export obligations and government approvals; these approvals were needed for nearly 60% of new FDI in the industrial sector. The restrictions ensured that FDI averaged only around US$200 million annually between 1985 and 1991; a large percentage of the capital flows consisted of foreign aid, commercial borrowing and deposits of non-resident Indians. India's exports were stagnant for the first 15 years after independence, due to the predominance of tea, jute and cotton manufactures, demand for which was generally inelastic. Imports in the same period consisted predominantly of machinery, equipment and raw materials, due to nascent industrialization.

Since liberalization, the value of India's international trade has become more broad-based and has risen to Rs. 63,080,109 crores in 2003–04 from Rs.1,250 crores in 1950–51. India's major trading partners are China, the US, the UAE, the UK, Japan and the EU. The exports during April 2007 were $12.31 billion up by 16% and import were $17.68 billion with an increase of 18.06% over the previous year. In 2006-07, major export commodities included engineering goods, petroleum products, chemicals and pharmaceuticals, gems and jewellery, textiles and garments, agricultural products, iron ore and other minerals. Major import commodities included crude oil and related products, machinery, electronic goods, gold and silver.

India is a founding-member of General Agreement on Tariffs and Trade (GATT) since 1947 and its successor, the WTO. While participating actively in its general council meetings, India has been crucial in voicing the concerns of the developing world. For instance, India has continued its opposition to the inclusion of such matters as labour and environment issues and other *non-tariff barriers* into the WTO policies.

Balance of Payments

Since independence, India's balance of payments on its current account has been negative. Since liberalisation in the 1990s (precipitated by a balance of payment crisis), India's exports have been consistently rising, covering 80.3% of its imports in 2002–03, up from 66.2% in 1990–91. India's growing oil import bill is seen as the main driver behind the large current account deficit. In 2007-08, India imported 120.1 million tonnes of crude oil, more than 3/4th of the domestic demand, at a cost of $61.72 billion.

Although India is still a net importer, since 1996–97 its overall balance of payments (i.e., including the capital account balance) has been positive, largely on account of increased foreign direct investment and deposits from non-resident Indians; until this time, the overall balance was only occasionally positive on account of external assistance and commercial borrowings. As a result, India's foreign currency reserves stood at $285 billion in 2008.

Due to the global late-2000s recession, both Indian exports and imports declined by 29.2% and 39.2% respectively in June 2009. The steep decline was because countries hit hardest by the global recession, such as United States and members of the European Union, account for more than 60% of Indian exports. However, since the decline in imports was much sharper compared to the decline in exports, India's trade deficit reduced to 252.5 billion rupee.

India's reliance on external assistance and commercial borrowings has decreased since 1991–92, and since 2002–03, it has gradually been repaying these debts. Declining interest rates and reduced borrowings decreased India's debt service ratio to 4.5% in 2007. In India, External Commercial Borrowings (ECBs) are being permitted by the Government for providing an additional source of funds to Indian corporates. The Ministry of Finance monitors and regulates these borrowings (ECBs) through ECB policy guidelines.

Foreign Direct Investment in India

As the fourth-largest economy in the world in PPP terms, India is a preferred destination for foreign direct investments (FDI); India has strengths in telecommunication, information technology and other significant areas such as auto components, chemicals, apparels, pharmaceuticals, and jewellery. Despite a surge in foreign investments, rigid FDI policies resulted in a significant hindrance. However, due to some positive economic reforms aimed at deregulating the economy and stimulating foreign investment, India has positioned itself as one of the front-runners of the rapidly growing Asia Pacific Region. India has a large pool of skilled managerial and technical expertise. The size of the middle-class population stands at 300 million and represents a growing consumer market.

The inordinately high investment from Mauritius is due to routing of international funds through the country given significant capital gains tax advantages; double taxation is avoided due to a tax treaty between India and Mauritius, and Mauriitus is a capital gains tax haven, effectively creating a zero-taxation FDI channel.

India's recently liberalized FDI policy (2005) allows up to a 100% FDI stake in ventures. Industrial policy reforms have substantially reduced industrial licensing requirements, removed restrictions on expansion and facilitated easy access to foreign technology and foreign direct investment FDI.

The upward moving growth curve of the real-estate sector owes some credit to a booming economy and liberalized FDI regime. In March 2005, the government amended the rules to allow 100 percent FDI in the construction business. This automatic route has been permitted in townships, housing, built-up infrastructure and construction development projects including housing, commercial premises, hotels, resorts, hospitals, educational institutions, recreational facilities, and city-and regional-level infrastructure.

A number of changes were approved on the FDI policy to remove the caps in most sectors. Fields which require relaxation in FDI restrictions include civil aviation, construction development, industrial parks, petroleum and natural gas, commodity exchanges, credit-information services and mining.

But this still leaves an unfinished agenda of permitting greater foreign investment in politically sensitive areas such as insurance and retailing. FDI inflows into India reached a record $19.5 billion in fiscal year 2006-07 (April-March), according to the government's Secretariat for Industrial Assistance.

This was more than double the total of US$7.8bn in the previous fiscal year. The FDI inflow for 2007-08 has been reported as $24 billion and for 2008-09, it is expected to be above $35 billion. A critical factor in determining India's continued economic growth and realizing the potential to be an economic superpower is going to depend on how the government can create incentives for FDI flow across a large number of sectors in India.

Currency

The Indian rupee is the only legal tender accepted in India. The exchange rate as on 1 February 2010 is 46.18 INR the USD, 64.03 to a EUR, and 73.82 to a GBP. The Indian rupee is accepted as legal tender in the neighbouring Nepal and Bhutan, both of which peg their currency to that of the Indian rupee. The rupee is divided into 100 paise.

The highest-denomination bank note is the 1,000 rupee note; the lowest-denomination coin in circulation is the 25 paise coin (it earlier had 1, 2, 5, 10 and 20 paise coins which have been discontinued by the Reserve Bank of India).

The Rupee hit a record low during early 2009 on account of global recession. However, due to a strong domestic market, India managed to bounce back sooner than the western countries. Since September 2009 there has been a constant appreciation in Rupee versus most Tier 1 currencies. On 11 January 2010 Rupee went as high as 45.50 to a United states dollar and on 10 January 2010 as high as Rupee 73.93 to a British Pound. A rising rupee also prompted Government of India to buy 200 tonnes of Gold from IMF.

The RBI, the country's central bank was established on 1 April 1935. It serves as the nation's monetary authority, regulator and supervisor of the financial system, manager of exchange control and as an issuer of currency. The RBI is governed by a central board, headed by a governor who is appointed by the Central government of India.

Income and Consumption

- 77.7% of the population lives on less than $2.50 (PPP) a day, down from 92.5% in 1981. This compares with 80.5% in Sub-Saharan Africa.
- 65.6% of the population lives on less than $2 a day (PPP), which is around 20 rupees or $0.5 a day in nominal terms. It was down from 86.6% and compares with 73.0% in Sub-Saharan Africa.
- 24.3% of the population earned less than $1 (PPP, around $0.25 in nominal terms) a day in 2005, down from 42.1% in 1981.

- 41.6% of its population is living below the new international poverty line of $1.25 (PPP) per day, down from 59.8% in 1981. The World Bank further estimates that a third of the global poor now reside in India.

Today, more people can afford a bicycle than ever before. Some 40% of Indian households owns a bicycle, with ownership rates ranging from around 30% to 70% at state level. Housing is modest.

According to Times of India, "a majority of Indians have per capita space equivalent to or less than a 10 feet x 10 feet room for their living, sleeping, cooking, washing and toilet needs." and "one in every three urban Indians lives in homes too cramped to exceed even the minimum requirements of a prison cell in the US." The average is 103 sq ft (9.6 m^2) per person in rural areas and 117 sq ft (10.9 m^2) per person in urban areas.

Around half of Indian children are malnourished. The proportion of underweight children is nearly double that of Sub-Saharan Africa. However, India has not had famines since the Green Revolution in the early 1970s. While poverty in India has reduced significantly, official figures estimate that 27.5% of Indians still lived below the national poverty line of $1 (PPP, around 10 rupees in nominal terms) a day in 2004-2005.

A 2007 report by the state-run National Commission for Enterprises in the Unorganised Sector (NCEUS) found that 65% of Indians, or 750 million people, lived on less than 20 rupees per day with most working in "informal labour sector with no job or social security, living in abject poverty."

Since the early 1950s, successive governments have implemented various schemes, under planning, to alleviate poverty, that have met with partial success. All these programmes have relied upon the strategies of the *Food for work* programme and *National Rural Employment Programme* of the 1980s, which attempted to use the unemployed to generate productive assets and build rural infrastructure.

In August 2005, the Indian parliament passed the *Rural Employment Guarantee Bill,* the largest programme of this type in terms of cost and coverage, which promises 100 days of minimum wage employment to every rural household in all the India's 600 districts.

The question of whether economic reforms have reduced poverty or not has fuelled debates without generating any clear cut answers and has also put political pressure on further economic reforms, especially those involving the downsizing of labour and cutting agricultural subsidies.

Employment

Agricultural and allied sectors accounted for about 60% of the total workforce in 2003 same as in 1993–94. While agriculture has faced stagnation in growth, services have seen a steady growth. Of the total workforce, 8% is in the organised sector, two-thirds of which are in the public sector.

The NSSO survey estimated that in 1999–2000, 106 million, nearly 10% of the population were unemployed and the overall unemployment rate was 7.3%, with rural areas doing marginally better (7.2%) than urban areas (7.7%). India's labour force is growing by 2.5% annually, but employment only at 2.3% a year.

Official unemployment exceeds 9%. Regulation and other obstacles have discouraged the emergence of formal businesses and jobs. Almost 30% of workers are casual workers who work only when they are able to get jobs and remain unpaid for the rest of the time. Only 10% of the workforce is in regular employment. India's labour regulations are heavy even by developing country standards and analysts have urged the government to abolish them.

Unemployment in India is characterized by chronic underemployment or disguised unemployment. Government schemes that target eradication of both poverty and unemployment (which in recent decades has sent millions of poor and unskilled people into urban areas in search of livelihoods) attempt to solve the problem, by providing financial assistance for setting up businesses, skill honing, setting up public sector enterprises, reservations in governments, etc.

The decreased role of the public sector after liberalization has further underlined the need for focusing on better education and has also put political pressure on further reforms.

Child labour is a complex problem that is basically rooted in poverty. The Indian government is implementing the world's largest child labour elimination program, with primary education targeted for 250 million.

Numerous non-governmental and voluntary organizations are also involved. Special investigation cells have been set up in states to enforce existing laws banning employment of children (under 14) in hazardous industries.

The allocation of the Government of India for the eradication of child labour was $10 million in 1995-96 and $16 million in 1996-97. The allocation for 2007 is $21 million. In 2006, remittances from Indian migrants overseas made up $27 billion or about 3% of India's GDP.

Economic Trends

In the revised 2007 figures, based on increased and sustaining growth, more inflows into foreign direct investment, Goldman Sachs predicts that "from 2007 to 2020, India's GDP per capita in US$ terms will quadruple", and that the Indian economy will surpass the United States (in US$) by 2043. In spite of the high growth rate, the report stated that India would continue to remain a low-income country for decades to come but could be a "motor for the world economy" if it fulfills its growth potential. Goldman Sachs has outlined 10 things that it needs to do in order to achieve its potential and grow 40 times by 2050.

These are:

1. improve governance
2. raise educational achievement
3. increase quality and quantity of universities
4. control inflation
5. introduce a credible fiscal policy
6. liberalize financial markets
7. increase trade with neighbours
8. increase agricultural productivity
9. improve infrastructure and
10. improve environmental quality.

Issues

Agriculture

Slow agricultural growth is a concern for policy makers as some two-thirds of India's people depend on rural employment for a living. Current agricultural practices are neither economically nor environmentally sustainable and India's yields for many agricultural commodities are low. Poorly maintained irrigation systems and almost universal lack of good extension services are among the factors responsible.

Farmers' access to markets is hampered by poor roads, rudimentary market infrastructure, and excessive regulation.– *World Bank: "India Country Overview 2008"*. The low productivity in India is a result of the following factors:

- According to "India: Priorities for Agriculture and Rural Development" by World Bank, India's large agricultural subsidies are hampering productivity-enhancing investment. Overregulation of agriculture has increased costs, price risks and uncertainty. Government interventions in labour, land, and credit markets are hurting the market. Infrastructure and services are inadequate.
- Illiteracy, slow progress in implementing land reforms and inadequate or inefficient finance and marketing services for farm produce.
- The average size of land holdings is very small (less than 20,000 m^2) and is subject to fragmentation, due to land ceiling acts and in some cases, family disputes. Such small holdings are often overmanned, resulting in disguised unemployment and low productivity of labour.
- Adoption of modern agricultural practices and use of technology is inadequate, hampered by ignorance of such practices, high costs and impracticality in the case of small land holdings.
- World Bank says that the allocation of water is inefficient, unsustainable and inequitable. The irrigation infrastructure is deteriorating. Irrigation facilities are inadequate, as revealed by the fact that only 52.6% of the land was irrigated in 2003–04, which result in farmers still being dependent

on rainfall, specifically the Monsoon season. A good monsoon results in a robust growth for the economy as a whole, while a poor monsoon leads to a sluggish growth. Farm credit is regulated by NABARD, which is the statutory apex agent for rural development in the subcontinent.

India has many farm insurance companies that insure wheat, fruit, rice and rubber farmers in the event of natural disasters or catastrophic crop failure, under the supervision of the Ministry of Agriculture. One notable company that provides all of these insurance policies is Agriculture Insurance Company of India and it alone insures almost 20 million farmers.

India's population is growing faster than its ability to produce rice and wheat. The most important structural reform for self-sufficiency is the ITC Limited plan to connect 20,000 villages to the Internet by 2013. This will provide farmers with up to date crop prices for the first time, which should minimise losses incurred from neighbouring producers selling early and in turn facilitate investment in rural areas.

Corruption

Corruption has been one of the pervasive problems affecting India. The economic reforms of 1991 reduced the red tape, bureaucracy and the *Licence Raj* that had strangled private enterprise and was blamed by Chakravarthi Rajagopalachari for the corruption and inefficiencies. Yet, a 2005 study by Transparency International (TI) India found that more than half of those surveyed had firsthand experience of paying bribe or peddling influence to get a job done in a public office.

The Right to Information Act (2005) and equivalent acts in the Indian states, that require government officials to furnish information requested by citizens or face punitive action, computerisation of services and various central and state government acts that established vigilance commissions have considerably reduced corruption or at least have opened up avenues to redress grievances. The 2009 report by Transparency International ranks India at 84th place and states that significant improvements were made by India in reducing corruption.

Government

The current government has concluded that most spending fails to reach its intended recipients. Lant Pritchett calls India's public sector "one of the world's top ten biggest problems — of the order of AIDS and climate change". The Economist's article about Indian civil service (2008) says that Indian central government employs around 3 million people and states another 7 million, including "vast armies of paper-shuffling peons". Million dollar bureaucracies can be run without a single computer in the management.

At local level, administration can be worse. It is not unheard of that most state assembly seats are held by convicted criminals. One study found out that 25% of public sector teachers and 40% of public sector medical workers could not be found at the work place. India's absence rates are one of the worst in the world.

The Reserve Bank of India has warned that India's public-debt to GDP ratio is over 70%. The government of India is highly indebted and its former investment-grade status has deteriorated near junk status. India's current public-debt to GDP ratio is 58.2% (US has 60.8%).

Education

India has made huge progress in terms of increasing primary education attendance rate and expanding literacy to approximately two thirds of the population. The right to education at elementary level has been made one of the fundamental rights under the Eighty-Sixth Amendment of 2002. However, education is still far behind developing countries such as China and continues to face challenges.

Despite growing investment in education, 40% of the population is illiterate and only 15% of the students reach high school. An optimistic estimate is that only one in five job-seekers in India has ever had any sort of vocational training.

Infrastructure

Development of infrastructure was completely in the hands of the public sector and was plagued by corruption, bureaucratic inefficiencies, urban-bias and an inability to scale investment. India's low spending on power, construction, transportation, telecommunications and real estate, at $31 billion or 6% of GDP in 2002 had prevented India from sustaining higher growth rates. This has prompted the government to partially open up infrastructure to the private sector allowing foreign investment which has helped in a sustained growth rate of close to 9% for the past six quarters.

Some 600 million Indians have no mains electricity at all. While 80% of Indian villages have at least an electricity line, just 44% of rural households have access to electricity. According to a sample of 97,882 households in 2002, electricity was the main source of lighting for 53% of rural households compared to 36% in 1993.

Some half of the electricity is stolen, compared with 3% in China. The stolen electricity amounts to 1.5% of GDP. Almost all of the electricity in India is produced by the public sector. Power outages are common. Many buy their own power generators to ensure electricity supply. As of 2005 the electricity production was at 661.6 billion kWh with oil production standing at 785,000 bbl/day. In 2007, electricity demand exceeded supply by 15%. Multi Commodity Exchange has tried to get a permit to offer electricity future markets.

Indian Road Network is developing. Trucking goods from Gurgaon to the port in Mumbai can take up to 10 days. India has the world's third largest road network. Container traffic is growing at 15% a year.

Some 60% of India's container traffic is handled by the Jawaharlal Nehru Port Trust in Mumbai. Internet use is rare; there were only 7.57 million broadband lines in India in November 2009, however it is still growing at slower rate and is expected to boom after the launch of 3G and wimax services.

Most urban cities have good water supply water 24 hours a day, while some smaller cities face water shortages in summer season. A World Bank report says it is an institutional problem in water agencies, or "how the agency is embedded in the relationships between politics and the citizens who are the consumers."

Labour Laws

India's labour regulations – among the most restrictive and complex in the world – have constrained the growth of the formal manufacturing sector where these laws have their widest application.

Better designed labour regulations can attract more labour-intensive investment and create jobs for India's unemployed millions and those trapped in poor quality jobs. Given the country's momentum of growth, the window of opportunity must not be lost for improving the job prospects for the 80 million new entrants who are expected to join the work force over the next decade.– *World Bank: India Country Overview 2008.*

India's restrictive labour regulations hamper the large-scale creation of formal industrial jobs. A recent report highlights a growing labour unrest all over India which is hampering the industrial output. India ranked 133th on the Ease of Doing Business Index 2010, behind countries such as China (89th), Pakistan (85th), and Nigeria (125th).

Economic Disparities

Lagging states need to bring more jobs to their people by creating an attractive investment destination. Reforming cumbersome regulatory procedures, improving rural connectivity, establishing law and order, creating a stable platform for natural resource investment that balances business interests with social concerns, and providing rural finance are important.– *World Bank: India Country Overview 2008.*

One of the critical problems facing India's economy is the sharp and growing regional variations among India's different states and territories in terms of per capita income, poverty, availability of infrastructure and socioeconomic development. Seven low-income states-Bihar, Chhattisgarh, Jharkhand, Madhya Pradesh, Orissa, Rajasthan, and Uttar Pradesh-are home to more than half of India's population.

Between 1999 and 2008, the analysed growth rates for Maharashtra (9%), Gujarat (8.8%), Haryana (8.7%), or Delhi (7.4%) were much higher than for Bihar (5.1%), Uttar Pradesh (4.4%), or Madhya Pradesh (3.5%). Poverty rates in rural Orissa (43%) and rural Bihar (40%) are some of the worst in the world. On the other hand, rural Haryana (5.7%) and rural Punjab (2.4%) compare well with middle-income countries.

The five-year plans have attempted to reduce regional disparities by encouraging industrial development in the interior regions, but industries still tend to concentrate around urban areas and port cities. After liberalization, the more advanced states are better placed to benefit from them, with infrastructure like well developed ports, urbanisation and an educated and skilled workforce which attract manufacturing and service sectors. The union and state governments of backward regions are trying to reduce the disparities by offering tax holidays, cheap land, etc., and focusing more on sectors like tourism, which although being geographically and historically determined, can become a source of growth and is faster to develop than other sectors.

Environment and Health

On Yale and Columbia's Environmental Performance Index, India's score is 21/100 on sanitation, compared with 67/100 for the region and 48/100 for the country income group.

6

Voluntary Action, Voluntary Organization and Management

Volunteering

Volunteering is the practice of people working on behalf of others or a particular cause without payment for their time and services. Volunteering is generally considered an altruistic activity, intended to promote good or improve human quality of life, but people also volunteer for their own skill development, to meet others, to make contacts for possible employment, to have fun, and a variety of other reasons that could be considered self-serving.

Volunteering takes many forms and is performed by a wide range of people. Many volunteers are specifically trained in the areas they work in, such as medicine, education, or emergency rescue. Other volunteers serve on an as-needed basis, such as in response to a natural disaster or for a beach-cleanup.

Social Capital

The *social capital* represented by volunteering plays a key role in economic regeneration. Where poverty is endemic to an area, poor communities lack friends and neighbours able to help. This, voluntary mutual aid or self-help is an important safety net. This model works well within a state because there is a national solidarity in times of adversity and more prosperous groups will usually make sacrifices for the benefit of those in need.

Skills-based Volunteering

Skills-based volunteering refers to volunteering in which the volunteer is specifically trained in the area they are volunteering in. This is in contrast to traditional volunteering, where specific training is not required. The average hour of traditional volunteering is valued by the Independent Sector at between $18–20 an hour. Skills-based volunteerism is valued at $40–500 an hour depending on the market value of the time.

Virtual-Volunteering

Virtual volunteering, also sometimes called as eVolunteering, online volunteering or micro-volunteering, is a term describing a volunteer who completes tasks, in whole or in part, offsite from the organization being assisted, using the Internet and a home, school, tele centre or work computer or other Internet-connected device, such as a PDAs or smart phone. Virtual volunteering is also known as cyber service, tele mentoring, and tele tutoring, and various other names. Virtual volunteering is similar to tele commuting, except that, instead of online employees who are paid, these are online volunteers who are not paid.

Environmental-Volunteering

Environmental volunteering refers to volunteers who contribute towards environmental management. Volunteers conduct a range of activities including environmental monitoring, ecological restoration such as re-vegetation and weed removal, and educating others about the natural environment.

Volunteering in Schools

School systems around the world rely heavily on volunteers and donations in order to run effectively. Whenever the economy is down, the need for volunteers and resources increases greatly. There are many opportunities available in the school system for volunteers to take advantage of, especially if you have a special skill or trade. There are not many requirements in order to become a volunteer in the school system. Whether you are a parent, grandparent or just a community member most schools just require a volunteer form be completed. Much like the benefits of any type of volunteerism there are great rewards for the volunteer, student, and school.

These benefits include but are not limited to: School Benefits-Provided with additional service without having to have added costs, Teachers are given extra time for educational purposes and planning, A positive relationship between the community and the school. Volunteer Benefits-Parents become involved in their child's school and education, New talents that one never knew they had are discovered, A sense of personal satisfaction, Ability to meet new people and develop new friendships. Student Benefits-Students are given a positive role model, Educational success is encouraged and improved.

Politics

Further Information: Gift Economy

In almost all modern societies, the most basic of all values is people helping people and, in the process, helping themselves. But a tension can arise between volunteerism and the state-provided services, so most countries develop policies and enact legislation to clarify the roles and relationships among stockholders and identify and allocate the necessary legal, social, administrative, and financial support.

This is particularly necessary when some voluntary activities are seen as a challenge to the authority of the state, e.g. on 29 January 2001, President Bush cautioned that volunteer groups should supplement, not replace, the work of government agencies. Volunteerism that benefits the state but challenges paid counterparts raises the ire of labour unions representing the paid counterparts as in the case of volunteer fire departments, particularly in combination departments.

Difficulties in Cross-National Aid

Difficulties in this model of volunteering can arise when this is applied across national borders. A state sending volunteers to another state can be viewed as a breach of sovereignty and a lack of respect towards the national government of the proposed recipients. Thus, when states negotiate the offer and acceptance of aid, motivations become important, particularly if donors may postpone assistance or stop it altogether. Three types of conditionality have evolved:

1. Financial accountability: Transparency in the management of funding to ensure that what is done by the volunteers is properly targeted.

2. Policy reform: Requesting governments of developing countries adopt certain social, economic, or environmental policies, the most controversial relating to the privatization of services traditionally offered by the state.
3. Development objectives: Asking developing countries to adjust specific time-bound economic objectives.

Some international volunteer organisations define their primary mission altruistically as fighting poverty and improving the living standards of people in the developing world, e.g. Voluntary Services Overseas has almost 2,000 skilled professionals working as volunteers to pass on their expertise to local people so that, when they return home, their skills remain. When these organisations work in partnership with governments, the results can be impressive. But when other organisations or individual First World governments support the work of volunteer groups, there can be questions as to whether their real motives are poverty alleviation or wealth creation for some of the poor or policies intended to benefit the donor states.

This confusion exists because experience shows that what is volunteered can distort the foreign and economic policy of the country receiving the aid. The economies of many low-income countries suffer from "industrialisation without prosperity" and "investment without growth". This arises because "development assistance" guides many Third World governments to pursue "development" policies that have been wasteful, ill-conceived, unproductive or even so positively destructive that they could not have been sustained without outside support.

Indeed, some of the offers of aid have distorted the general spirit of volunteerism, treating local voluntary action as "contributions in kind", i.e. as conditions requiring local people to earn the right to donor "largesse" by modifying their behaviour. This can be seen as patronising and offensive to the recipients because the aid expressly serves the policy aims of the donors rather than the needs of the recipients.

The track record shows that making any aid conditional on policy reforms is often ineffective. Conditionality only works when there is a strong domestic commitment to reform and the recipient governments are democratic, i.e. they are accountable to their own electorates. Volunteer organizations and their funding donors should respect the governments of the countries they wish to help and build on the deep-rooted traditions of people to help one another, and thereby provide an important ingredient for social and democratic development.

Criticism

In the 1960s Ivan Illich offered an analysis of the role of American volunteers in Mexico in his speech entitled, "To Hell With Good Intentions". His concerns, along with critics such as Paulo Freire and Edward Said, revolve around the notion of altruism as an extension of Christian missionary ideology and the sense of responsibility/obligation driving the concept of noblesse oblige, first developed by the French aristocracy as a moral duty derived from their wealth. Simply stated, these both propose the extension of power and authority over indigenous cultures around the world.

Recent critiques of volunteerism come from Westmier and Kahn (1996) and bell hooks (2004). There is also growing concern about the effects of neoliberalism in the field of volunteerism, as witnessed by the increasing influence of corporations on the social programming of non-profit community organizations, particularly through youth work.

The field of medical tourism (referring to volunteers travelling overseas to deliver care) has recently attracted negative criticism vis-a-vis the alternative notion of sustainable capacities (working in the context of long-term, locally-run but foreign-supported infrastructures). A preponderance of this criticism has appeared largely in the scientific and peer-reviewed literature. Recently, media outlets with more general readerships have published such criticisms, as well.

Non-Governmental Organization

Non-governmental organization (NGO) is a term that has become widely accepted as referring to a legally constituted, non-governmental organization created by natural or legal persons with no participation or representation of any government. In the cases in which NGOs are funded totally or partially by governments, the NGO maintains its non-governmental status and excludes government representatives from membership in the organization. Unlike the term *intergovernmental organization*, "non-governmental organization" is a term in general use but is not a legal definition. In many jurisdictions these types of organization are defined as "civil society organizations" or referred to by other names.

The number of internationally operating NGOs is estimated at 40,000. National numbers are even higher: Russia has 277,000 NGOs. India is estimated to have between 1 million and 2 million NGOs.

History

National NGOs go back to antiquity. International non-governmental organizations have a history dating back to at least 1839. Rotary, later Rotary International, was founded in 1905. It has been estimated that by 1914 there were 1083 NGOs. International NGOs were important in the anti-slavery movement and the movement for women's suffrage, and reached a peak at the time of the World Disarmament Conference. The definition of "international NGO" (INGO) is first given in resolution 288 (X) of ECOSOC on February 27, 1950: it is defined as "any international organization that is not founded by an international treaty".

Rapid development of the non-governmental sector occurred in western countries as a result of the processes of restructurization of the welfare state. Further globalization of that process occurred after the fall of the communist system and was an important part of the Washington consensus.

Globalization during the 20th century gave rise to the importance of NGOs. Many problems could not be solved within a nation. International treaties and international organizations such as the World Trade Organization were perceived as being too centred on the interests of capitalist enterprises. Some argued that in an attempt to counterbalance this trend, NGOs have developed to emphasize humanitarian issues, developmental aid and sustainable development. A prominent example of this is the World Social Forum which is a rival convention to the World Economic Forum held annually in January in Davos, Switzerland. The fifth World Social Forum in Porto Alegre, Brazil, in January 2005 was attended by representatives from more than 1,000 NGOs. Some have argued that in forums like these, NGOs take the place of what should belong to popular movements of the poor. Others argue that NGOs are often imperialist in nature, that they sometimes operate in a racialized manner in dominant countries, and that they fulfil a similar function to that of the clergy during the high colonial era. The philosopher Peter Hallward argues that they are an aristocratic form of politics. However, this philosophy would suggest that organizations of indigenous peoples are not represented, which is untrue. Whatever the case, NGO transnational networking is now extensive.

Types of NGOs

Apart from "NGO", often alternative terms are used as for example: independent sector, volunteer sector, civil society, grassroots organizations, transnational social movement organizations, private voluntary organizations, self-help organizations and non-state actors (NSA's).

Non-governmental organizations are a heterogeneous group. A long list of acronyms has developed around the term "NGO". These include:

- CSO, short for civil society organization;
- DONGO: Donor Organized NGO;
- ENGO: short for environmental NGO, such as Global 2000;
- GONGOs are government-operated NGOs, which may have been set up by governments to look like NGOs in order to qualify for outside aid or promote the interests of the government in question;
- INGO stands for international NGO; Oxfam is an international NGO
- QUANGOs are quasi-autonomous non-governmental organizations, such as the International Organization for Standardization (ISO). (The ISO is actually not purely an NGO, since its membership is by nation, and each nation is represented by what the ISO Council determines to be the 'most broadly representative' standardization body of a nation. That body might itself be a non-governmental

organization; for example, the United States is represented in ISO by the American National Standards Institute, which is independent of the federal government. However, other countries can be represented by national governmental agencies; this is the trend in Europe.)

- TANGO: short for technical assistance NGO;
- GSO: Grassroots Support Organization
- MANGO: short for market advocacy NGO
- CHARDS: Community Health and Rural Development Society.

There are also numerous classifications of NGOs. The typology the World Bank uses divides them into Operational and Advocacy:

The primary purpose of an operational NGO is the design and implementation of development-related projects. One frequently used categorization is the division into *relief-oriented* versus *development-oriented* organizations; they can also be classified according to whether they stress service delivery or participation; or whether they are religious or secular; and whether they are more public or private-oriented. Operational NGOs can be community-based, national or international. The primary purpose of an Advocacy NGO is to defend or promote a specific cause. As opposed to operational project management, these organizations typically try to raise awareness, acceptance and knowledge by lobbying, press work and activist events.

USAID refers to NGOs as *private voluntary organisations*. However many scholars have argued that this definition is highly problematic as many NGOs are in fact state and corporate funded and managed projects with professional staff.

NGOs exist for a variety of reasons, usually to further the political or social goals of their members or funders. Examples include improving the state of the natural environment, encouraging the observance of human rights, improving the welfare of the disadvantaged, or representing a corporate agenda. However, there are a huge number of such organizations and their goals cover a broad range of political and philosophical positions. This can also easily be applied to private schools and athletic organizations.

Methods

NGOs vary in their methods. Some act primarily as lobbyists, while others primarily conduct programs and activities. For instance, an NGO such as Oxfam, concerned with poverty alleviation, might provide needy people with the equipment and skills to find food and clean drinking water, whereas an NGO like the FFDA helps through investigation and documentation of human rights violations and provides legal assistance to victims of human rights abuses. Others, such as Afghanistan Information Management Services, provide specialized technical products and services to support development activities implemented on the ground by other organizations.

Public Relations

Non-governmental organizations need healthy relationships with the public to meet their goals. Foundations and charities use sophisticated public relations campaigns to raise funds and employ standard lobbying techniques with governments. Interest groups may be of political importance because of their ability to influence social and political outcomes. A code of ethics was established in 2002 by The World Association of Non Governmental NGOs.

Consulting

Project Management

There is an increasing awareness that management techniques are crucial to project success in non-governmental organizations. Generally, non-governmental organizations that are private have either a community or environmental focus. They address varieties of issues such as religion, emergency aid, or humanitarian affairs. They mobilize public support and voluntary contributions for aid; they often have strong links with community groups in developing countries, and they often work in areas where government-to-government aid is not possible. NGOs are accepted as a part of the international relations landscape, and while they influence national and multilateral policy-making, increasingly they are more directly involved in local action.

Staffing

Not all people working for non-governmental organizations

are volunteers. The reasons people volunteer are not necessarily purely altruistic, and can provide immediate benefits for themselves as well as those they serve, including skills, experience, and contacts.

There is some dispute as to whether expatriates should be sent to developing countries. Frequently this type of personnel is employed to satisfy a donor who wants to see the supported project managed by someone from an industrialized country. However, the expertise these employees or volunteers may have can be counterbalanced by a number of factors: the cost of foreigners is typically higher, they have no grass root connections in the country they are sent to, and local expertise is often undervalued.

The NGO sector is an important employer in terms of numbers. For example, by the end of 1995, CONCERN worldwide, an international Northern NGO working against poverty, employed 174 expatriates and just over 5,000 national staff working in ten developing countries in Africa and Asia, and in Haiti.

Funding

Large NGOs may have annual budgets in the hundreds of millions or billions of dollars. For instance, the budget of the American Association of Retired Persons (AARP) was over US$540 million in 1999. Funding such large budgets demands significant fundraising efforts on the part of most NGOs. Major sources of NGO funding include membership dues, the sale of goods and services, grants from international institutions or national governments, and private donations. Several EU-grants provide funds accessible to NGOs.

Even though the term "non-governmental organization" implies independence from governments, most NGOs depend heavily on governments for their funding. A quarter of the US$162 million income in 1998 of the famine-relief organization Oxfam was donated by the British government and the EU. The Christian relief and development organization World Vision collected US$55 million worth of goods in 1998 from the American government. Nobel Prize winner Medecins Sans Frontieres (MSF) (known in the USA as Doctors Without Borders) gets 46% of its income from government sources.

Monitoring and Control

In a March 2000 report on United Nations Reform priorities, former U.N. Secretary General Kofi Annan wrote in favour of international humanitarian intervention, arguing that the international community has a "right to protect" citizens of the world against ethnic cleansing, genocide, and crimes against humanity. On the heels of the report, the Canadian government launched the Responsibility to Protect R2PPDF (434 KiB) project, outlining the issue of humanitarian intervention. While the R2P doctrine has wide applications, among the more controversial has been the Canadian government's use of R2P to justify its intervention and support of the coup in Haiti.

Years after R2P, the World Federalist Movement, an organization which supports "the creation of democratic global structures accountable to the citizens of the world and call for the division of international authority among separate agencies", has launched Responsibility to Protect-Engaging Civil Society (R2PCS). A collaboration between the WFM and the Canadian government, this project aims to bring NGOs into lockstep with the principles outlined under the original R2P project.

The governments of the countries an NGO works or is registered in may require reporting or other monitoring and oversight. Funders generally require reporting and assessment, such information is not necessarily publicly available. There may also be associations and watchdog organizations that research and publish details on the actions of NGOs working in particular geographic or program areas.

In recent years, many large corporations have increased their corporate social responsibility departments in an attempt to preempt NGO campaigns against certain corporate practices. As the logic goes, if corporations work *with* NGOs, NGOs will not work *against* corporátions.

In December 2007, The United States Department of Defence Assistant Secretary of Defence (Health Affairs) S. Ward Casscells established an International Health Division under Force Health Protection & Readiness. Part of International Health's mission is to communicate with NGOs in areas of mutual interest. Department of Defence Directive 3000.05, in 2005, requires DoD to regard stability-enhancing activities as a mission of importance equal to war fighting. In compliance with international law, DoD has necessarily built a capacity to improve essential services in areas of conflict such as Iraq, where the customary lead agencies (State Department and USAID) find it difficult to operate.

Unlike the "co-option" strategy described for corporations, the OASD(HA) recognizes the neutrality of health as an essential service. International Health cultivates collaborative relationships with NGOs, albeit at arms-length, recognizing their traditional independence, expertise and honest broker status. While the goals of DoD and NGOs may seem incongruent, the DoD's emphasis on stability and security to reduce and prevent conflict suggests, on careful analysis, important mutual interests.

Legal Status

The legal form of NGOs is diverse and depends upon homegrown variations in each country's laws and practices. However, four main family groups of NGOs can be found worldwide:

- Unincorporated and voluntary association
- Trusts, charities and foundations
- Companies not just for profit
- Entities formed or registered under special NGO or non-profit laws.

NGOs are not subjects of international law, as states are. An exception is the International Committee of the Red Cross, which is subject to certain specific matters, mainly relating to the Geneva Convention. The Council of Europe in Strasbourg drafted the European Convention on the Recognition of the Legal Personality of International Non-Governmental Organizations in 1986, which sets a common legal basis for the existence and work of NGOs in Europe. Article 11 of the European Convention on Human Rights protects the right to freedom of association, which is also a fundamental norm for NGOs.

Citizen Organization

There is a growing movement within the "non"-profit and "non"-government sector to define itself in a more constructive, accurate way. Instead of being defined by "non" words, organizations are suggesting new terminology to describe the sector. The term "civil society organization" (CSO) has been used by a growing number of organizations, such as the Centre for the Study of Global Governance. The term "citizen sector organization" (CSO) has also been advocated to describe the sector — as one of citizens, for citizens. This labels and positions the sector as its own entity, without relying on language used for the government or business sectors. However some have argued that this is not particularly helpful given that most NGOs are in fact funded by governments and business and that some NGOs are clearly hostile to independently organized people's organizations.

National Policy on the Voluntary Sector

Preamble

This Policy is a commitment to encourage, enable and empower an independent, creative and effective voluntary sector, with diversity in form and function, so that it can contribute to the social, cultural and economic advancement of the people of India.

The voluntary sector has contributed significantly to finding innovative solutions to poverty, deprivation, discrimination and exclusion, through means such as awareness raising, social mobilization, service delivery, training, research, and advocacy. The voluntary sector has been serving as an effective non-political link between the people and the Government. This policy recognizes the important role that the voluntary sector has to play in various areas and affirms the growing need for collaboration with the voluntary sector by the Government, as well as by the private sector, at the local, provincial and national levels.

Scope of the Policy

In the Policy, voluntary organizations (VOs) mean to include organizations engaged in public service, based on ethical, cultural, social, economic, political, religious, spiritual, philanthropic or scientific & technological considerations. VOs include formal as well as informal groups, such as: community-based organizations (CBOs); non-governmental development organizations (NGDOs); charitable organizations; support organizations; networks or federations of such organisations; as well as professional membership associations. To be covered under the Policy, VOs should broadly have the following characteristics:

a) They are private, *i.e.,* separate from Government
b) They do not return profits generated to their owners or directors
c) They are self-governing, *i.e.,* not controlled by Government
d) They are registered organizations or informal groups, with defined aims and objectives.

Objectives of the Policy

The specific objectives of the policy are listed below:

To create an enabling environment for VOs that stimulates their enterprise and effectiveness, and safeguards their autonomy;

To enable VOs to legitimately mobilize necessary financial resources from India and abroad;

To identify systems by which the Government may work together with VOs, on the basis of the principles of mutual trust and respect, and with shared responsibility; and,

To encourage VOs to adopt transparent and accountable systems of governance and management.

The following paragraphs describe how these objectives are to be achieved.

Establishing an Enabling Environment for the Voluntary Sector

The independence of VOs allows them to explore alternative paradigms of development to challenge social, economic and political forces that may work against public interest and to find new ways to combat poverty, deprivation and other social problems. It is therefore crucial that all laws, policies, rules and regulations relating to VOs categorically safeguard their autonomy, while simultaneously ensuring their accountability.

Voluntary organizations may be registered as societies, as charitable trusts, or as non-profit companies under Central or State laws. Some States have adopted the Societies Registration Act (1860), with amendments, while others have independent laws. Similarly, laws relating to charitable trusts vary across States. Over time, many of these laws and their corresponding rules have become complex and restrictive, thus leading to delays, harassment and corruption. As the nodal agency for interface between the Government and the Voluntary Sector, the Planning Commission will encourage State Governments to review prevailing laws & rules and simplify, liberalise and rationalise them as far as possible. In order to facilitate registration of non-profit companies, the Government will examine measures to simplify procedures under section 25 of the Companies Act (1956), including those for license, registration, and remuneration to member-employees.

The Government will also examine the feasibility of enacting a simple and liberal central law that will serve as an alternative all-India statute for registering VOs, particularly those that wish to operate in different parts of the country and even abroad. Such a law would co-exist with prevailing central and state laws, allowing a VO the option of registering under one or more laws, depending on the nature and sphere of its activities.

There has been much public debate on the voluntary sector, particularly its governance, accountability, and transparency. It is widely believed that the voluntary sector must address these issues through suitable self-regulation. The Government will encourage the evolution of, and subsequently accord recognition to, an independent, national level, self-regulatory agency for the voluntary sector.

At the same time, there is need to bolster public confidence in the voluntary sector by opening it up to greater public scrutiny. The Government will encourage Central and State level agencies to introduce norms for filing basic documents in respect of VOs, which have been receiving funding by Government agencies and placing them in the public domain (with easy access through the internet) in order to inculcate a spirit of public oversight.

Public donation is an important source of funds for the voluntary sector and one that can and must increase substantially. Tax incentives play a positive role in this process. Stocks and shares have become a significant form of wealth in the country today. In order to encourage transfer of shares and stock options to VOs, the Government will consider suitable tax rebates for this form of donation. The Government will also simplify and streamline the system for granting income tax exemption status to charitable projects under the Income Tax Act. At the same time, the Government will consider tightening administrative and penal procedures to ensure that these incentives are not misused by paper charities for private financial gain.

International funding of voluntary organizations plays a small, but significant part in supporting such organizations and their work in the country. An organization seeking foreign funding must be registered under the Foreign Contribution (Regulation) Act. This law prescribes stringent screening norms that often restrict the ability of VOs to avail foreign funds. When approved, there are problems like funds must be held in a single bank account, thus presenting enormous difficulties to VOs working at different locations. The Government will review the FCRA and simplify its provisions that apply to VOs, from time to time, in consultation with the joint consultative group to be set up by the concerned Ministry (as suggested under para 5.4).

The Central Government has framed guidelines for bilateral agencies to give direct assistance to voluntary organizations for projects of social and economic importance. It controls access to such funds and their utilisation, both through the FCRA and through regulation by the Department of Economic Affairs. This system needs to be simplified in consultation with the joint consultative group to be set up by the concerned Ministry.

The Government will encourage all relevant Central and State Government agencies to introduce pre-service and in-service training modules on constructive relations with the voluntary sector. Such agencies should introduce time bound procedures for dealing with the VOs. These would cover registration, income tax clearances, financial assistance, etc. There would be formal systems for registering complaints and for redressing grievances of VOs.

Partnership in Development

The voluntary sector can play an important role in the development process, particularly through community participation. VOs can offer alternative perspectives; committed expertise; an understanding of the local opportunities and constraints; and perhaps most importantly, the capacity to conduct a meaningful dialogue with communities, particularly those that are disadvantaged. It is therefore essential that the Government and the Voluntary Sector work together. Where feasible, such partnership may also include other entities such as *panchayati raj* institutions, municipalities, academic institutions, and private sector organizations.

Partnership between Government and VOs implies identifying shared goals and defining complementary roles. It must be based on the basic principles of mutual trust and respect, with shared responsibility and authority. These principles must be explicit in the terms and conditions of the partnership. They must also be evident in the formal and informal systems of collaboration.

This Policy recognizes three instruments of partnership, viz., (i) consultation, through a formal process of interaction at the Centre, State and District level; (ii) strategic collaboration to tackle complex interventions where sustained social mobilization is critical over the long term; and (iii) project funding through standard schemes. The Government will ensure that these three instruments of partnership are given due attention in Annual Plans prepared by Ministries and States. The action that will be taken in respect of each of the three instruments is discussed in the following paragraphs.

The Government will encourage setting up of Joint Consultative Groups/Forums or Joint Machineries of government and voluntary sector representatives, by relevant Central Departments and State Governments. It will also encourage district administrations, district planning bodies, district rural development agencies, *zilla parishads* and local governments to do so. These groups will be permanent forums with the explicit mandate to share ideas, views and information and to identify opportunities and mechanisms of working together. The Government will introduce suitable mechanisms for involving a wide cross-section of the voluntary sector in these Groups/Forums.

The expertise of the voluntary sector will also be utilized, by including experts from VOs in the committees, task forces, and advisory panels constituted by the Government from time to time to help address important issues.

The country faces a number of complex problems that require adaptive, multi-sectoral solutions where sustained social mobilization is particularly important. These include poverty alleviation, skill promotion, entrepreneurship development, empowerment of women, population stabilization, combating HIV/AIDS, managing water resources, elementary education and forest management, to name a few. Such areas urgently require strategic collaboration between the Government and VOs, through national level programmes that are long-term in duration, and utilize multiple strategies, methodologies and activities to achieve their objectives. The Government will identify national collaborative programmes to be implemented in partnership with VOs. Each national collaborative programme will involve a finite set of reputed, medium or large VOs with a proven track record, and the ability to work on a reasonably large scale. The Government will ensure that such national collaborative programmes are given due importance in Plan documents.

The third instrument of partnership between the Government and the voluntary sector is project funding. A large number of Government agencies operate schemes for financial assistance to VOs. These schemes usually deal with activities such as surveys, research, workshops, documentation, awareness raising, training, creation and running of public welfare facilities, and so on. Project grants are a useful means for the Government to promote its activities without its direct involvement. They are also a valuable source of support to small and medium VOs. Nevertheless, there are legitimate concerns regarding the effectiveness of grant-in-aid schemes. Out-dated design of funding schemes, arbitrary procedures, selection of unsuitable VOs, poor quality of implementation, and misuse of funds are some of the reasons for the possible defeat of the objectives of such funding. Concerned Government agencies would be encouraged to ensure proper accountability and monitoring of public funds distributed to VOs.

Some Central agencies have achieved good results by decentralizing the process of project funding. Rather than administering various schemes directly, they appoint regional or State level intermediary organizations to do so on their behalf. This allows for closer interaction for better selection and monitoring of VOs. Intermediaries could include umbrella VOs, professional or academic institutes, State Government agencies, or multi-stockholder standing committees. The Government will review the experience of such decentralized funding and make suitable recommendations to Central agencies.

There is reason to believe that accreditation of VOs will lead to better funding decisions and make the funding processes more transparent. Further, accreditation may provide incentives for better governance, management and performance of VOs. No reliable accreditation system is in place at present. The Government will encourage various agencies, including those in the voluntary sector, to develop alternative accreditation methodologies. It will allow time for such methodologies to be debated and gain acceptability in the voluntary sector, before considering their application to Government funding of VOs.

Strengthening the Voluntary Sector

The Indian society has a well-established tradition of philanthropy. While a regime of tax concessions facilitates donations to charitable organizations, there is considerable untapped potential to channelise private wealth for public service. The Government will support and encourage existing, as well new, independent philanthropic institutions and private foundations to provide financial assistance to deserving VOs. It will also promote a dialogue among public and private grant makers so that they may take advantage of the best practices in grant making and fund-raising strategies.

Accountability to all stockholders and transparency in functioning are key issues in good governance. The voluntary sector is expected to set its own benchmarks in these areas. Since VOs vary in their objectives and activities, it would be impractical to expect uniform norms for accountability and transparency. The Government will encourage support organizations, and VO networks & federations to facilitate discussion and consensus building on these issues. It will also encourage such agencies to advise and assist VOs to adopt norms that they find acceptable and useful. The Government will recognize excellence in governance among VOs by publicizing best practices.

Training is a crucial requirement for people working in the voluntary sector. However, this is often neglected on account of limited availability of good quality training courses that are reasonably priced. The Government will support and encourage organizations that train aspirants to enter the voluntary sector, as well as those already working in the sector. It will make available physical facilities currently available with its training institutes as a measure of such support.

Innovation in institutional, technical and social approaches to development problems is an essential ingredient of voluntary action. The Government will encourage and recognize innovative & pioneering work.

Databases of VOs working in different fields and at different levels are useful for communication within the voluntary sector, as well as between the voluntary sector and the public & private sector. The Government will commission suitable agencies to prepare and update such databases.

Information on Government policies and programmes is often difficult for VOs to access. The websites of various Government agencies will be re-designed to provide links to key documents and databases, including those related to project funding schemes.

The Government will encourage involvement of volunteers in public services, such as, at family welfare centres, primary health centres, hospitals, schools, vocational training centres, sanitation campaigns, etc.

This National Policy on the Voluntary Sector-2007 is the beginning of a process to evolve a new working relationship between the Government and the Voluntary Sector, without affecting the autonomy and identity of VOs.

7

Human Resource Development

Human Resources

Human resources is a term used to refer to how employees are managed by organizations, or to the personnel department charged with that role. The field has moved from a traditionally administrative function to a strategic one that allegedly recognizes the link between talented and engaged people and organizational success. The field draws upon concepts developed in Industrial/ Organizational Psychology and System Theory. Human resources has at least two related interpretations depending on context. The original usage derives from political economy and economics, where it was traditionally called labour, one of four factors of production although this perspective is changing as a function of new and ongoing research into more strategic approaches at national levels.

This first usage is used more in terms of 'human resources development', and can go beyond just organizations to the level of nations. The more traditional usage within corporations and businesses refers to the individuals within a firm or agency, and to the portion of the organization that deals with hiring, firing, training, and other personnel issues, typically referred to as 'human resources management'. This article addresses both definitions.

Development

Human resource management's objective, on the other hand, is to maximize the return on investment from the organization's human capital and minimize financial risk. It is the responsibility of human resource managers in a corporate context to conduct these activities in an effective, legal, fair, and consistent manner. Management is the process of getting things done effectively and efficiently with and through other people to achieve the objective of the organization.

Human Resource Management is the organizational function that deals with issues related to people such as compensation, hiring, performance management, organization development, safety, wellness, benefits, employee motivation, communication, administration, and training.

Key Functions

Human Resource Management serves these key functions:

1. Recruitment and Selection
2. Redundancy
3. Industrial and Employee Relations
4. Record keeping of all personal data
5. Total Rewards: Employee benefits and compensation
6. Confidential advice to internal 'customers' in relation to problems at work
7. Career development
8. Competency Mapping (Competency mapping is a process an individual uses to identify and describe competencies that are the most critical to success in a work situation or work role.)
9. Performance Appraisal.

Modern Analysis

Modern analysis emphasizes that human beings are not "commodities" or "resources", but are creative and social beings in a productive enterprise. The 2000 revision of ISO 9001 in contrast requires to identify the processes, their sequence and interaction, and to define and communicate responsibilities and authorities. In general, heavily unionized nations such as France and Germany have adopted and encouraged such job descriptions especially within trade unions.

The International Labour Organization also in 2001 decided to revisit, and revise its 1975 Recommendation 150 on Human Resources Development. One view of these trends is that a strong social consensus on political economy and a good social welfare system facilitates labour mobility and tends to make the entire economy more productive, as labour can develop skills and experience in various ways, and move from one enterprise to another with little controversy or difficulty in adapting. Another view is that governments should become more aware of their national role in facilitating human resources development across all sectors.

Labour Mobility

An important controversy regarding labour mobility illustrates the broader philosophical issue with usage of the phrase "human resources": governments of developing nations often regard developed nations that encourage immigration or "guest workers" as appropriating human capital that is rightfully part of the developing nation and required to further its growth as a civilization. They argue that this appropriation is similar to colonial commodity fiat wherein a colonizing European power would define an arbitrary price for natural resources, extracting which diminished national natural capital.

The debate regarding "human resources" versus human capital thus in many ways echoes the debate regarding natural resources versus natural capital. Over time the United Nations have come to more generally support the developing nations' point of view, and have requested significant offsetting "foreign aid" contributions so that a developing nation losing human capital does not lose the capacity to continue to train new people in trades, professions, and the arts.

An extreme version of this view is that the historical inequities such as African slavery must be compensated by current developed nations, which benefited from stolen "human resources" as they were developing. This is an extremely controversial view, but it echoes the general theme of converting human capital to "human resources" and thus greatly diminishing its value to the host society, i.e. "Africa", as it is put to narrow imitative use as "labour" in the using society.

Human Resources of a business are its employees, Organisations look after all their staff on the basis that if they are all well trained and committed to the aims of the business, the organisation is more likely to be successful. In a series of reports of the UN Secretary-General to the General Assembly [e.g. A/56/162 (2001)], a broad inter-sectoral approach to developing human resourcefulness has been outlined as a priority for socioeconomic development and particularly anti-poverty strategies. This calls for strategic and integrated public policies, for example in education, health, and employment sectors that promote occupational skills, knowledge and performance enhancement.

Perceptions

Terms like "human resources" and "human capital" may be perceived as insulting to people. They create the impression that people are merely commodities, like office machines or vehicles, despite assurances to the contrary.

Corporate Management

In the very narrow context of corporate "human resources" management, there is a contrasting pull to reflect and require work place diversity that echoes the diversity of a global customer base. Foreign language and culture skills, ingenuity, humour, and careful listening, are examples of traits that such programs typically require. It would appear that these evidence a general shift through the human capital point of view to an acknowledgment that human beings do contribute much more to a productive enterprise than "work": they bring their character, their ethics, their creativity, their social connections, and in some cases even their pets and children, and alter the character of a work place. The term corporate culture is used to characterize such processes at the organizational level.

The traditional but extremely narrow context of hiring, firing, and job description is considered a 20th century anachronism. Most corporate organizations that compete in the modern global economy have adopted a view of human capital that mirrors the modern consensus as above. Some of these, in turn, deprecate the term "human resources" as useless. Yet the term survives, and if related to `resourcefulness', has continued and emerging relevance to public policy.

In general the abstractions of macro-economics treat it this way-as it characterizes no mechanisms to represent choice or ingenuity. So one interpretation is that "firm-specific human capital" as defined in macro-economics is the modern and correct definition of "human resources"-and that this is inadequate to represent the contributions of "human resources" in any modern theory of political economy.

Human Resources Management Trends and Influences

In organizations, it is important to determine both current and future organisational requirements for both core employees and the contingent workforce in terms of their skills/technical abilities, competencies, flexibility etc. The analysis requires consideration of the internal and external factors that can have an effect on the resourcing, development, motivation and retention of employees and other workers. The external factors are those largely out-with the control of the organization and include issues such as the economic climate, current and future trends of the labour market e.g. skills, education level, government investment into industries etc. On the other hand internal influences are broadly within the control of the organization to predict determine and monitor, for example the organizational culture underpinned by management behaviours (or style), environmental climate and the approach to ethical and corporate social responsibilities.

Major Trends

In order to know the business environment in which any organization operates, three major trends should be considered:

Demographics the characteristics of a population/workforce, for example, age, gender or social class. This type of trend may have an effect in relation to pension offerings, insurance packages etc.

Diversity the variation within the population/work place. Changes in society now mean that a larger proportion of organizations are made up of "baby-boomers" or older employees in comparison to thirty years ago. Advocates of "work place diversity" simply advocate an employee base that is a mirror reflection of the make-up of society insofar as race, gender, sexual orientation, etc.

Skills and qualifications as industries move from manual to a more managerial professions so does the need for more highly skilled graduates. If the market is "tight" (i.e. not enough staff for the jobs), employers will have to compete for employees by offering financial rewards, community investment, etc.

Individual Responses

In regard to how individuals respond to the changes in a labour market the following should be understood:

Geographical spread how far is the job from the individual? The distance to travel to work should be in line with the pay offered by the organization and the transportation and infrastructure of the area will also be an influencing factor in deciding who will apply for a post.

Occupational structure the norms and values of the different careers within an organization. Mahoney 1989 developed 3 different types of occupational structure namely craft (loyalty to the profession), organization career (promotion through the firm) and unstructured.

Generational difference different age categories of employees have certain characteristics, for example their behaviour and their expectations of the organization.

Framework

Human Resources Development is a framework for the expansion of human capital within an organization or (in new approaches) a municipality, region, or nation. Human Resources Development is a combination of training and education, in a broad context of adequate health and employment policies, that ensures the continual improvement and growth of both the individual, the organisation, and the national human resourcefulnes.

Adam Smith states, "The capacities of individuals depended on their access to education". Human Resources Development is the medium that drives the process between training and learning in a broadly fostering environment. Human Resources Development is not a defined object, but a series of organised processes, "with a specific learning objective" (Nadler,1984) Within a national context, it becoms a strategic approach to inter sectoral linkages between health, education and employment.

Structure

Human Resources Development is the structure that allows for individual development, potentially satisfying the organization's, or the nation's goals. The development of the individual will benefit both the individual, the organization, or the nation and its citizens. In the corporate vision, the Human Resources Development framework views employees, as an asset to the enterprise whose value will be enhanced by development, "Its primary focus is on growth and employee development...it emphasises developing individual potential and skills" (Elwood, olton and Trott 1996) Human Resources Development in this treatment can be in-room group training, tertiary or vocational courses or mentoring and coaching by senior employees with the aim for a desired outcome that will develop the individual's performance. At the level of a national strategy, it can be a broad inter sectoral approach to fostering creative contributions to national productivity.

Training

At the organizational level, a successful Human Resources Development program will prepare the individual to undertake a higher level of work, "organized learning over a given period of time, to provide the possibility of performance change" (Nadler 1984). In these settings, Human Resources Development is the framework that focuses on the organizations competencies at the first stage, training, and then developing the employee, through education, to satisfy the organizations long-term needs and the individuals' career goals and employee value to their present and future employers. Human Resources Development can be defined simply as developing the most important section of any business its human resource by, "attaining or upgrading the skills and attitudes of employees at all levels in order to maximise the effectiveness of the enterprise" (Kelly 2001).

The people within an organization are its human resource. Human Resources Development from a business perspective is not entirely focused on the individual's growth and development, "development occurs to enhance the organization's value, not solely for individual improvement. Individual education and development is a tool and a means to an end, not the end goal itself". The broader concept of national and more strategic attention to the development of human resources is beginning to emerge as newly independent countries face strong competition for their skilled professionals and the accompanying brain-drain they experience.

Recruitment

Employee recruitment forms a major part of an organization's overall resourcing strategies which seek to identify and secure the people needed for the organisation to survive and succeed in the short to medium-term. Recruitment activities need to be responsive to the ever-increasingly competitive market to secure suitably qualified and capable recruits at all levels. To be effective these initiatives need to include how and when to source the best recruits internally or externally. Common to the success of either are; well-defined organisational structures with sound job design, robust task and person specification and versatile selection processes, reward, employment relations and human resource policies, underpinned by a commitment for strong employer branding and employee engagement strategies.

Internal recruitment can provide the most cost-effective source for recruits if the potential of the existing pool of employees has been enhanced through training, development and other performance-enhancing activities such as performance appraisal, succession planning and development centres to review performance and assess employee development needs and promotional potential.

Increasingly, securing the best quality candidates for almost all organizations will rely, at least occasionally if not substantially, on external recruitment methods. Rapid changing business models demand skills of experiences which cannot be sourced or rapidly enough developed from the existing employee base. It would be unusual for an organisation today to undertake all aspects of the recruitment process without support from third-party dedicated recruitment firms. This may involve a range of support services, such as; provision of CVs or resumes, identifying recruitment media, advertisement design and media placement for job vacancies, candidate response handling, short-listed, conducting aptitude testing, preliminary interviews or reference and qualification verification. Typically, small organisations may not have in-house resources or, in common with larger organisations, may not possess the particular skill-set required to undertake a specific recruitment assignment. Where requirements arise these will be referred on an adhoc basis to government job centres or commercially run employment agencies.

Except in sectors where high-volume recruitment is the norm, an organization faced with an unexpected requirement for an unusually large number of new recruits at short notice will often hand over the task to a specialist external recruiter to manage the end-to-end resourcing programme. Sourcing executive-level and senior management as well as the acquisition of scarce or 'high-potential' recruits has been a long-established market serviced by a wide range of 'search and selection' or 'head-hunting' consultancies which typically form long-standing relationships with their client organizations.

Finally, certain organizations with sophisticated HR practices have identified there is a strategic advantage in out sourcing complete responsibility for all workforce procurement to one or more third-party recruitment agencies or consultancies. In the most sophisticated of these arrangements the external recruitment services provider may not only physically locate, or 'embed', their resourcing team(s) within the client organization's offices but will work in tandem with the senior human resource management team in developing the longer-term HR resourcing strategy and plan.

Modern Concept of Human Resources

Though human resources have been part of business and organizations since the first days of agriculture, the modern concept of human resources began in reaction to the efficiency focus of Taylorism in the early 1900s. By 1920, psychologists and employment experts in the United States started the human relations movement, which viewed workers in terms of their psychology and fit with companies, rather than as interchangeable parts. This movement grew throughout the middle of the 20th century, placing emphasis on how leadership, cohesion, and loyalty played important roles in organizational success. Although this view was increasingly challenged by more quantitatively rigorous and less "soft" management techniques in the 1960s and beyond, human resources development had gained a permanent role within organizations, agencies and nations, increasingly as not only an academic discipline, but as a central theme in development policy.

Human Resource Planning

Need for Human Resource Planning

Human Resource Planning is the process by which a management determines how an organization should move from its current manpower position to its desire manpower position. This way a management strives to have the right number and the right kind of people at the right places at the right time. Human Resource Planning consists of a series of activities:

1. Forecasting future manpower requirements
2. Making an inventory of present manpower resources.
3. Anticipating manpower problems by projecting present resources into the future.
4. Planning the necessary programs of requirement, selection, training & development to ensure that future manpower requirements are properly met.

Human Resource Planning is necessary for one or more of the following reasons:

1. Effective manpower planning is required for every organization to carry on the work efficiently.
2. There is a constant need for replacing personnel who have grown old or who retire so that the work doesn't suffer.
3. Human Resource Planning is essential because of frequent labour turnover that arises from social & economical factors like voluntary quits, marriage, promotions etc.
4. Due to rising standards of living large quantities of goods are required because of which human resource planning is unavoidable.
5. The present workforce has to be changed in relation to the challenging needs of technology & production.
6. Manpower planning is needed in order to identify areas of surplus personnel or areas in which there is shortage of personnel.

Process of Human Resource Planning:

1. Deciding goals or objectives
2. Estimating future organizational structure & manpower requirements
3. Auditing Human Resources
4. Planning job requirements & job descriptions
5. Developing a human resource plan.

Assessment of Available HR in the Organization

The assessment of available HR in the organization is an important step to human resource planning. This assessment of manpower requirement depends on the manpower assumptions and the organizational corporate strategy.

1. Zero Budgeting – The total operation begins from zero where the objective of the managers is to lay importance on their current activities.
2. Ideal Approach – Decision like off-loading, sub-contracting, maintenance, production, technology is kept in mind while assessing human resource in the organization.
3. Realistic Approach – Based on existing information manpower assessment is determined.

Work Load Analysis

It's the method of studying & analysing a job to prepare the manning norms.

Work load analysis is used to understand the methods & processes of doing a particular job. It thus helps in improving the productivity of an organization.

Human Development Index and Gender Development Index of India

The human development index (HDI) compiled by the UNDP, is a summary measure of a country's human development. It measures the average achievements in a country in three basic dimensions:

- a long and healthy life, as measured by life expectancy at birth;

- access to knowledge, as measured by the adult literacy rate and the combined gross enrolment (sic) ratio in education; and
- a decent standard of living, as measured by GDP per capita in purchasing power parity (PPP) US dollars.

These three dimensions are standardized to values between 0 and 1, and the simple average is taken to arrive at the overall HDI value in the range 0 to 1. Countries are then ranked on the basis of this value with a rank of 1 representing the highest HDI value. India ranks 134 among 182 countries and is classified as a medium HDI country. Between 1980 and 2007, India's HDI increased by about 1.3% every year. Many African countries show even higher growth rates in HDI, reflecting the very low levels they were at in 1980. Most high income countries show growth rates between 0.25 to 0.5% per year over this period.

The ranking clearly showed India has slipped in comparative terms in ensuring a better quality of life for its citizens as in the previous index, compiled together for 2007 and 2008, it ranked 128, while the position the year before was 126.

Norway, Australia and Iceland top the HDI while Afghanistan, Sierra Leone and Niger are the bottom of the HDI.

Gender Development Index of India

In terms of the Gender Development Index, India ranks 113 out of 157 countries. Gender Development Index is calculated with the use of 3 variables:

- Life Expectancy
- Education
- Estimated Earned Income.

Government Expenditure in Social Sector

The government to improve these parameters that affect the HDI and GDI has increasingly been spending higher on social services as a proportion of total expenditure and was 22.5% for 2008. Expenditure on education and health care has also increased.

Poverty Index of India

There are concerns about vulnerability of people who have crossed the poverty line (PL) and are at present above it.

Vulnerability is a relative term and could be gauged from the consumption pattern in the absence of a better available alternative.

The average per capita consumption expenditure for rural and urban population as per 61st Round (2004-05) is Rs. 558.78 and Rs.1052.36, respectively. NSSO data also reveals that rural population on an average spends about 55% of its consumption on food and the remaining 45% on non-food items.

The Essence of Human Development

Human biology deals with the bodily processes. Understanding how our body works will help us take care of ourselves more.

Human Biology was founded at the Stanford University in 1970. It is considered as an interdisciplinary field of medicine, nutrition, biological anthropology and biology, focusing in humans. It can be associated with primate biology as well as several other fields. Human development, on the other hand, deals with the process of growing to maturity. Biologically, this pertains to the growth from one-celled zygotes to adult human beings. The development begins, as we all know, with fertilization wherein the male gamete or sperm cell as well as the female gamete or the oocyte fuse actually gives rise to a diploid cell or the zygote. This would refer to the 3 stages such as the zygote, embryo and the fetus.

In modern medicine, pregnancy is characterized as the process wherein the fertilized zygote is implanted inside the woman's uterus, embedding on the endometrium or uterus lining. This will form a placenta, serving as the channel for the receiving of nutrients via the wall of the uterus. This is the umbilical cord of a newborn child, signifying the remnants of the implantation.

After this, the zygote will undergo rapid mitotic divisions having no significant growth (this process is referred to as cleavage) as well as cellular differentiation which will lead to the development of the embryo. Childbirth is a process wherein the baby is born. For many, it is regarded as the start of a person's life. In fact, in most cultures, the age is relative to this process.

The Physical Stages of One's Existence

There are different terms related to the age for the physical development. This would include the approximate age that ranges from many different terms. Prenatal is from fertilization to birth (from embryo to fetus stages). A child is that from birth to toddler years (from newborn or neonate to pre-pubescence or primary school age). Puberty and adolescence are the teenage years (from 13 up to 19 years old). An adult is from 20 years old to death (from young adult to senior citizen or advanced adult stages).

Death occurs at different ages, usually depending on the person (this is the stage of decomposition or the body's breakdown after death). The heart stops beating and all the other organs stop functioning.

Factors Affecting the Parent's Desire to know their Unborn Child's Sex

Most parents feel the urge to know the sex of their unborn child immediately. One good reason is so that they can already prepare themselves. This can range to the things they will be buying for the baby or to prepare themselves psychologically and emotionally on the child's future.

Other reasons include conceiving accidentally, not planning to breastfeed, finding out the child's sex in a prior pregnancy, the influence of sex on futuristic childbearing plans, specific parental preference for the child's sex and the plans for renovation or moving associated with the wanting to learn the child's sex.

Studies show that both socioeconomic and demographic factors really affect a parent's desire to know the sex of their unborn child. The ones who prefer to know this are the ones with a lower socioeconomic status. Hence, at this point, the best way to determine the sex of an unborn child is through prenatal ultrasound examinations.

Another common reason is to be able to come up with the baby's name. Parents think about it carefully, wanting it to be very meaningful, for the child will carry the name for the rest of his life.

Human Development Report-2009

Increasing mobility is not a new phenomenon. The process which started slowly with the developments in the fields of science and technology gradually evolved into lightning speed around the world. It had its repercussions both – good and bad. Alvin

Toffler had conducted a detailed study on increasing mobility and shared the information with the readers in his widely acclaimed book "The Future Shock".

Increasing mobility and migration are interdependent. No one is going to disagree with this truth. Immigration-its positive and negative aspects-has become a subject for study and research at the international level.

The other day there was a news item in 'The Hindu' by the noted journalist and correspondent Vidya Subramaniam on Human Development Reports (HDR) released simultaneously across the world by Deputy Chairman, Planning Commission: Montek Singh Ahluwalia and United Nations Co-ordinator Patrice Coeur Bizot: Overcoming Barriers: Human mobility and development and the salutary effects of migration between countries-from developing countries to developed countries, developing countries to other developing countries and migration within countries and the enormous potential, social, financial and cultural brought about by the latter.

The report is based on statistics and on going through it a citizen has much to feel cheerful about it. The report also mentions about certain areas of a country which are left behind in the field of education resulting in the reluctance of the inhabitants of these areas to emigrate to other parts of the country or to other countries. A country like India, where lack of adequate education facilities even 62 years after Independence has a lot to be ashamed of.

While feeling happy and elated about the positive aspects migration brings about in the world, we feel equally sad on going through news reports emanating from different countries on a regular basis – the harassment, hardships and torture the immigrants suffer at the hands of the citizens of a particular country.

The "Sons of the soil" policy and racist attacks escalate on a daily basis. Right below the news report on emigration, with a feeling of sadness I came across a news item on the racist attacks by Australians against the Indians who live and lead peaceful lives working as cabbies, bartendenders, such menial jobs and the students for the purpose of higher studies and dreaming of a bright future. These attacks on Indians even after government's strong protests and despite Australian Prime Minister Kevin Rudd's assurances to the Government of India on adopting a zero tolerance towards the attackers continue unabated. Recently Juliet Gillard, the Education Minister of Australia on her visit to India also gave an assurance on these lines. All in vain. Now it is learnt that the Indian immigrants having lost their patience have started to hit back in the same coin. As somebody put it, "A confident resistance will make a thug flee".

Xenophobia has become a bane across world. More and more protectionist tendencies are the root causes. Even a few developed countries are prone to protectionist tendencies and intolerant towards the immigrants.

Nicholas Sarkozy, French President, was the Interior Minister under the regime of Jacques Chirac, before becoming President. Sarkozy was a pain in the neck of Chirac for his xenophobic policies. Jacques Chirac favoured Dominique De Villipine, the former Prime Minister according to the media reports to be his successor. Sarkozy could swing the mandate to his side, for he adopted a more protectionist policy and it had many takers then. The infamous racist attacks, the widely condemned electrocution of two African teenagers and his reported justification for the suppression of racist violence consequent upon it, his intolerance towards burqa-clad muslim women, even Sikhs sporting turbans following their religious beliefs during that period and even after that, was widely condemned.

Anyhow the highest position of President later somewhat made him show more maturity and he even played the role of a master diplomat in arriving at an amicable solution to the war between Russia and Georgia over South Ossetia, thus averting a catastrophe which would have reached an unimaginable dimension with USA intervening under the belligerent George Bush, the then President. Xenophobia still stares in the face of immigrants though. Economic recession across the world has a damaging contribution to this nagging problem.

Xenophobia and protectionist tendencies to a large extent are prevalent in various corners of the world. Not only between countries but even in a particular country itself. Take for example our own "Incredible Nation". The financial capital of India,

"Mumbai" (sorry, not Bombay) is a glaring example of the "Sons of the soil". The emigrants from the States of Uttar Pradesh, Bihar, Orissa always live in perpetual fear of the "policy holders", the "Marathi mannoos". About a year ago, the North Indian inhabitants were brutally attacked, robbed of their belongings, their properties destroyed and forced them to flee to their States. Some even succumbed to injuries on being badly mauled. Poor men, women and children leaving their beloveds in their respective native States catch trains and after three or four days of ardous train journeys reach the city not for leading a pompous life but for earning something to have atleast a square meal per day. They don't stay in flats, bungalows or five-star hotels but in slums, chawls and railway platforms. Mumbai is nobody's monopoly. It is a part of our nation and it should remain as such.

I do not know whether the HDR (Human Development Reports) took into account while preparing it with the deserving significance. Anyhow as long as immigration remains a smooth affair and mobility undisturbed, happy days are here to stay. Otherwise get doomed.

Low Human Resource Development Directly Proportional to Economic Growth!

Human rights is one factor that is much more instrumental than it is thought to be for the growth and development of a country. In the times when most of the countries in the world are democratic, human rights is a fundamental factor that needs to be addressed to.

These rights are not to be decided and written down in the constitution alone but they are to be equally implemented and practiced as they are the determinant and underlying factor behind another very important factor namely human development. Human resource is the aspect that is one of the most important in the overall condition of the concerned country. Human resource development should be and in fact is the most primary concern of most of the countries of the world. In some other countries democracy is just there for name, a decorative element to ordain the constitution. Some surveys conducted by the UN has showed that most of the countries that are low on human development and human rights are Muslim countries.

The interesting fact is however that this is not exclusive to the Muslim countries. Be it the Muslim countries or the non Muslim ones human development is imperative for the overall growth and development of any country. And it has also been noticed that the places where human development is poor and human resource is not as progressive as it ought to be, the issue of human rights was also in dire straits. Human rights are not practiced ideally as they ought to be in a democracy. This condition is very much prominent in the Muslim countries though there are a few non Muslim countries also included in the list. The bottom line is that Muslim or non Muslim growth is unattainable without appropriate human rights and subsequent development.

This trend is more cornmon with the Muslim countries as they have a very arbitrary lifestyle. Gender inequality, fanaticism, religious, political and social bias are some the factors that have made the correct exercise of human rights very difficult in these countries. As a result human resource is at a very pathetic low in these nations. Economics, politics, society everything are man made. It is vital that human development is at an optimum for upliftment in these departments. Poor human resource results in low economy, disturbing politics and a society that cannot be called fit to survive in and these facts are not just bookish. The result can be seen in the current political and socio economic conditions of the countries that find a presence in this list.

When human resource is at the prime and in a good condition anything can be accomplished. The able, smart, and acumen friendly employees especially in the line of information technology have pushed the traders from the developed countries to hire the software company based in countries like India, China and Malaysia. These companies provide every solution from web application development to ecommerce solution and that too at extremely affordable rates.

8

Development of Women and Children

The Constitution of India authorizes the Government to take measures for the protection of women and children. In accordance with these provisions several progressive steps have been taken by Government of Karnataka with a view to ensure the care and protection of women and children.

The Department of Probation and After Care Services was established in 1956 and was functioning under the Social Welfare Department wherein focus was on giving services to children and women admitted under various social legislations in correctional institutions. A separate directorate of Women and Child Development was created in 1975, during the "International Year of Women", with the objective of giving the much needed impetus to the holistic development of women and children. The major thrust of the programmes and schemes of the directorate of Women and Child Development is to ensure a state of well being for women and children especially those of the weaker sections of society.

The Department formulates plans, policies and programmes, guides and co-ordinates the efforts of both governmental and non-governmental organizations working in the field of women and child development.

The Department of Women and Child Development has promoted and assisted the voluntary sector significantly in the implementation of the government policies and programmes for women and children.

The focus of the Department is the all round development of women and children and empowerment of women. The activities of the department can be broadly classified into 3 categories

Programmes for Women Development

The strategy adopted for the programmes in the areas of women development involves empowerment of women through education and awareness generation and greater emphasis on vocational training and employment so as to enable them to enter the mainstream of economic development as equal partners. The department implements programmes in the areas of employment, training for women, awareness generation and gender sensitization. The emphasis is on helping women to become self sufficient and economically independent with the help of training and income generating activities so as to enhance their earning capacity and to bring up their status in life. The department aims at the economic development and integration of women into the main stream of society and also as individuals with a right to human dignity. Besides expanding the on-going programmes, the department has evolved some innovative schemes such as "Stree Shakthi" for empowerment of women and "Santhwana" for providing assistance to victims of various atrocities in the society.

Stree Shakti

The scheme was launched during 2000-01 with an objective to empower rural women and make them self reliant by inculcating the habit of savings and proper utilization of financial resources.

Anganwadi workers and supervisors are instrumental in organizing rural women in self help groups. About 15 to 20 women who belong to below poverty line families, landless agricultural labourers, SC/ST join together to form one self help group.

In addition to the existing one lakh groups, an additional 20,000 new self help groups were formed at the village level through Anganwadi workers in the state. As at the end of 2006-07, 17.80 lakh women have been organised in 1.20 lakh groups.

Objectives :

1. To strengthen the process of economic development of rural women and create a conducive environment for social change.

2. To form one lakh Self Help Women Groups based on thrift and credit principles which builds self reliance and enable women to have greater access to control over resources.
3. To create self confidence in rural women by involving them in income generating activities thereby contributing to poverty alleviation.
4. To provide opportunities to the members of the groups to avail the benefits of other departmental schemes by converging the services of various departments and lending institutions to ensure women's access to credit financing.

Savings and Inter Loaning

The self help groups conduct regular weekly meetings and save minimum of Rs. 10/-.So far these women self help groups have saved an amount of Rs. 444.91 crores and have lent Rs. 1251.98 crores internally to the members. This enthusiastic savings activity has weaned them away from the clutches of money lenders and take up income generating activities.

Revolving Fund

To help SHGs to take up income generating activities, the department has contributed an amount of Rs.-5,000/-as revolving fund to add to the corpus of each group which is used for taking up income generating activities. So far 1,13,478 SHGs have been given this revolving fund

Kit Materials

Each group is given kit materials worth of Rs.600/- consisting of registers and a zinc trunk for keeping the registers and other documents of the group.

Training

Training to members of women SHGs constitutes an important component in Stree Shakthi Programme. The first phase of training for 11 lakh members was taken up to orient SHG members about the Stree Shakthi Programme. In the second phase training in gender issues, leadership qualities, communication skills were taken up. In the third phase training in book keeping, credit management and social issues were taken up. So far 92,709 groups have been trained in credit management, 97,213 groups have been trained in book keeping and 94,819 groups have been trained in social issues.

In co-ordination with Nabard and Myrada a capacity building training programme for Supervisors of Women and Child Development Department was conducted.

Total cost of the training programme is Rs.6.00 Lakhs. 50% of the training cost is borne by the Department and 50% by Nabard. Training in Fashion Designing was given to 30 members from stree shakthi groups through National Institute of Fashion Technology.

Credit Linkages to Shgs

As at the end of March 99,969 groups were eligible for credit linkage with banks and also to take up income generating activities. So far 90,182 groups have been credit linked and given financial assistance to the extent of Rs. 496.13 crores.

Income Generating Activities

74,896 SHGs have taken up various IGA programmes available in other Government Departments namely, Animal Husbandry, Nirmithi Kendras etc., A few of these groups have been given training and technical support under Giriraja Scheme of Animal Husbandry Department.

The department has also assisted the SHGs to procure Giriraja birds. So far 14,718 groups have taken up this activity and invested Rs.3.81 lakh towards purchase of Giriraja birds. The different activities taken up are as follows:

1. Dairying
2. Production and sale of readymade garments
3. Blanket marketing
4. Marketing of seeds and manure
5. Production and sale of.
    a. Papad
    b. Sambar Powder
    c. Agarbathi etc.
6. Production and sale of composite manure
7. Production and sale of soap and detergent.

New Swarnima Programme

SHGs who belong to backward classes are given financial assistance from Backward Class and Minorities Development Corporation for taking up income generating activities. So far, 17,007 members have been given financial assistance of Rs.1,657.99 lakhs.

Incentives to Groups

As announced by the Hon'ble Chief Minister in the budget speech for 2003-04, the SHGs who have saved Rs. 75000/- to Rs.1.00 lakh and groups who have saved Rs. 1.00 lakh and above are given incentives of Rs.15,000 and Rs.20,000/- respectively. So far 1571 groups which had saved Rs.75,000 and above and 449 groups which had saved Rs.1.00 lakh and above have been given incentives as above.

Programmes for Child Development

To ensure that children get protection against neglect, abuse and exploitation, the department has taken up programmes and schemes to guarantee the basic human rights including survival, development and full participation in social, cultural, educational and other endeavours for their individual growth and well being.

Children below 6 years constitute 17% of the total population of India i.e. about 17 crores. As compared to other developed countries, infant mortality rate in our country is very high. At the beginning of 1980s, 120 out of every 1000 newly born children were dying even before completing one year. Even after 50 years of independence, more than 40% of the Indian population live below poverty line.

Ignorance and illiteracy are still rampant among the rural people. Severe malnutrition on account of acute poverty which gives room for low-resistance and the consequential early childhood diseases are the main causes for this alarming situation.

The emphasis on child development has been on improving the quality of services under Integrated Child Development Services and also to improve the delivery of the programmes, components through the convergence of services meant for women and children.

Integrated Child Development Services Scheme

Having realized the utmost urgency and importance of giving highest priority to develop human resources, the Government of India found it most essential to evolve a national programme for the overall development of children. The result of this concern is the emergence of a national programme called Integrated Child Development Services Scheme in the year 1975, with a modest coverage of 33 projects in the country with one pilot project at T. Narsipur in Karnataka, which has been expanded to cover all the taluks in the State. The welfare of pregnant and nursing mothers and children below 6 years has acquired a prime place in the programme.

Objectives of the Scheme

The main objectives of the scheme broadly are to :

- Improve the nutritional and health status of children in the age group 0-6 years.
- Lay the foundation for proper psychological, physical and social development of the child
- Reduce the incidence of mortality, morbidity, malnutrition and school drop-out.
- Achieve effective co-ordination of policy and implementation amongst the various departments to promote child development; and to.
- Enhance the capability of the mother to look after the normal health and nutritional needs of the child through proper nutrition and health education.

Expansion of ICDS in Karnataka

The Integrated Child Development Services Scheme was started in Karnataka on 2nd October 1975 with a pilot project at T.Narasipura in Mysore District with just 100 Anganwadi Centres. Since then, the programme has been expanded to cover all the revenue taluks and 10 urban areas in the state. At present 185 projects are in operation covering all the 175 taluks and 10 urban areas.

All the 185 Integrated Child Development Services Scheme projects are now operational under the Central Sector.

The Profile of Projects and Anganwadis in Karnataka

	Rural	*Urban*	*Tribal*	*Total*
Icds Projects:				
Sanctioned	166	10	9	185
Operational	166	10	9	185
Anganwadi Centres				
Sanctioned	46369	1819	3426	51614
Functioning as on Mar. 2007	45940	1799	3411	51150

2646 additional Anganwadi centres and 405 mini-anganwadi centres sanctioned by the Government of India on 21st December 2006 will be operationlised during 2007-08.

Targeted Beneficiaries

The benefits of the scheme are provided to children below 6 years, pregnant women and nursing mothers belonging to socially and economically disadvantaged families living in backward rural and tribal areas, urban slums and places where SC/ST/minority populations are concentrated.

Services Under Icds

The package of six services provided are;

- Supplementary Nutrition
- Nutrition and Health Education for women.
- Immunization
- Health check up
- Referral services
- Non formal preschool education.

These services are delivered to all the eligible beneficiaries through Anganwadi centre which is the focal point of Integrated Child Development Services scheme, between 9.30 a.m. and 1.30 p.m.

Supplementary Nutrition

Supplementary Nutrition programme is provided in Anganwadi Centres to the eligible children below 6 years of age, pregnant women and nursing mothers and 2 adolescent girls percentre in the age group of 11-18 years. This supplementary feeding is in addition to what they get at home with an intention to fill the gap between what is required in terms of calories, proteins, vitamins, minerals, fats etc., and what is available through their regular intake of food at home. Each beneficiary is provided 300 calories of energy and 8-10 gms of protein as supplements, for a minimum of 300 days in a year. For children in the age group 0-6 years supplementary nutrition is being given at the cost of Rs. 2.00 per beneficiary per day for normal children including transportation charges w.e.f. 01.04.2006. In all ICDS projects severely malnourished children, adolescent girls, pregnant women, nursing mothers, anganwadi workers & helpers are provided food @ Rs. 3.00 per beneficiary per day for 300 days in a year.

Present Intervention

Amylase Rich Energy food is given to the to the beneficiaries after mixing it with lukewarm water and made into Laddus/ porridge. The composition of Amylase rich energy food is whole wheat (toasted), soya dhal (steamed), defatted soya flour (toasted), bengal gram (toasted), powdered sugar, vitamins and minerals (premix) and malted ragi.

1. 0-3 children-Amylase Rich Energy food (AREF) prepared by M/S. Christy Fried Gram Industries is supplied to 96 ICDS projects and in remaining districts local food is given.
2. 3-6 children-Amylase Rich Energy food is given for 2 days and rice based local food for 4 days.
3. for Pregnant women and nursing mothers- rice and green gram are given as "take home" food for four days and AREF for 2 days.

Nutrition and Health Education

With a view to create awareness about personal hygiene and health and to inculcate basic knowledge of nutritious food, child care to mothers in ICDS areas, trained Supervisors/Anganwadi Workers, ANMs/LHVs jointly conduct Nutrition and Health Education Sessions with Audio Visual Aids. Matters relating to child care, care of pregnant women and nursing mothers, dietary needs, immunization, supplementary nutrition for children, better child bearing and rearing practices, sanitation/hygiene, etc. are included in NHED. Nutrition Camps and demonstrations are also conducted by the Food & Nutrition Board, Government of India. Anganwadi workers and Supervisors are trained in conducting nutrition camps by the Food & Nutrition Board.

Immunization

As per the immunization schedule, children are protected against 6 vaccine preventable diseases like diphtheria, whooping cough, tetanus, poliomyelitis, pertusis, tuberculosis and measles. Pregnant women are given Tetanus Toxoid and immunization is carried out with the co-ordination of Health department.

Health Check up

Health Check up includes;

- ante-natal care of expectant mothers
- post-natal care of nursing mothers and care of new born infants
- care of children under six years of age especially 'at risk' children like those born with low birth weight/congenital defects and severely malnourished.

Jurisdictional Medical officers of PHC/CHC/PHU conduct health check up of all the children, pregnant women and nursing mothers coming to each anganwadi, once in a quarter. Medicine kits are provided by the Department of Women and Child Development to anganwadi centres to provide primary health care of a simple nature.

Referral Services

Severely malnourished Children (Grade III and IV), pregnant women and nursing mothers during the course of health check up, if necessary are referred for treatment to nearby government hospitals for specialized intervention. Referral Slips are provided in each Anganwadi Centre. Beneficiaries with referral slips are attended to on priority and follow up action is initiated by Anganwadi Workers.

Non-Formal Pre-School Education

Integrated Approach to pre-school Education" has been introduced in the state for children in the age group of 3-6 years who attend anganwadi centres in order to provide a better linkage between primary schools and the Anganwadi centres and also to achieve proper co-ordination between all those involved in pre-school activities. An exhaustive "Activity Bank" with 100 stories/ songs/with colourful illustrations has been provided to each anganwadi centre.

Expenditure on ICDS

The Central Government bears the entire administrative expenditure. The expenditure towards supplementary nutrition is borne by the State Government and the central Government on 50: 50 basis.

Budgetary allocation and expenditure 2006-07

I. Administration Cost (Rs. in lakhs);

Description	*Central Funds*	*State funds for Additional* Honorarium
Allocation	18960.74	5291.01
Expenditure Up to end of Mar. 2007	14099.58	4311.65

II. Supplementary Nutrition (Rs. in lakhs);

Description	*Plan*	*Non Plan*	*Total*
Allocation	11196.66	13039.26	242325.92
Expenditure (Up to end of Mar. 2007)	8244.41	10872.35	19116.76

Community Participation

The fulcrum of Integrated Child Development Services Scheme is community awareness and participation. Community is assisting in the implementation of the scheme by providing buildings locally grown vegetables, fuel, organizing health check up, immunization and conducting health and nutrition education camps. In some places the community has come forward to donate toys, uniforms, utensils and furniture also for use in Anganwadi centres. The participation from community has enhanced after setting up Balavikas Samithis in each of the villages. Members of women self-help groups also assist in the implementation of the programme.

Monitoring of ICDS Programme

Monthly and quarterly progress reports under the Integrated Child Development Services programme are being consolidated through NIC NET with the co-ordination of the National Informatics Centre, Bangalore.

Impact of ICDS

The Integrated Child Development Services Scheme has proved to be a very effective child survival scheme in the country and state as well. Infant Mortality Rate in Integrated Child Development Services areas has come down from 120/1000 live births in 1975 to 55/1000 in 2006. Likewise, the percentage of severely malnourished children has also come down considerably. The community has fully accepted the programme and actively participating in the implementation. The School dropout rate has come down considerably. Elected representatives, local organizations and public have realized the importance of the Integrated Child Development Services scheme.

ICDS Training Programme

The training component of the Integrated Child Development Services Programme has now been recognized as the most important key to achieve the aims and objectives of Integrated Child Development Services scheme with the ultimate aim of moulding the functionaries into "Agents of social and behavioural change."

The Southern Regional Centre of the National Institute of Public Cooperation and Child Development (NIPCCD) located at Bangalore is an apex body catering to the training needs of senior level Integrated Child Development Services functionaries like Deputy Directors/Programme Officers/CDPOs/ACDPOs etc., besides undertaking Research and Evaluation studies.

At present there is one Middle Level Training Centre (MLTC) at Ujire (Dakshina Kannada) which is catering to the training needs of ICDS supervisors. The state has 19 Anganwadi Workers Training Centres (AWTCs) which are run by NGOs for training anganawadi workers and helpers. The rates of honorarium as well as course grants as per GOI guidelines have been sanctioned by the State Government to implement various training programmes.

During 2006-07 an amount of Rs 216.29 lakhs was released and Rs. 196.73 lakhs was incurred under the ICDS training programme to train 595 supervisors, 6658 Anganwadi Workers and 8595 Anganwadi Helpers (Job/Refresher training/orientation training).

State Training Task Force (Sttf)

For regular monitoring and evaluation of the training component of Integrated Child Development Services scheme, the state Government has constituted the State Training Task Force.

The basic function of this Task Force is to integrate and coordinate all aspects of ICDS training at all levels and to recommend changes in the curriculum, strategies and methodology. The ultimate goal is to reorient and re-utilise ICDS training to turn it into a dynamic, responsive and human resource development programme.

Construction of Anganwadi Buildings

Out of 51150 Anganwadi centres functioning in the State, 29020 anganwadi centres have their own buildings. The remaining centres are functioning in rented buildings, temples, community halls, etc. Zilla Panchayats have been requested to take up construction of buildings on a priority basis.

Departmental Contribution: The department contributes an amount of Rs.50,000/- per building and the remaining amount is met out of funds of various schemes under Zilla Panchayath or public contribution. During the year 2006-07 an allocation of Rs. 173.55 lakhs was made, and expenditure of Rs. 168.20 lakhs was incurred.

Nabard Assistance: During 2006-07 an amount of Rs.800.00 lakhs was initially allocated for this purpose. Subsequently additional amount of Rs 900.00 lakhs was provided. The proposal to construct 692 buildings has been approved by NABARD along with a sanction of Rs. 1445.76 lakhs as loan. The construction of these buildings will be taken up during 2007-08.

Nutrition Programme for Adolescent Girls (NPAG)

Nutrition programme for adolescent girls (NPAG) is a Government of India scheme through which special nutrition is provided to adolescent girls from families living below poverty line. Two backward districts of Karnataka i.e. Kolar and Gulbarga have been selected for implementing this programme on an experimental basis. An amount of Rs.516.40 lakhs was earmarked as "additional central assistance". Out of this, an amount of Rs. 234.15 lakhs to Kolar district and Rs. 282.25 lakhs to Gulburga district has been released during March 2005-06. For the year 2006-07 an amount of Rs. 259.55 lakhs to Kolar district and Rs. 268.15 lakhs to Gulburga district has been released.

Under this Scheme, Adolescent girls who weigh less than 35 kg are identified and 6 kgs of rice is distributed every month through fair price shops to identified card holders. 65833 adolescent girls in Kolar district and 66399 adolescent girls in Gulbarga district have availed this benefit during the year 2006-07.

Kishori Shakti Yojana

Kishori Shakti Yojana was being implemented in 38 ICDS blocks in the state from 2001-02 and during 2005-06 the scheme was extended to cover all the 185 ICDS blocks in the state. Under KSY, 180 Adolescent Girls in the block are given 5-days residential training from funds released exclusively for the scheme and supplementary Nutrition is being provided to 2 adolescent girls in each anganwadi centre. During the current year, all the Deputy Directors have been given one days orientation training regarding Taluk level Trainers Training and the implementation of KSY. Taluk level TOT members conduct the 5-days residential training for adolescent girls.

An amount of Rs. 203.50 lakhs is provided in the budget for the year and up to the end of March 2007 an amount of Rs. 138.165 lakhs was spent.

Bhagyalakshmi

Objective As per 2001 census, the sex ratio in Karnataka is 964 females to 1000 males. Though this is better than the national average, the current situation is strong argument for according higher value to the life of a girl child. There are several socio economic reasons for the 'strong preference for a male pregnancy' that is seen to be present in society at large which adversely affects the girl child's access to nutrition, health care and education and her overall development. In order to show the state government's concern for the girl child and change society's attitudes towards her, and promote birth of girl children in below poverty line families, a new welfare scheme called Bhagyalakshmi was launched during the year.

Eligibility

This scheme is restricted to two girl children born after 31.03.2006 in BPL families. This benefit will be available if the father or mother of the beneficiary girl has undergone terminal family planning methods so that the total number of children of the BPL family does not exceed three in the said family.

In order to be eligible for the maturity amount, it is compulsory that the beneficiary completes 8th standard and she should not have been married off before she reaches the age of 18. Otherwise, the maturity amount will be forfeited. If the beneficiary dies within 18 years, the amount will be forfeited.

Pattern of Assistance Certain interim payments such as annual scholarships and insurance benefits will be made available to the beneficiary on continued fulfillment of the eligibility criteria outlined in the scheme. The annual scholarship slab is as given below:

Class	*Amount of Annual Scholarship*
I-III	Rs.300/-per annum for each class
IV	Rs. 500/-
V	Rs. 600/-
VI-VII	Rs. 700/-
VIII	Rs. 800/-
IX-X	Rs.1,000/-

When the girl child is enrolled after due verification by the Dept., each girl child will be given an amount of Rs. 10,000/- deposited in her name in fixed deposit.

The amount deposited in the financial institution will be maximized and paid along with interest to the beneficiary on her attainment of 18 years.

During the year 2006-07 Rs. 234 crores had been earmarked to cover 2.30 lakh beneficiaries under the scheme.

Anganwadi Workers and Helpers Death/Medical Relief Fund

The Government of Karnataka has launched this scheme during 2002-03. to provide financial assistance to the families of Anganwadi workers and helpers who die while in service and medical expenses to those workers/helpers suffering from serious illnesses like cancer, heart diseases and renal problems. Anganwadi workers and helpers who have completed a minimum of one year service are eligible for reimbursement up to Rs 20,000/- in case of anganwadi workers and Rs. 10,000/- in case of anganwadi helpers During 2006-07 families of 72 anganwadi workers and 138 helpers have been provided financial assistance at a cost of Rs. 28.19 lakhs.

Attendance Scholarship for Girls from Rural Areas

Objectives To encourage girls from rural areas to pursue their education and improve their educational level and also to prevent school drop outs among rural girls.

Eligibility A girl child who hails from educationally backward districts like Chamarajanagar, Bijapur, Bagalkot, Raichur, Bidar, Koppal, Gulbarga and Bellary wit a minimum 80% attendance in previous class and successful completion of examination is eligible for scholarship subject to the conditions that she must be a resident of a village with a population of less than 20,000 and the family income must be as per IRDP norms. In 10 districts only renewal of old cases is done and no fresh sanctions given.

Pattern of Assistance: Each girl student will get scholarship for 10 months at the following rates:

5th to 7th Std -Rs. 25/-p.m.

8th to 10th Std. -Rs. 50/-p.m.

During the year 2006-07, an amount of Rs 110.44 lakhs was provided, of which an expenditure of Rs.98.70 lakhs was incurred to extend the benefit to 28207 eligible girls. An amount of Rs. 123.78 lakhs is allocated for the year 2007-08. The scheme is being implemented in 18 districts.

Scheme For Welfare of Children in Need of Care and Protection

Objective To provide care, protection and near family atmosphere for orphan and destitute children and to provide food, clothing, shelter, education, vocational training, medical and recreational facilities.

Eligibility Registered voluntary organizations working in the field of child welfare for at least 3 years are eligible to get grant-in-aid for a unit of 25 children. Orphan Children or children from single parent families below 18 years of age (boys and girls). Family income should be less than Rs.6,000/- p.a. Income certificate from Tahsildars to be obtained. Pattern of assistance Maintenance grant of Rs.400/-per month per child, Rent of Rs.50/-p.m. per child is provided where the cottage is housed in rented building. Construction grant of Rs.10,000/ per child for construction and the non-recurring grant of Rs.500/-per child for starting the destitute cottage is provided. 90% of the estimated cost is met by State govt and 10% by the organization.

During the year 2006-07, an amount of Rs 378.54 lakhs was allocated and an expenditure of Rs. 338.98 lakhs was incurred to provide grant in aid to 315 destitute cottages. A budgetary allocation of Rs 393.94 lakhs is made during 2007-08.

Scheme of Assistance to Voluntary Organizations for Creches for Children of Working Mothers

Objective To provide day care services for children of working mothers between the age group of 0-3 years for a better and safe environment and to ensure a healthy growth and there by lower the mortality rate. Services provided are health care, supplementary nutrition, sleeping facilities, immunization, play and recreation for the children.

Eligibility Registered voluntary organization with suitable building is eligible for financial assistance from the Govt. The children of working women in the rural areas who are engaged in agriculture and other occupations are benefited. Universities and Stree Shakti SHGs can also avail the assistance under the scheme.

Scheme for Combating Trafficking of Women and Children

Trafficking of women and children has been increasing in an alarming rate. This evil has to be inevitably tackled at local levels. It is the duty of the civilized society to prevent this and rehabilitate women and children who are being trafficked. In order to contain this organized menace, the department felt the need to create awareness at district, taluk and village level. The new scheme was sanctioned during 2006-07.

Committees have been constituted at state level, district level, taluk level and grama panchayat level. In order to see that these committees at the grass root level function in a proper manner it was felt that these members of the committees are to be sensitized.

Accordingly training programmes were conducted to create awareness regarding the issue among these committee members at taluk and Grama Panchayat level and also one day awareness programme for the general public through Jathas, ralleys, street plays etc. were organized at taluk level.

During 2006-07, an amount of Rs. 15.00 lakhs was allocated. Training for 4280 Gram Panchayat members, 1640 Taluk level members were organized and awareness camps for general public in 164 blocks.

Hoysala and Keladi Chennamma Bravery Awards

The new scheme of giving bravery awards to children both boys and girls in the age group of 6-15 years who have shown exemplary courage in saving the life of others was accorded sanction during 2006-07. Two boys from each district are identified under Hoysala Award and two girls are identified under Keladi Chennamma Award. It carries a cash prize of Rs.10,000/-and a citation. These children are also given scholarship of Rs.2000/-till their schooling. An amount of Rs.100 lakhs was provided during 06-07 and Rs.0.85 lakhs was utilized for giving awards to 7 brave children.

Financial Assistance for Children Especially under Difficult Circumstances

Under the scheme financial assistance is extended to the children of ex-Devadasis, ex-prostitutes and prisoners and to the children of women who are the victims of atrocities, for continuing education the financial assistance will be given to the girls till the age of 20 and boys till the age of 18. The details of the financial assistance provided under the scheme is as follows:

1. I and II std. Rs.50/-for ten months (Children of Devadasis and children of women victims of atrocities only)

2. III and IV std. Rs. 75/-for ten months (Children of Devadasis and children of women who are the victim of atrocities only)
3. V to VII std. Rs. 100/-p.m. for 10 months.
4. VIII to X Std. Rs. 150/-p.m. for 10 months.
5. X Std. onwards Rs. 300/-p.m. for 10 months.

The school Headmaster should certify that the student has passed in the previous class and is continuing the education. Rs. 17.00 lakhs was provided and 1622 children were given the benefit.

State Awards in the Field of Child Welfare

On the lines of the National Awards instituted by the Government of India as a part of International Year of the Child in 1979, the State Government has instituted State Awards for the best work done in the field of child welfare in the past 5 years. Two awards are conferred to institutions and one award to an individual.

I Award : To an institution engaged in the field of child welfare, cash award of Rs. 1,00,000/-and a citation.

II Award : To an institution engaged in the field of child welfare, cash award of Rs. 1,00,000/-and a citation.

Individual Award : To an individual who has done best work in the field of child welfare, cash award of Rs. 50,000/- and a citation. During the year 2006-07 two institutions and one individual were honoured for their yeomen service in the field of child welfare. Exceptional Awards in the field of academy, culture, art and sports were given to 8 children besides bravery award to 6 children. 3 Anganwadi Workers who rendered exceptional service for the welfare of children were also given awards. An amount of Rs. 4.12 lakhs was spent during the year 2006-07.

Government of India Schemes

Scheme for Welfare of Working Children in Need of Care and Protection

Objective : Provision of opportunities including non-formal education, vocational training, etc. to working children to facilitate their entry/re-entry into the mainstream of education in cases where they have either not attended any learning system or where for some reasons their education has been discontinued with a view to preventing their continued or future exploitation.

Target Group : The programme will lend support to projects in urban areas not already being covered by the existing schemes of Ministry of Labour, which provide support for the whole development of child workers and potential child workers especially those who have none or ineffective family support such as children of slum/pavement dwellers/drug addicts, children living on railway platforms, children working in shops, dhaba, children engaged as domestic workers, children whose parents are in jail, children of migrant labourers, sex workers, leprosy patients etc.

Eligibility : Non-Governmental Organizations meeting the following requirements are eligible for the assistance under this programme.

- It is a registered body under an appropriate act for at least two years so that it gets a corporate status and a legal personality and a group of liability for its activities.
- It has an appropriate administrative structure and a duly constituted managing/executive committee.
- Aims and objectives of Organization's Memorandum of Association should include the basic objectives of this scheme namely the welfare of child.

Pattern of Assistance 90% of the cost will be borne by Govt. of India and 10% will be met by the concerned voluntary organization.

Scheme of Assistance to Voluntary Organization to Combat Trafficking of Children for Commercial Sexual Exploitation

Objective This project aims to test the efficacy of certain approaches and methods to combat sexual abuse of children and rehabilitate them.

Eligibility NGO working for the cause must be a registered Voluntary Organization possessing by law Infrastructure facilities, Board of Management and possess the pattern of staff, specified as per guidelines. Project area for A specific red light area of a city or town, a village in a source assistance : district.

National Award for Individuals and Institutions

Government of India has instituted this award to recognize voluntary efforts of individuals/institutions rendering services in the field of child welfare and development. Five institutional awards of Rs. 3 lakh each and three individual awards of Rs. 1 lakh each and a citation is given.

The awards will be given to institutions and individuals who have rendered outstanding services in the field of child welfare for a period of 5 years. The committee constituted by the state government will select and recommend the names to Government of India.

National Award to Children for Exceptional Achievement

Government of India has instituted the award to be given to children with exceptional abilities and who have shown outstanding achievement in any field such as academics, arts, culture and sports. Children between the age group of 4-15 years will be selected for this award. The National Award consists of a Gold Medal, Rs.20,000/-cash and citation for one child. In addition to this, a Silver Medal with a cash prize of Rs.10,000/-and citation is given for one child per State.

The committee constituted by the state government will select and recommend such exceptional children to government of India. The selected children will be declared and awarded by Government of India.

Rajiv Gandhi Manav Seva Award

Rajiv Gandhi Manav Seva Award identifies an individual who has made outstanding contribution while rendering services for children for a period of 10 years. Service in the field of child welfare including the care of children with disabilities will be considered. The name of the selected individual will be announced on the birthday of late Sri. Rajiv Gandhi i.e., on 20th August every year. The award carries a cash prize of Rs. 1,00,000 and a citation. The committee constituted by the State government select and recommend the names to Government of India.

9

Social Defence Programmes

The Department of Women and Child Development is implementing programmes under several social legislations to ensure that women and children from the marginalised sections of the society are protected against abuse and exploitation. Programmes have been formulated to guarantee their basic human rights which include care, protection and rehabilitation. The legislations and programmes implemented in the Programme Development Monitoring Cell are:

1. The Juvenile Justice (Care and Protection of Children) Act, 2000 amendment 2006 and Rules 2002
2. The Immoral Traffic (Prevention) Act, 1956 and Rules 1989
3. The Probation of Offenders Act, 1958 and Rules 1960
4. The Orphanages & Charitable Homes (Supervision & Control) Act, 1960 and Rules 2000.
5. Adoption
6. Child Line Services
7. Scheme of assistance to voluntary organisations for homes (Shishugruha)
8. Sponsorship Programme for Placing Children in Families.

The Juvenile Justice (Care and Protection of Children) Act, 2000

The Juvenile Justice (Care and Protection of Children) Act, 2000 came into force with effect from 1st April 2001. The objective of the Act is to make effective provision in law for juveniles in conflict with law and children in need of care and protection, by providing proper care, protection and treatment by catering to their development needs, and by adopting a child-friendly approach in the adjudication and disposition of matters in the best interest of children and for their ultimate rehabilitation through various institutions established under this enactment. The Government of Karnataka has framed the Rules and published vide Notification No.WCD 40 SBB 2001 (P) dated 26th September 2002. Government of India have further amended the act in August 2006.

Salient Features of Juvenile Justice (Care and Protection of Children) Act, 2000

- To provide an uniform legal framework of justice for children who have not completed their eighteenth year of age throughout the country.
- To attempt to provide a new juvenile jurisprudence as the basis for the delivery of juvenile justice, moving away from an adult and criminal approach to children
- To shift the focus of inquiry into alleged crimes committed by children from intent to motive.
- To provide and strengthen infrastructure for the care, protection, treatment, development and rehabilitation of children coming into the system.
- To separate children alleged to be in conflict with law from children in need of care and protection.
- To try and socially integrate child victims to the extent possible without resorting to judicial proceedings.
- To upgrade and coordinate the police treatment of children under the Act by setting up Special Juvenile Police Units.
- To identify and build compliance with standards for the administration of justice through monitoring systems such as Advisory Boards, Social Audit and Inspection.
- To refer children in need of alternate care outside their biological family to non-institutional rehabilitative options such as adoption, foster care and sponsorship.
- To develop a greater co-ordination and collaboration between the Government and non-government agencies,

the family, the community and corporate agencies through joint management ventures and other forms of linkages.

A Selection Committee has been constituted for the nomination of members of the Juvenile Justice Boards and the Child Welfare Committees.

The Members are :

(1) A retired District and Sessions Judge	Chairperson
(2) A representative from the National Law School of India University not below the rank of a Professor	Member
(3) The Secretary, Women and Child Development or her nominee not below the rank of a Deputy Secretary	Member
(4) The Secretary, Parliamentary Affairs and Legislation or his nominee not below the rank of a Deputy Secretary	Member
(5) Director, Department of Women and Child Development	Member Secretary

Juvenile Justice Boards

The Juvenile Justice Boards have been constituted in 8 districts vide Government Notification dated 4-01-2007. The list of Juvenile Justice Boards is given in contacts link.

Child Welfare Committees

Government has constituted 28 Child welfare committees in 27 districts, one additional for Bangalore district considering the gravity of the problem of neglected and orphaned children vide notification dated 26-02-2007. The list of committees constituted are given in contacts link.

Training of Functionaries Under J J Act

To implement Juvenile Justice (Care and Protection of Children) Act, 2000 effectively, it is considered highly imperative to provide training for all staff members working in children Homes. Training was organized to house mothers/fathers, guards and cooks working in children homes in Chitradurga district. One day orientation programme on J.J.Act was organized on 5.3.07 to create awareness on provisions of the Act for the newly nominated Juvenile Justice Board members and Probation Officers, Superintendents and Women Welfare Officers of 8 districts where Observation Homes are functioning.

Observation Homes

Observation Homes are meant for the temporary reception of any juvenile in conflict with the law during the pendency of any inquiry regarding them under the Act.

Only children in conflict with law brought under the purview of the Indian Penal Code and other legislations are produced before the Juvenile Justice Board. The Probation Officers obtain information regarding the antecedents and family background of the juveniles and other material circumstances likely to be of assistance to the Board. Based on the findings of the report the Boards decide to

(a) restore the child to the care of the parents or relatives.

(b) commit the child to the Special Home till he/she ceases to be a child i.e. 18 years for proper care, protection, treatment and rehabilitation.

Juveniles in conflict with law are admitted to these Homes by Police. The apprehended children are normally detained for a period of 4 months for observation during the period of enquiry.

During the period of stay in the Observation Home the children are provided accommodation, facilities for medical examination and treatment. They are also engaged in informal education, training in some skills and play activities by staff of the Home and some NGOs besides children are also given counselling to bring them to the main stream of life. Food, clothing and bedding is provided as per the prescribed scale 8 Observation Homes are functioning in the State.

Children's Homes

Children's Homes are homes meant for the reception of children in need of care and protection.. Children who are produced before the Child Welfare Committee. and committed by the committee are admitted to these homes. The Committee disposes cases in the interest of providing care, protection, treatment, education and rehabilitation of children

The Homes provide not only accommodation, maintenance and facilities for education, training and rehabilitation of children but also ensure all round development to their fullest abilities. Food, clothing and bedding as per the scale prescribed is provided.

Children are provided education up to VII Std. in the institution itself and training in various crafts is also given. Children studying in high schools and colleges are sent to outside schools and colleges. Three seats in each of the ITIs/Polytechnics over and above the sanctioned strength are reserved for the children of these homes to pursue technical education and to improve on their job opportunities.

There is one Home at Bangalore exclusively for the mentally retarded boys .and one home for Mentally retarded girls at Hubli. Children admitted in these homes suffer from mental retardation/ mental illness with multiple disabilities. They are generally orphan, abandoned or neglected children. In addition to mental retardation they are found to be suffering from various illness like malnutrition, scabies, tuberculosis, epilepsy etc. Medical examination is regularly conducted by expert doctors from NIMHANS.

There are 45 Children's Homes in the State, of which 26 are for boys and 18 are for girls and one Shishumandir for 0-6 years.

Special Homes

Special Homes are meant for the reception and rehabilitation of children in conflict with law after they are released from Observation Homes and provide accommodation, maintenance, education, and rehabilitation as well as for their all-round development to ensure growth and development of their individual personality. Two Special Homes one for boys attached to Observation Home, Dharwad and another for girls attached to Observation Home, Madiwala, Bangalore have been set up. So far no admissions have been made in these homes since children are committed to the care of parents/guardians.

After Care Homes for Men

After Care Homes have been set up for taking care of juveniles discharged from Children's Homes or Special Homes for the purpose of enabling them to lead an honest, industrious and useful life. This is done with a view to bridge the gap between institutional treatment and a process of reintegration in the society.

There are 5 After Care Homes for Men, 1 at Hubli, 1 at Belgaum, 1 at Mysore and 2 at Bangalore, one is attached to the Children's Home for Boys and another is attached to the Children's Home for Mentally Retarded Children. The After Care Home admit the inmates discharged from the Children's Homes who are totally orphans even after completing 18 years of age and are continuing their education in High Schools, Colleges, ITIs, Polytechnics etc. Efforts are made to rehabilitate them by securing jobs.

Constitution of Inspection Committees

District level Inspection Committee have been constituted by government under the Chairmanship of Deputy Commissioner for the welfare and rehabilitation of children with the following members:

(a)	Deputy Commissioner of the District	Chairperson
(b)	Deputy Director of Women and Child Development	Member
(c)	A member of the Juvenile Justice Board/Child Welfare Committee	Member
(d)	District Health Officer/District Surgeon	Member
(e)	NGO to be decided by the Deputy Commissioner	Member

The tenure of this committee is three years.

Constitution of the State Level Advisory Board

The State Level Advisory Board has been constituted to advise on matters relating to the establishment and maintenance of the homes, mobilization of resources, provision of facilities for education, training and rehabilitation of children in need of care and protection and juvenile in conflict with law. In other words the SLAB will monitor and oversee the functioning of the Homes and administration of juvenile justice Act in the state.

Fit Institutions

Institutions managed by voluntary organizations have been recognized as Fit Institutions under the Juvenile Justice (Care & Protection of Children) Act, 2000. These institutions receive and take care of children committed through Child Welfare Committee and provide them education and training facilities for their future rehabilitation.

16 institutions are managed by voluntary organizations. 9 Voluntary organizations are receiving grants from government towards the maintenance of children.

Immoral Traffic (Prevention) Act 1986

Salient Features of the Act:

- Punishment for keeping a brothel or allowing premises to be used as brothel.
- Punishment for living on the earnings of prostitution
- Punishment for procuring a person for prostitution
- Punishment for a person for immoral purpose.
- Punishment for prostitution in the vicinity of public place.
- Punishment for seducing or soliciting for prostitution.
- Punishment for custodial seduction.

Reception Centres

Reception Centres are short stay homes meant for the temporary shelter and care to women who are socially deprived in the society such as widows, destitute and deserted women till some suitable rehabilitation arrangements are made or till they are transferred to State Home for long term stay and rehabilitation.

Women are given care, shelter, protection, training, and recreational activities. Food, clothing and bedding is provided as per the scale prescribed.

There are 11 Reception Centres for Women in the State. Out of 11 Reception Centres 5 are functioning in own buildings and 6 are functioning in rented buildings

State Homes for Women

State Homes for Women are meant to receive such of those women and girls who are in moral danger, destitute, unmarried mothers, widows who are ostracised and also voluntary cases who are in need of care and shelter. Even those cases sent by the Courts for temporary custody under the Immoral Traffic (Prevention) Act 1986 are also admitted.

The State Home for Women at Bangalore has been started exclusively for the admission of cases under the Immoral Traffic (Prevention) Act. It receives cases sent by court as well as committed cases transferred from other State Homes and Reception Centres. In these Homes, care, shelter, protection, education, training in skill development and recreational facilities are provided. Food, clothing and bedding as per the scale prescribed is given.

There are 8 State Homes in the State. Out of 8 State Homes, 6 are functioning in own buildings and 2 are functioning in rented buildings.

After Care Homes for Mentally Retarded Women

There are 2 After Care Homes for Mentally Retarded Women one at Bangalore and another at Hubli to provide care, shelter, protection, medical and psychiatric treatment and training (wherever possible).. These two Homes are functioning in own buildings.

Women and girls who are above 18 years of age and mentally retarded girls who come under the purview of the Juvenile Justice (Care and Protection of Children) Act below 18 years of age are admitted.

These women and girls are provided food, clothing and bedding as per the scale prescribed. Medical care is provided either at NIMHNS or cases referred to other Govt. hospitals for treatment.

Marriage of Inmates

Financial assistance of Rs. 7,000/- is being given for the marriage of destitute and orphan inmates, above 18 years of age from Reception Centres, State Homes for Women or voluntary organisations who are receiving grant in aid from Govt. for a period of not less than one year. The suitor should be above 21 years of age at the time of submission of application for marriage. Rs.2,000/-is given to the couple to meet the expenses of the marriage and the remaining amount of Rs.5,000/- is kept in the fixed deposit in any Nationalized Bank in the name of the couple for a period of two years. During 2005-06 13 marriages of inmates were conducted.

The Probation of Offenders Act, 1958

The department is the nodal agency for the implementation of this central act in the state. Under this Act, first offenders below 21 years of age are kept under probation of good conduct. There is one Probation Officer in each district who conducts enquiries in respect of cases on juvenile delinquency, cases entrusted by the Juvenile Justice Boards and Child Welfare Committees and also cases under Immoral Traffic (Prevention) Act. There are 27 Probation Officers in the State.

A State level Probation Advisory Committee has been constituted with High Court Judge as Chairman with official and non-officials as members.

A District level Probation Advisory Committee has been constituted in each district consisting of the District and Sessions Judge as Chairman with official and non-officials as members.

Non-Institutional Services

The new approach to child welfare also believes that the institution can not be a substitute for the individualized care that a family can provide.

This approach recognizes that the right to a family encompasses that all child welfare activities should ensure that the physical, social, emotional and educational needs of the child are met in a secure nurturing family environment. The primary focus of institutional intervention lies in strengthening of the family, prevention of family disintegration and abandonment of children.

These could take the form of foster care, sponsorship, Juvenile Service Bureaus, Family support and other community based services. The non-institutional services implemented by the Department are detailed below.

Juvenile Service Bureaus

This is a programme of non institutional services which aims at the prevention of juvenile delinquency in urban slums by providing health, recreation through play centres. Juvenile Service Bureaus extend guidance and counselling services to the children in slums and schools particularly those with psychological and social problems.

The services aim to reach the children with the help of voluntary organizations and local bodies. Play Centres are located in slum areas and children both boys and girls from 6-16 yrs. of the area are enrolled. The recreational activities both indoor and outdoor are conducted wherever playground facilities and community buildings are available. A daily programme of organized games, physical training etc. are taken up. There are 9 Juvenile Service Bureaus covering 50 Play Centres in the State.

Adoption

Adoption is a recognized best way for providing a substitute family for an abandoned, orphaned child deprived of love, care and affection of parents. To promote this cause, the department has established an Adoption Cell to coordinate, develop and regulate activities relating to adoption. A State level Adoption Advisory Committee has been constituted with the Secretary, Women and Child Development as Chairperson and members from among the Adoption Coordinating Agency, the Scrutinizing Agency, Adoption Placement Agencies and experts in the field of child development. This Committee meets regularly to oversee the placement of children in adoption.

Currently, placement of children in adoption is done according to the provisions of the two Acts mentioned below:

1. Hindu Adoption and Maintenance Act, 1956
2. Guardianship and Wards Act, 1890.

The Department receives its mandate to regulate placement of children in adoption from the guidelines framed by the Central Adoption Resource Agency (CARA), an apex body set up under the Ministry of Welfare, Government of India. These guidelines are based on the norms, principles and procedures laid down by the Supreme Court in their judgement in petition no. 1171 of 1982. As per the provisions under the J J Act 2000, Child Welfare Committees are empowered to release the child for placing in adoption.

Role of State Government:

- Recognition and licensing of adoption agencies for placing children in in-country and inter-country adoption.
- Recommending the release of grants to Adoption Co-coordinating Agency.

In Karnataka 11 NGOs have been recognized to do adoption activities. of them are doing only in-country adoption and 7 involved in both in-country and inter country adoption. During the year 2006-07, 180. children were placed in in-country adoption and 52 children in inter country adoption.

Child Line Services

A programme initiated by the Ministry of Social Justice and Empowerment, Government of India, aims to build partnership between NGOs and society by responding to children in distress and who are in need of care and protection. It provides 24 hours emergency phone service for children in difficult circumstances. The main objective of the child line services is to help children in distress by calling a Toll Free No. 1098. A City Advisory Board has been constituted comprising of members of various departments of government and NGOs working for the welfare of the children. In addition to this, a steering committee has been constituted for proper functioning and transparency in the system. The Bangalore City Child Line has been launched with the help of Bangalore Telecom Department on 9th May 2002.

NIMHANS, Bangalore has been identified as a nodal agency. The city is divided into 3 zones and operated by 3 collaborative voluntary agencies namely APSA, BOSCO and Makkala Sahayavani. 40055 calls were received up to March 2007. Mangalore Child line was started in 2001. 26,650 calls were received up to March 2007.

Sponsorship Programme for Placing Children in Families

As per provisions under section 43 of the Juvenile Justice (Care and Protection of Children Act, 2000, the state government accorded approval for sponsorship programme with the objective of deinstitutionalising children and enable parents to bring up their children in a family environment.

Sponsorship services are considered:

1. to supplement the resources of the child coming under the purview of the Act.
2. to finance his/her education, vocational training, health care etc.
3. to provide supplementary support to the family.
4. to provide for sponsorship of the children based on their needs when they are discharged from the homes.

The Child Welfare Committees are empowered to sanction financial benefit to the beneficiaries as per the conditions laid down in the scheme. Under this scheme financial assistance is also given to children who have extraordinary talent in the field of education, music, art, literature and sports considering them as special cases.

During the year 2006-07 an amount of Rs. 10 lakhs was allocated and Rs 7.88 lakhs was spent to proved financial assistance to children.

Government of India Schemes

A Programme for Juvenile Justice (Centrally Sponsored Scheme)

Funds are shared equally by Government of India and the State in the ratio of 50:50 for the maintenance and staff salary of Children's Homes and maintenance of all children's Homes in the State. Government of India has enhanced the cost of maintenance of children admitted in Children's Homes and Observation Homes from Rs.300/- p.m. to Rs.500/-p.m. from the year 2003-04. An expenditure of Rs.190.56 lakhs was incurred up to the end of March 2006-07.

Scheme of Assistance to Voluntary Organizations for Homes (Shishugruha) for Infants for Promoting in-Country Adoption

Objective :

- To regulate adoption within the country to ensure minimum standards in care of children
- To provide support for institutional care within the country for care and protection of infants and children up to 6 years of age who are either abandoned or orphaned/ destitute and their rehabilitation through in-country adoption.

To Promote in-Country Adoptions

Eligibility:

- It should be registered with the State Government under the Orphanages and other Charitable Homes (supervision and Control) Act, 1960 or any other Act/Rule/Law as may be prevalent in the State.

- It should be registered under the Societies Registration Act, 1860
- A public trust registered under the law for the time being in force: or
- A Government run Institution/Home for children.
- Any other organization, which may be approved by the Secretary, Ministry of Social Justice and Empowerment.

Target Group : ***Children in the age group of 0-6 years.***

Pattern of	: A) Recurring expenditure	-Rs. 6,08,000-00
Assistance	: B) Non-recurring expenditure of	-Rs. 55,000-00
		Total-Rs. 6,63,000-00

90% of grant is borne by Govt. of India and remaining 10% met by the voluntary organizations. As regards Govt. run institutions 100% grant would be provided subject to a ceiling of Rs. 6,00,000 in a financial year. Grants are released in two half yearly installments.

Government of India has sanctioned 3 Shishu Gruhas to the department. One each of these Shishu Gruhas are attached to Shishumandir, Bangalore, Children's Home, Hubli and Children's Home, Gulbarga. These Shishu Gruhas are also licensed to give children in adoption.

Orphanages and other Charitable Homes (Supervision and Control) Act, 1960

Salient features of the act:

- Fix minimum standards for orphanages and other children's homes run by private agencies with reference to conditions regarding boarding, lodging, clothing, sanitation, health, hygiene and also regarding facilities provided for the education and training of the inmates.
- Grant certificate of recognition for those orphanages who fulfil the requirements.
- Monitor the performance of all the orphanages and other children's homes run by private agencies and to revoke the certificate when situation warrant.

The Board of Control is being constituted to give recognition to children homes as required under the act.

Development of Women and Children

The strategy of women's development comprises social and economic empowerment of women through attitudinal change towards girl child, and education, training, employment, support services and emphasis on women' rights and law. Similarly, for the child, various schemes to raise nutritional and early childhood care and pre-school educational status have been implemented. A provision of Rs.1226 crore has been provided in 1998-99 (BE) as against Rs.1026 crore in 1997-98 (RE), for implementation of various welfare schemes for women and children.

Under the scheme of Balika Samridhi Yojana launched on October 2, 1997 with a specific objective to encourage the enrolment and retention of girl child in the schools, the mother of a girl child born on or after August 15, 1997 in a family, below the poverty line in rural and urban areas is given a grant of Rs.500 besides a scholarship for education of the girl child when she attends school. 12 lakh girl children were benefited during 1997-98. A sum of Rs.60 crore has been provided in 1998-99 (BE) under the scheme.

The scheme for school drop-out adolescent in the age group of 11-18 year is being implemented in 507 blocks of ICDS projects. So far four lakh adolescent girls have been benefited. Six projects under Support to Training and Employment Programme (STEP) were sanctioned to benefit 53325 women during 1997-98. A sum of Rs.16 crore has been provided during 1998-99 (BE).

Under Indira Mahila Yojana (IMY) for empowerment of women, 28000 small homogeneous women's groups were formed up to 1997-98. A sum of Rs.10 crore has been provided in 1998-99 (BE). The scheme of Mahila Samridhi Yojana (MSY) to inculcate habit of saving among rural women is being revised and merged into IMY to have an integrated package of 5 components including formation of viable women's group.

Under the scheme of Employment and Income Generating Training-cum-Production centres, partially funded by Norwegian Agency for International Development and Cooperation (NORAD), 178 projects were sanctioned to benefit 36095 women in 1997-98. A budgetary provision of Rs.18 crore has been provided in 1998-99 (BE) under this programme.

The Rashtriya Mahila Kosh (RMK) set up for meeting the credit needs of the poor women has sanctioned loan to 250312 women during 1997-98. Under the scheme of Short Stay Home for Women and Girls, there are 361 short homes running in the various parts of the country to benefit 10830 women. Since inception, 811 working women hostels have been sanctioned to benefit 56974 women for single, divorced, married and widowed women who migrate to towns and cities in need of employment.

For the welfare and development of the children, the Integrated Child Development Services (ICDS) scheme aims to provide an integral package of services of health checkup, immunisation, supplementary nutrition, referral services, pre-school education, nutrition and health education to children, pregnant women and nursing mothers. The scheme which started in 1975-76 on an experimental basis in 33 projects has been extended to 5614 centrally sponsored ICDS projects of which 4200 projects are now operational.

The programme benefited 3.81 million expectant and nursing mothers and 21.0 million children under six years of age. A sum of Rs.603 crore has been provided in 1998-99 (BE). Apart from ICDS the other programme for child development are day-care centres for children below five years belonging to weaker sections of the society, Balwadi Nutrition Programme, Early Childhood Education and National Institute of Public Cooperation and Child Development.

Education in India

Education in India has a history stretching back to the ancient urban centres of learning at Taxila and Nalanda. Western education became ingrained into Indian society with the establishment of the British Raj. Education in India falls under the control of both the Union Government and the states, with some responsibilities lying with the Union and the states having autonomy for others. The various articles of the Indian constitution provide for education as a fundamental right. Most universities in India are Union or State Government controlled.

India has made a huge progress in terms of increasing primary education attendance rate and expanding literacy to approximately two thirds of the population. India's improved education system is often cited as one of the main contributors to the economic rise of India. Much of the progress in education has been credited to various private institutions. The private education market in India is estimated to be worth $40 billion in 2008 and will increase to $68 billion by 2012. However, India continues to face challenges. Despite growing investment in education, 40% of the population is illiterate and only 15% of the students reach high school.

As of 2008, India's post-secondary high schools offer only enough seats for 7% of India's college-age population, 25% of teaching positions nationwide are vacant, and 57% of college professors lack either a master's or PhD degree. As of 2007, there are 1522 degree-granting engineering colleges in India with an annual student intake of 582,000, plus 1,244 polytechnics with an annual intake of 265,000. However, these institutions face shortage of faculty and concerns have been raised over the quality of education.

Three Indian universities were listed in the Times Higher Education list of the world's top 200 universities — Indian Institutes of Technology, Indian Institutes of Management, and Jawaharlal Nehru University in 2005 and 2006. Six Indian Institutes of Technology and the Birla Institute of Technology and Science-Pilani were listed among the top 20 science and technology schools in Asia by *Asiaweek*. The Indian School of Business situated in Hyderabad was ranked number 12 in global MBA rankings by the *Financial Times* of London in 2010 while the All India Institute of Medical Sciences has been recognized as a global leader in medical research and treatment.

History

Monastic orders of education under the supervision of a *guru* was a favoured form of education for the nobility in ancient India. The knowledge in these orders was often related to the tasks a section of the society had to perform. The priest class, the *Brahmins*, were imparted knowledge of religion, philosophy, and other ancillary branches while the warrior class, the *Kshatriya*, were trained in the various aspects of warfare. The business class, the *Vaishya*, were taught their trade and the lowest class of the *Shudras* was generally deprived of educational advantages. The book of laws, the *Manusmriti*, and the treatise on statecraft the *Arthashastra* were among the influential works of this era which reflect the outlook and understanding of the world at the time.

Apart from the monastic orders, institutions of higher learning and universities flourished in India well before the common era, and continued to deliver education into the common era. Secular Buddhist institutions cropped up along with monasteries. These institutions imparted practical education, e.g.. medicine. A number of urban learning centres became increasingly visible from the period between 200 BCE to 400 CE. The important urban centres of learning were Taxila and Nalanda, among others. These institutions systematically imparted knowledge and attracted a number of foreign students to study topics such as logic, grammar, medicine, metaphysics, arts and crafts. By the time of the visit of the Islamic scholar Alberuni (973-1048 CE), India already had a sophisticated system of mathematics and science in place, and had made a number of inventions and discoveries.

With the arrival of the British Raj in India a class of Westernized elite was versed in the Western system of education which the British had introduced. This system soon became solidified in India as a number of primary, secondary, and tertiary centres for education cropped up during the colonial era. Between 1867 and 1941 the British increased the percentage of the population in Primary and Secondary Education from around 0.6% of the population in 1867 to over 3.5% of the population in 1941. However this was much lower than the equivalent figures for Europe where in 1911 between 8 and 18% of the population were in Primary and Secondary education. Additionally literacy was also improved. In 1901 the literacy rate in India was only about 5% though by Independence it was nearly 20%.

Following independence in 1947, Maulana Azad, India's first education minister envisaged strong central government control over education throughout the country, with a uniform educational system. However, given the cultural and linguistic diversity of India, it was only the higher education dealing with science and technology that came under the jurisdiction of the central government. The government also held powers to make national policies for educational development and could regulate selected aspects of education throughout India. The central government of India formulated the National Policy on Education (NPE) in 1986 and also re-enforced the Programme of Action (POA) in 1986. The government initiated several measures the launching of DPEP (District Primary Education Programme) and SSA (Sarva Shiksha Abhiyan, India's initiative for Education for All) and setting up of *Navodaya Vidyalaya* and other selective schools in every district, advances in female education, inter-disciplinary research and establishment of open universities.

India's NPE also contains the National System of Education, which ensures some uniformity while taking into account regional education needs. The NPE also stresses on higher spending on education, envisaging a budget of more than 6% of the Gross Domestic Product. While the need for wider reform in the primary and secondary sectors is recognized as an issue, the emphasis is also on the development of science and technology education infrastructure.

Overview

The National Council of Educational Research and Training (NCERT) is the apex body for curriculum related matters for school education in India. The NCERT provides support and technical assistance to a number of schools in India and oversees many aspects of enforcement of education policies. In India, the various curriculum bodies governing school education system are:

- The state government boards, in which the majority of Indian children are enrolled.
- The Central Board of Secondary Education (CBSE) board.
- The Council for the Indian School Certificate Examinations (CISCE) board.
- The National Institute of Open Schooling (NIOS) board.
- International schools affiliated to the International Baccalaureate Programme and/or the Cambridge International Examinations.
- Islamic Madrasah schools, whose boards are controlled by local state governments, or autonomous, or affiliated with Darul Uloom Deoband.

- Autonomous schools like Woodstock School, Auroville, Patha Bhavan and Ananda Marga Gurukula.

In addition, NUEPA (National University of Educational Planning and Administration) and NCTE (National Council for Teacher Education) are responsible for the management of the education system and teacher accreditation.

Primary Education

The Indian government lays emphasis to primary education up to the age of fourteen years (referred to as Elementary Education in India.) The Indian government has also banned child labour in order to ensure that the children do not enter unsafe working conditions. However, both free education and the ban on child labour are difficult to enforce due to economic disparity and social conditions. 80% of all recognized schools at the Elementary Stage are government run or supported, making it the largest provider of education in the Country. However, due to shortage of resources and lack of political will, this system suffers from massive gaps including high pupil teacher ratios, shortage of infrastructure and poor level of teacher training. Education has also been made free for children up to the age of 14 or class VIII under the Children's Right to Free and Compulsory Education Act 2009.

There have been several efforts to enhance quality made by the government. The District Primary Education Programme (DPEP) was launched in 1994 with an aim to universalize primary education in India by reforming and vitalizing the existing primary education system. 85% of the DPEP was funded by the central government and the remaining 15 percent was funded by the states. The DPEP, which had opened 160000 new schools including 84000 alternative education schools delivering alternative education to approximately 3.5 million children, was also supported by UNICEF and other international programmes.

This primary education scheme has also shown a high Gross Enrollment Ratio of 93–95% for the last three years in some states. Significant improvement in staffing and enrollment of girls has also been made as a part of this scheme. The current scheme for universalization of Education for All is the Sarva Shiksha Abhiyan which is one of the largest education initiatives in the world.

Enrollment has been enhanced, but the levels of quality remain low.

Secondary Education

The National Policy on Education (NPE), 1986, has provided for environment awareness, science and technology education, and introduction of traditional elements such as Yoga into the Indian secondary school system. Secondary education covers children 14-18 which covers 88.5 million children according to the Census, 2001. A significant feature of India's secondary school system is the emphasis on inclusion of the disadvantaged sections of the society. Professionals from established institutes are often called to support in vocational training. Another feature of India's secondary school system is its emphasis on profession based vocational training to help students attain skills for finding a vocation of his/her choosing. A significant new feature has been the extension of SS to secondary education in the form of the Madhyamik Shiksha Abhiyan.

A special Integrated Education for Disabled Children (IEDC) programme was started in 1974 with a focus on primary education., but which was converted into Inclusive Education at Secondary Stage Another notable special programme, the *Kendriya Vidyalaya* project, was started for the employees of the central government of India, who are distributed throughout the country. The government started the *Kendriya Vidyalaya* project in 1965 to provide uniform education in institutions following the same syllabus at the same pace regardless of the location to which the employee's family has been transferred.

Tertiary Education

Our university system is, in many parts, in a state of disrepair...In almost half the districts in the country, higher education enrollments are abysmally low, almost two-third of our universities and 90 percent of our colleges are rated as below average on quality parameters... I am concerned that in many states university appointments, including that of vice-chancellors, have been politicised and have become subject to caste and communal considerations, there are complaints of favouritism and corruption.– *Prime Minister Manmohan Singh in 2007.*

India's higher education system is the third largest in the world, after China and the United States. The main governing body at the tertiary level is the University Grants Commission (India), which enforces its standards, advises the government, and helps coordinate between the centre and the state. Accreditation for higher learning is overseen by 12 autonomous institutions established by the University Grants Commission.

As of 2009, India has 20 central universities, 215 state universities, 100 deemed universities, 5 institutions established and functioning under the State Act, and 13 institutes which are of national importance. Other institutions include 16000 colleges, including 1800 exclusive women's colleges, functioning under these universities and institutions. The emphasis in the tertiary level of education lies on science and technology. Indian educational institutions by 2004 consisted of a large number of technology institutes. Distance learning is also a feature of the Indian higher education system.

Some institutions of India, such as the Indian Institutes of Technology (IITs), have been globally acclaimed for their standard of education. The IITs enroll about 8000 students annually and the alumni have contributed to both the growth of the private sector and the public sectors of India.

Besides top rated universities which provide highly competitive world class education to their pupil, India is also home to many universities which have been founded with the sole objective of making easy money. Regulatory authorities like UGC and AICTE have been trying very hard to extirpate the menace of private universities which are running courses without any affiliation or recognition. Students from rural and semi urban background often fall prey to these institutes and colleges.

Technical Education

From the first Five Year Plan onwards India's emphasis was to develop a pool of scientifically inclined manpower. India's National Policy on Education (NPE) provisioned for an apex body for regulation and development of higher technical education, which came into being as the All India Council for Technical Education (AICTE) in 1987 through an act of the Indian parliament.

At the level of the centre the Indian Institutes of Technology and the Indian Institutes of Information Technology are deemed of national importance. The Indian Institutes of Management are also among the nation's premier education facilities. Several Regional Engineering Colleges (REC) have been converted into National Institutes of Technology. The UGC has inter-university centres at a number of locations throughout India to promote common research, e.g. the Nuclear Science Centre at the Jawaharlal Nehru University, New Delhi.

Literacy

2001 government statistics hold the national literacy to be around 64.84%. Government statistics of 2001 also hold that the rate of increase of literacy is more in rural areas than in urban areas. Female literacy was at a national average of 53.63% whereas the male literacy was 75.26%. Within the Indian states, Kerala has shown the highest literacy rates of 90.02% whereas Bihar averaged lower than 50% literacy, the lowest in India. The 2001 statistics also indicated that the total number of 'absolute non literates' in the country was 304 million.

Attainment

World Bank statistics found that fewer than 40 percent of adolescents in India attend secondary schools. *The Economist* reports that half of 10-year-old rural children could not read at a basic level, over 60% were unable to do division, and half dropped out by the age 14.

Only one in ten young people have access to tertiary education. Out of those who receive higher education, *Mercer Consulting* estimates that only a quarter of graduates are "employable". An optimistic estimate is that only one in five job-seekers in India has ever had any sort of vocational training.

Private Education

According to current estimates, 80% of all schools are government schools making the government the major provider of education. However, because of poor quality of public education, 27% of Indian children are privately educated.

According to some research, private schools often provide superior results at a fraction of the unit cost of government schools.

However, others have suggested that private schools fail to provide education to the poorest families, a selective being only a fifth of the schools and have in the past ignored Court orders for their regulation In their favour, it has been pointed out that private schools cover the entire curriculum and offer extra-curricular activities such as science fairs, general knowledge, sports, music and drama. The pupil teacher ratios are much better in private schools (1:31 to 1:37 for government schools and more teachers in private schools are female. There is some disagreement over which system has better educated teachers. According to the latest DISE survey, the percentage of untrained teachers (paratechers) is 54.91% in private, compared to 44.88% in government schools and only 2.32% teachers in unaided schools receive inservice training compared to 43.44% for government schools. The competition in the school market is intense, yet most schools make profit.

Even the poorest often go to private schools despite the fact that government schools are free. A study found that 65% of schoolchildren in Hyderabad's slums attend private schools.

Private schools are often operating illegally. A 2001 study found that it takes 14 different licenses from four different authorities to open a private school in New Delhi and could take years if done legally. However, operation of unrecognized schools has been made illegal under the Children's Right to Free and Compulsory Education Act.

Women's Education

Women have much lower literacy rate. Compared to boys, far fewer girls are enrolled in the schools, and many of them drop out. According to a 1998 report by U.S. Department of Commerce, the chief barrier to female education in India are inadequate school facilities (such as sanitary facilities), shortage of female teachers and gender bias in curriculum (majority of the female characters being depicted as weak and helpless).

The number of literate women among the female population of India was between 2-6% from the British Raj onwards to the formation of the Republic of India in 1947. Concerted efforts led to improvement from 15.3% in 1961 to 28.5% in 1981. By 2001 literacy for women had exceeded 50% of the overall female population, though these statistics were still very low compared to world standards and even male literacy within India. Recently the Indian government has launched Saakshar Bharat Mission for Female Literacy. This mission aims to bring down female illiteracy by half of its present level.

Sita Anantha Raman outlines the Progress of Women's Education in India

Since 1947 the Indian government has tried to provide incentives for girls' school attendance through programs for midday meals, free books, and uniforms. This welfare thrust raised primary enrolment between 1951 and 1981. In 1986 the National Policy on Education decided to restructure education in tune with the social framework of each state, and with larger national goals. It emphasized that education was necessary for democracy, and central to the improvement of women's condition.

The new policy aimed at social change through revised texts, curricula, increased funding for schools, expansion in the numbers of schools, and policy improvements. Emphasis was placed on expanding girls' occupational centres and primary education; secondary and higher education; and rural and urban institutions. The report tried to connect problems like low school attendance with poverty, and the dependence on girls for housework and sibling day care. The National Literacy Mission also worked through female tutors in villages. Although the minimum marriage age is now eighteen for girls, many continue to be married much earlier. Therefore, at the secondary level, female dropout rates are high.

Sita Anantha Raman also maintains that while the educated Indian women workforce maintains professionalism, the men outnumber them in most fields and, in some cases, receive higher income for the same positions.

Rural Education

Following independence, India viewed education as an effective tool for bringing social change through community development. The administrative control was effectively initiated in the 1950s, when, in 1952, the government grouped villages under a Community Development Block—an authority under national programme which could control education in up to 100 villages. A Block Development Officer oversaw a geographical area of 150 square miles which could contain a population of as many as 70000 people.

Setty and Ross elaborate on the role of such programmes, themselves divided further into *individual-based, community based,* or the *Individual-cum-community-based,* in which microscopic levels of development are overseen at village level by an appointed worker:

The community development programmes comprise agriculture, animal husbandry, cooperation, rural industries, rural engineering (consisting of minor irrigation, roads, buildings), health and sanitation including family welfare, family planning, women welfare, child care and nutrition, education including adult education, social education and literacy, youth welfare and community organisation. In each of these areas of development there are several programmes, schemes and activities which are additive, expanding and tapering off covering the total community, some segments, or specific target populations such as small and marginal farmers, artisans, women and in general people below the poverty line.

Despite some setbacks the rural education programmes continued throughout the 1950s, with support from private institutions. A sizable network of rural education had been established by the time the *Gandhigram Rural Institute* was established and 5, 200 Community Development Blocks were established in India. Nursery schools, elementary schools, secondary school, and schools for adult education for women were set up. The government continued to view rural education as an agenda that could be relatively free from bureaucratic backlog and general stagnation.

However, in some cases lack of financing balanced the gains made by rural education institutes of India. Some ideas failed to find acceptability among India's poor and investments made by the government sometimes yielded little results. Today, government rural schools remain poorly funded and understaffed. Several foundations, such as the Rural Development Foundation (Hyderabad), actively build high-quality rural schools, but the number of students served is small.

Issues

One study found out that 25% of public sector teachers and 40% of public sector medical workers were absent during the survey. Among teachers who were paid to teach, absence rates ranged from 15% in Maharashtra to 71% in Bihar. Only 1 in nearly 3000 public school head teachers had ever dismissed a teacher for repeated absence. A study on teachers by Kremer etc. found that 'only about half were teaching, during unannounced visits to a nationally representative sample of government primary schools in India.'.

Modern education in India is often criticized for being based on rote learning rather than problem solving. *Business Week* denigrates the Indian curriculum saying it revolves around rote learning. and Express India suggests that students are focused on cramming.

A study of 188 government-run primary schools found that 59% of the schools had no drinking water and 89% had no toilets. 2003-04 data by National Institute of Educational Planning and Administration revealed that only 3.5% of primary schools in Bihar and Chhattisgarh had toilets for girls. In Madhya Pradesh, Maharashtra, Andhra Pradesh, Gujarat, Rajasthan and Himachal Pradesh, rates were 12-16%.

Fake degrees are a problem. One raid in Bihar found 0.1 million fake certificates. In February 2009, the University Grant Commission found 19 fake institutions operating in India. Only 16% of manufacturers in India offer in-service training to their employees, compared with over 90% in China.

Initiatives

Following India's independence a number of rules were formulated for the backward Scheduled Castes and the Scheduled Tribes of India, and in 1960 a list identifying 405 Scheduled Castes and 225 Scheduled Tribes was published by the central government. An amendment was made to the list in 1975, which identified 841 Scheduled Castes and 510 Scheduled Tribes. The total percentage of Scheduled Castes and Scheduled Tribes combined was found to be 22.5 percent with the Scheduled Castes accounting for 17 percent and the Scheduled Tribes accounting for the remaining 7.5

percent. Following the report many Scheduled Castes and Scheduled Tribes increasingly referred to themselves as *Dalit*, a Marathi language terminology used by B. R. Ambedkar which literally means "oppressed".

The Scheduled Castes and Scheduled Tribes are provided for in many of India's educational programmes. Special reservations are also provided for the Scheduled Castes and Scheduled Tribes in India, e.g. a reservation of 15% in *Kendriya Vidyalaya* for Scheduled Castes and another reservation of 7.5% in *Kendriya Vidyalaya* for Scheduled Tribes. Similar reservations are held by the Scheduled Castes and Scheduled Tribes in many schemes and educational facilities in India. The remote and far-flung regions of North East India are provided for under the Non Lapsable Central pool of Resources (NLCPR) since 1998-1999. The NLCPR aims to provide funds for infrastructure development in these remote areas.

The government objective for the *Sarva Shiksha Abhiyan* (SSA), started in 2001, is to provide education to children between 6–14 years by 2010. The programme focuses specially on girls and children with challenged social or financial backgrounds.

The SSA also aims to provide practical infrastructure and relevant source material in form of free textbooks to children in remote areas. The SSA also aims at widening computer education in rural areas. SSA is currently working with Agastya International Foundation-an educational NGO-to augment its efforts in making science curriculum current and exciting. However, some objectives of the SSA, e.g. enrolment of all children under the scheme in schools by 2005 remain unfulfilled. Education Guarantee Scheme and Alternative and Innovative Education are components of the SSA.

Women from remote, underdeveloped areas or from weaker social groups in Andra Pradesh, Assam, Bihar, Jharkhand, Karnataka, Kerala, Gujarat, Uttar Pradesh, and Uttarakhand, fall under the *Mahila Samakhya Scheme*, initiated in 1989. Apart from provisions for education this programme also aims to raise awareness by holding meetings and seminars at rural levels. The government allowed 340 million rupees during 2007–08 to carry out this scheme over 83 districts including more than 21, 000 villages.

Currently there are 68 *Bal Bhavans* and 10 *Bal Kendra* affiliated to the *National Bal Bhavan*. The scheme involves educational and social activities and recognising children with a marked talent for a particular educational stream. A number of programmes and activities are held under this scheme, which also involves cultural exchanges and participation in several international forums. India's minorities, especially the ones considered 'educationally backward' by the government, are provided for in the 1992 amendment of the Indian National Policy on Education (NPE). The government initiated the Scheme of Area Intensive Programme for Educationally Backward Minorities and Scheme of Financial Assistance or Modernisation of Madarsa Education as part of its revised Programme of Action (1992). Both these schemes were started nationwide by 1994. In 2004 the Indian parliament allowed an act which enabled minority education establishments to seek university affiliations if they passed the required norms.

Central Government Involvement

Budget

As a part of the tenth Five year Plan (2002–2007), the central government of India outlined an expenditure of 65.6% of its total education budget of Rs. 438250 million, or (Rs. 287500 million) on elementary education; 9.9% (Rs. 43250 million) on secondary education; 2.9% (Rs. 12500 million) on adult education; 9.5% (Rs. 41765 million) on higher education; 10.7% (Rs. 47000 million) on technical education; and the remaining 1.4% (Rs. 6235 million) on miscellaneous education schemes.

According to the United Nations Educational, Scientific and Cultural Organization (UNESCO), India has the lowest public expenditure on higher education per student in the world.

Public Expenditure on Education in India

In recent times, several major announcements were made for developing the poor state of affairs in education sector in India, the most notable ones being the National Common Minimum Programme (NCMP) of the United Progressive Alliance (UPA) government. The announcements are;

(a) To progressively increase expenditure on education to around 6 percent of GDP.

(b) To support this increase in expenditure on education, and to increase the quality of education, there would be an imposition of an education cess over all central government taxes.

(c) To ensure that no one is denied of education due to economic backwardness and poverty.

(d) To make right to education a fundamental right for all children in the age group 6–14 years.

(e) To universalize education through its flagship programmes such as Sarva Siksha Abhiyan and Mid Day Meal.

However, even after five years of implementation of NCMP, not much progress has been done on these promises or announcements. The public expenditure on education has actually declined from around 3.23 percent of GDP in 2000-2001 to 2.88 percent in the recent times. As a proportion of total government expenditure, it has declined from around 11.1 percent in 2000-2001 to around 9.98 percent during UPA rule. A policy brief issued by [Network for Social Accountability (NSA)] titled "[NSA Response to Education Sector Interventions in Union Budget: UPA Rule and the Education Sector]" provides significant revelation to this fact. Due to a declining priority of education in the public policy paradigm in India, there has been an exponential growth in the private expenditure on education also. [As per the available information, the private out of pocket expenditure by the working class population for the education of their children in India has increased by around 1150 percent or around 12.5 times over the last decade].

Legislative Framework

"The State shall endeavour to provide, within a period of ten years from the commencement of this Constitution, for free and compulsory education for all children until they complete the age of fourteen years."

This article was a directive principle of state policy within India, effectively meaning that it was within a set of rules that were meant to be followed in spirit and the government could not be held to court if the actual letter was not followed. However, the enforcement of this directive principle became a matter of debate since this principle held obvious emotive and practical value, and was legally the only directive principle within the Indian constitution to have a time limit. Following initiatives by the Supreme Court of India during the 1990s the Ninety-third amendment bill suggested three separate amendments to the Indian constitution:

- The constitution of India was amended to include a new article, 21A, which read: "The State shall provide free and compulsory education to all children of the age of six to fourteen years in a such manner as the State may, by law, determine."
- Article 45 was proposed to be substituted by the article which read: "Provision for early childhood care and education to children below the age of six years: The State shall endeavour to provide early childhood care and education for all children until they complete the age of sixteen years."
- Another article, 51A, was to additionally have the clause:"...a parent or guardian shall provide opportunities for education to his child or, as the case may be, a ward between the age of six to fourteen years." The bill was passed unanimously in the *Lok Sabha,* the lower house of the Indian parliament, on November 28, 2001. It was later passed by the upper house—the *Rajya Sabha*—on May 14, 2002. After being signed by the President of India the Indian constitution was amended formally for the eighty sixth time and the bill came into effect. Since then those between the age of 6–14 have a *fundamental right* to education.

Article 46 of the Constitution of India holds that: "The State shall promote, with special care, the education and economic interests of the weaker sections of the people, and in particular of the Scheduled Castes and Scheduled Tribes, and shall protect them from social injustice and all forms of social exploitation'."

Other provisions for the Scheduled Castes and Scheduled Tribes can be found in Articles 330, 332, 335, 338–342. Both the 5th and the 6th Schedules of the Constitution also make special provisions for the Scheduled Castes and Scheduled Tribes.

10

Urban Community Development

As the world moves into the year 2008, there will be more number of people living in urban areas than rural areas. In fact, the 20th century witnessed a rapid growth in urban population. The next few decades will see unprecedented scale of urban growth in the developing world including those in Asia and Africa continents. The urban population in these two continents will double in a period of 30 years. Asia has been witnessing the triple dynamics of growth, rapid urbanisation and growing poverty. While many Asian countries witnessed higher economic growth, the growth pattern brought about enormous disparities across and within nations.

India has shared the growth pattern and rapid urbanisation with some of the fastest growing regions in Asia. The Country has witnessed around 8% growth in GDP in the last couple of years and has planned to achieve a target of over 9% growth by the end of 11th plan period. India's urban population is also increasing at a faster rate than its total population. With over 575 million people, India will have 41% percent of its population living in cities and towns by 2030 AD from the present level of 286 million and 28%.

Economic development and urbanisation are closely linked. In India, cities contribute over 55 % to country's GDP and urbanisation has been recognised as an important component of economic growth. With India becoming increasingly globalized and urban, there is also an increase in the number of poor people living here. As per the latest NSSO survey reports there are over 80 million poor people living in the cities and towns of India. The

Slum population is also increasing and as per TCPO estimates 2001, over 61.80 million people were living in slums.

It is interesting to note that the ratio of urban poverty in some of the larger states is higher than that of rural poverty leading to the phenomenon of 'Urbanisation of Poverty'. Urban poverty poses the problems of housing and shelter, water, sanitation, health, education, social security and livelihoods along with special needs of vulnerable groups like women, children and aged people. Poor people live in slums which are overcrowded, often polluted and lack basic civic amenities like clean drinking water, sanitation and health facilities. Most of them are involved in informal sector activities where there is constant threat of eviction, removal, confiscation of goods and almost non-existent social security cover.

With growing poverty and slums, Indian cities have been grappling with the challenges of making the cities sustainable i.e. inclusive, productive, efficient and manageable. The sustainability of urban development in India is seen in the context of shelter and slums, Basic urban services, Financing urban development and Governance and Planning. India has entered the Eleventh Plan period with an impressive record of economic growth.

However, the incidence of decline of urban poverty has not accelerated with GDP growth. In fact, urban poverty will become a major challenge for policy makers in our country as the urban population in the country is growing, so is urban poverty. Therefore, a need has arisen to develop new poverty reduction tools and approaches to attack the multidimensional issues of urban poverty. For this, policy makers at the national and local levels should have a good understanding of the nature of urban poverty as well as accurate data on various issues relating to it, in order to develop programme/policies to manage urban poverty in a systematic manner. Urban poverty with over 25% of urban population is largely concentrated in small and medium towns. Though the incidence of poverty is lower in larger cities, the poor face acute shortage of basic amenities there.

It is mentioned that the level of urbanisation in India and its pace over time has been amongst the lowest in the world. It has in fact been lower than the previous decade in 1991-2001. The slow growth of urbanisation is also due to the structure of employment in India where a large proportion of total number of workers continue to be engaged in agriculture in spite of its slow growth and declining share in the GDP. Growth rate of metro and bigger cities has been higher than the small and medium towns. The poverty line used by the planning commission has limitations in view of the change in consumer behaviour, compulsion of life style change, housing expenses in cities, shrinking access to health and education facilities etc.and expenses on such activities not included in the poverty line calculations.

Higher degree of urbanisation is seen associated with lower levels of poverty with exception of states like Karnataka and West Bengal. Poverty levels in small size towns are higher than medium and large towns. Quality of employment, productivity and returns on education are likely to be better in large cities than small towns.

Urban poverty is not a spill-over of rural poverty as generally perceived and the manufacturing sector in India has not been able to provide necessary pull to rural workers. Migrants in cities are economically better off and are placed at higher economic stratum than the natives of cities on poverty indices. Rural Migrants into urban areas have been found to have a lower probability of being poor than the local population.

Though urbanisation is generally associated with lower levels of poverty, certain aspects of economic development and changes associated strongly with the process of urbanisation in India have created a backwash effect for poor urban communities. This includes re-structuring and dismantling of larger industries in big cities like Mills due to higher land prices in cities leaving a large number of workforce jobless forcing them into informal sector activities. Similarly, slum demolition drive in some cities has made urban poor more deprived and stressed.

The relationship between economic development and urban poverty is complex. Though large cities have lower levels of poverty the backwash effect of new development may become even harsher on the urban poor. Cities do need blue collar workers and in the interest of an orderly and inclusive development, cities need to integrate the poor and informal sector workers into the main city system.

Gender Dimensions of Urban Poverty

There are various Dimensions of urban poverty that affect the urban women. Women constitute a larger set with their own characteristics that require further explorations. However, it is clear that the single women, unmarried, divorces/separated and widowed are more vulnerable among the FHHs.

More importantly, other dimensions over and above income and consumption requirements can be instrumental in identifying urban poverty. Women's employment is increasing over time.

Unless this accompanies betterment in their human capital endowments, labour market participation is likely to be unprotected and extremely vulnerable. Lower human capital endowments, in terms of the differentials in educational access and attainments across income categories has direct implications for the nature of labour market participation made feasible and the returns earned by the poor women in most cases.

Women's concentration in certain jobs/tasks, the wages received and insights from the literature on the barriers for entry into certain newly opening employment avenues for women will be elucidated. Given the significance of women's labour based economic contributions to the households among the poor, improvements or reflecting on aspects concerning their educational and skill development gain tremendous importance for poverty amelioration.

Other issues that need focus are related to at least two broad heads: firstly, improving the access and availability of basic amenities and public provisioning related to water, fuel, toilets and sanitation, electricity and so on, in order to improve the conditions of living and well being for poor women and secondly, addressing factors involving external environment such as shelter spaces, transport, overall security levels and so on that can improve the standards of living for poor women and also facilitate their participation in the urban labour market.

Given the lower levels of support structures in urban locations for most poor households, the excessive monetization in urban areas as opposed to rural areas, implications for poor households food security, access to health care, especially child care, and creditworthiness or asset ownership all get linked to the extent of women's earning capacities and productivity as well.

Policy efforts towards provision of social security measures for the unorganised workers, with special emphasis on aspects concerning poor women Worker's rights, provision of maternity benefits, Toilets, Security from oppressive forms of employment, violence, protection from sexual harassment and improving mechanisms for provision of justice. Improving statistics on women in general, ensuring identification of data gaps and generation of gender disaggregated data systems is a special need.

Poverty and Migration: Does Moving Help?

It is found that the incidence of migration in India has shown an increase in 2001 as compared to consistent decline during 1961-1991. Increase in percentage of migration due to the new policy of liberalisation could not be established. Changes in administrative boundaries of various districts and states have also contributed to increase in percentage of migrants.

Migration towards urban areas has increased in inter state analysis and rural to urban migration shows a sizeable increase among male and female migrants whereas urban to urban migration has shown declining trend. The economic motive remains the main reason for migration among male interstate migrants. Economically backward states keep losing people to developed states.

The relationship between poverty and migration is not clearly established and it was observed that middle and higher income groups show higher propensity to move. Poverty incidence was found less among migrants as compared to non-migrants but it was higher among rural to urban migrants.

The most successful group of migrants is urban to urban migrants in terms of type of occupation they have and their income levels due to better education and skills they possessed. Influx of migration towards metropolitan cities indicates that economic reforms have not been able to create much employment opportunities in small and medium towns and in rural areas. Hence migration will continue towards large and metropolitan cities.

The Unorganised Sector and Urban Poverty: Issues of Livelihood

It is pointed out that the current model of urbanisation has less space and resources for the urban poor. It is resource and capital intensive and facilitates amenities to urban upper and elite classes in terms of large apartment complexes, shopping malls, multiplexes and parking lots. Capital intensity of urban growth creates divide between the rich and the poor raising prices of basic amenities and making these inaccessible to poor.

Urban casual informal workers have been left behind in grabbing the growing urban employment opportunities as they don't have adequate education and skills. The self-employed workers face specific problems of access to credit, markets and space and also incur various 'hidden costs'.

The self-employed among the urban workers in the 15-64 years group has shown higher poverty rates than the salaried but much lower than the casual workers. Urban policy of sealing drive has affected economic condition of a large number of poor families.

The social security and working conditions of the workers are important aspects and the report of the National Commission for enterprises in unorganised sector has suggested addressing these issues which is a welcome step. Skill is a form of security and it improves employability of the workers. A system of skill training for urban areas will be a useful way forward in promoting employment opportunities amongst the urban workers.

Changing Sectoral Profile of Urban Economy and Implications for Urban Poverty

It is mentioned that there is a significant change in the structure of employment over last two decades (NSSO 38th to 61st round) mainly, a sharp increase in self-employment for males and females during 1999-00 in 2004-05 and a decline in the proportion of casual labour employment for males and females. The author based on the data, states that 83 percent for males and 81 percent for females are either self-employed or casual labour. 60% of the self-employed find their income remunerative and they considered Rs.3000/month as remunerative. The proportion of self-employed vis-a-vis all India (45.4%) is higher in some of the poorer-states – Bihar (59.8%),

Madhya Pradesh (49.8%), Rajasthan (56.0%) and Uttar Pradesh (59.9%). The proportion of workers employed on regular or even on casual basis is gradually shrinking.

The wage rates are usually institutionally determined, rather than market driven. Many of the States that have lower casual wage rates vis-a-vis all India also have lower unemployment rates. In terms of sectoral allocation of employment at all India level about 43 percent of workers are engaged in commodity production (agriculture, manufacturing, electricity, etc. and construction) and the rest in the tertiary sector; A well-known feature of the Indian employment scene after globalisation and liberalisation is the domination of the unorganized sector with irregular and insecure jobs, low productivity and earnings and no social protection.

Proportion of workers having regular salary/wage employment rises with level of urbanization and has significant negative correlation with index of relative deprivation. The percentage of casual wage worker has significant negative correlation with the rate of urbanization, implying that as rate of urbanization rises, the weightage of casual wage workers declines and the Wage rates for regular employees or for casual workers do not show any significant relation with urbanization or relative deprivation.

It is seen that there has not been major shifts in the sectoral composition, though services have gained somewhat vis-a-vis directly productive activities. Major change is in the overall employment share of informal sector which from roughly one-third of employment in 1976-77 to now accounts more than three-fourth of total workforce. All this has happened with falling labour productivity as income share has risen far slower compared to informal sector's employment share. Another interesting factor is that the strong labour force that once belonged to the organized sector faced radically altered situation due to displacements after the closing down of industries.

The urban workforce usually does casual wage earner or self-employment work. The general profile of an owner of a home-based unit of 35 years of age with 6 years of schooling and 5 to 7 years of work experience in a brass factory as a labourer starts a unit investing about Rs 10,000 to Rs 12,000 borrowed from family, friends, and relatives, and earning about Rs 3000 a month to feed a family of about 6 persons. Lack of access to formal channels of credit facilities and training skills hinders the growth of his business.

Based on the assumption that the decrease in gainful unemployment and the labour force is on the increase, the author suggests that need of the hour is to convert this vast pool of human resources into productive assets by promoting entrepreneurship. This calls for an approach which develops people's enterprise in urban areas, and links the same with economically viable opportunities.

The prominent reason for urban informalisation is the reorganization or collapse of industrial structure in major industrial centres. Therefore a sizeable portion of displaced workers failed to find any gainful employment. The others, who were occupied as wage-earners or self-employed, got only meagre returns for their labour time. The above account highlights heavy concentration of poor households as self-employed and casual workers. But these people hardly able to raise their income due to the lack of business skills.

Urban Microfinance in the Context of Urban Poverty

The evolution of social banking concept in India is through the development of the Self Help Group–Bank Linkage Scheme. The genesis of the scheme was an experiment piloted by the National Bank for Rural Development (NABARD) in the late 1980s to link informal groups of low income individuals in rural areas with banks The experiment was main streamed by the Reserve Bank of India as the SHG-Bank Linkage Scheme in 1996 when linkage banking was included as an activity of banks under priority sector lending.

The institutional structure that facilitates rural financial intermediation was strengthened by the setting up of Regional Rural Banks in 1975 and the National Bank for Agriculture and Rural Development in 1982 with the mandate of developing the cooperative credit system.

The debate on financial services to the poor and low income households in India has revolved around the rural population since the time when banks were nationalized for the first time in the country. Unlike rural financial intermediation, flow of financial resources to urban populations was never a matter of serious debate in India. The tendency among microfinance intermediaries to move towards urban centres came only after it found that the rural markets coming to a saturation point. Still now the SHG-Bank Linkage model remains predominantly a rural phenomenon.

Economic Development Associates (2004) observed that about 80 percent of the micro finance clients are without any formal savings, and 91 percent, without formal credit. Nearly 77 percent of the micro credit clients are in the rural sector. The first targeted credit programme with focus on enterprise and self employment opportunities in urban areas was launched in 1989 during the Seventh Five Year Plan period (1985-90).

Various urban poverty alleviation schemes with a credit focus introduced in India since 1989 shows that they broadly followed a top-down approach. The Swarna Jayanti Shahari Rozgar Yojana (SJSRY) is the first such urban scheme launched by Government of India where community based organisations, especially poor urban women, were recognised as the critical points of delivery of benefits Indian Bank has started Microstate branches that are exclusive satellite branches for servicing micro loans (Business Line, 2007). Later State Bank of India has promoted about 7000 SHGs in the city of Mumbai of which nearly 2000 are bank linked.

Credit flow from formal financial institutions to the urban population groups steadily increased in India since the 1970s and this has come to be concentrated in large cities and larger sized credit brackets. Though the social banking efforts of the central bank and the government financial intermediation in rural areas too have gone through a phase of expansion but the low income asset holding segments of urban areas have largely been bypassed by such overall expansion in financial intermediation.

While the state's poverty alleviation approach has steadily expanded from mere provision of basic amenities and services to facilitating creation of income earning opportunities, it has failed to make any significant impact on the urban poor. The impact of microfinance interventions will be severely limited both in urban and rural locations unless well directed investments are made in physical and social infrastructure.

The Millennium Development Goals & Role of Cities

The MDG's have been generally accepted as a framework for measuring development progress. Government of India has launched various urban poverty alleviation programmes since independence. These include Economically Weaker Section Housing in 1952 to Jawaharlal Nehru National urban Renewal Mission in 2005.

Jnnurm provides a new paradigm for inclusive city development and building inclusive urban communities based on a holistic approach.

It is critical that cities devise institutional framework for themselves that satisfy the requirements of good urban governance. It is essential that urban local governments translate national policies and programmes into local action. one of the key requisites for sustained poverty alleviation is decentralization and capacity building at municipal level. Poverty Alleviation requires both attitudinal change and skill development among government and municipal officials. They need to regard poor as their partners, rather than the 'governed'. The role of municipal officials is to facilitate the creation of supportive institutional mechanism at local level. The skills of technical and managerial nature need to be strengthened.

Cities and urban local governments have major roles to play in making a differentiation in respect of MDGs 1 through 7: in education and health services, in environmental protection, in improving living conditions of slum dwellers, as well as providing a strong local governance framework supporting implementation of the MDGs through planning, local strategic processes, and local community engagement. The partnerships, as per the MDG 8, between communities, local authorities, national governments, NGOs, and world government represented by the UN and its institutions, will promote implementation of the MDGs at the local level, cement the interface between national governments and urban local governments, enhance civic capital and strengthen pro-poor governance.

Two factors have an extremely vital role to play-local decentralization and good urban governance. Local democratic decentralization is an important means of deepening the democratic process. ULBs must have political willingness & administrative capabilities to implement good governance principles within their entities-transparency, accountability and involvement of citizens in decision-making.

Thus, a key requisite for sustained poverty alleviation is decentralization and capacity building at municipal level and It is critical that cities devise organizational structures that satisfy the requirements of good urban governance on a city-specific basis.

The Poor and Morphology of Cities

As per 2001 census report the slum population of India was 42.6 million, which constitute 15 percent of the total urban population of the country. Only 12.7 percent of total Indian towns have reported slum. As per the data 11.2 million of the total slum population of the country is in Maharashtra followed by Andhra Pradesh 5.2, Uttar Pradesh 4.4 and West Bengal 4.1 million It is highlighted that while the slum population has increased, the number of slums recorded in the 58th round is lower than the 49th round which indicated densification of slums. The reason could be due to a number of factors, including resettlement process, the conversion of some of the non-notified slums into notified slums, measures relating to evacuation of the non-notified slums, consolidation of smaller clusters and the exhaustion of capacity within the city for the formation of new slums Since slums do not house all of the urban poor but most of the urban poor are found to be living in slums. Though there is reduction in the levels of urban poverty, the number of slum dwellers in India continues to remain high.

There is higher concentration of slum population in the large urban centres. Conversely in comparatively less developed states the phenomenon of slums is not as pronounced (Census, 2001). Since adequate, affordable formal housing supply for the urban poor is not a priority for most state Governments, squatting appears to be the only housing option for poor in near future. land values are escalating sharply, so the Govt. needs to be play a more proactive role to provide for the poor rather than relying solely on facilitating the 'Market driven system'. There is good potential for organising slum communities as the average size of size of slum is small.

A positive correlation is found between states' proportions of notified slums and slum amenities. Whereas, a few states have shown increase in percentage of notified slums, in several other states it has shown a decline. Logically, rationalising the slum notification process is therefore an important step to provide access to basic services to slum dwellers.

Steep increase in land values and the growing interest of reality sector in land is perhaps making less and less land available for slums. Resettlement policy should lay down guide lines to minimize development based, market induced displacements and insure rehabilitation of project affected persons based on human rights to adequate shelter.

State slum Legislation needs to be reviewed and revised in light of slum policies. Slum improvements are primarily State subjects. Interestingly enough, the jurisdiction of Local Body responsible for slum improvements have very limited jurisdiction over land issues. Concern for housing needs of slum dwellers can be seen throughout the five-year plans.

The Task Force set up Planning Commission (Government of India) in 1983 reviewed policies related to shelter of urban poor and. recognized Slums and squatter settlements as products of poverty and social injustice, slum improvement was emphasized by firmly linking improvement programme with security of tenure, social development programmes and house improvement loans with certain cost recovery. Until today, slums are not fully recognized and integrated in the city development framework.

The National Housing & Habitat Policy of 1998 recommended slum improvement/reconstruction programmes through land sharing, release of additional F.A.R. and use of Transferable development rights. The policy however stipulates that land/shelter rights provided to the poor/slum dweller would be non-transferable.

The objective of the draft National Slum Policy (2001) was to integrate slum settlements and the communities residing within them into the urban area and to strengthen the legal and policy framework to facilitate the process of slum development and improvement on a sustainable basis."

Slum improvement has broadly been done through the following channels:

- Central Government Policies for Slum Improvement and Poverty Alleviation.
- Slum Improvement in selected cities through international and bilateral aid.
- Slum Improvement & Tenure regularization through State Legislation/State Government Programs
- Slum Improvement/Redevelopment projects with private sector participation.
- City specific initiatives.

Since adequate, affordable formal housing supply for the urban poor is not a priority for most state Governments, squatting appears to be the only housing option for poor in near future. At the same time, land values are escalating so sharply, that the only housing that is formally coming up is the high-end variety.

Cities are getting spatially fragmented into high quality formal developments and informal areas marked by insecurity and acute deficiencies. Govt. needs to be play a more proactive role to provide for the poor rather than relying on and facilitating the 'Market".

Selection of slums for notification is done on ad-hoc basis and excludes many substandard areas resulting in gross underestimation There is a need to recognize variety of settlement typologies of slum and each informal settlement has different and unique characteristics and problems and hence needs different policies and improvement inputs.

Urban Land Market and Access of Poor

Last 10 years of economic reforms have observed the following features in the land market of the world metropolitan cities:

- Increase in land and property prices in metro cities;
- Land as a resource for infrastructure projects.
- Urban land diverted or given away cheaply for higher end real estate projects and townships.
- Permitting foreign direct investment in the real estate.
- Deregulation and land use zone conversions.
- Market based solution for slums.

- Introduction of new land management tools
- Slum evictions a displacement in metro cities.

There are various land legislations in India which are related to different dimensions of land. Each of these has influenced land supply in specific contexts of city for determining access of the urban poor to land. There are ownership related legislations and use related legislations. Land legislations in general have converted urban poor or informal housing occupants as illegal occupants of land the poor access land through variety of occupancy rights for instance easement rights.

The 11th Plan approach paper lays emphasis of increasing land supply and making processes of land conversion simpler. The urban housing and habitat policy of 2007 states that shelter is one of the basic human needs next to food and clothing. The Common Minimum Programme of the UPA Government commits itself to a comprehensive programme of urban renewal and to a massive expansion of social housing in towns and cities paying particular attention to the needs of slum dwellers.

The analysis shows that there are no realistic estimates of slum population living in urban areas and there have been vast fluctuations in these estimates. For housing rights activists', urban renewal is synonymous with slum demolitions. The legislative tools of the government have been used for converting urban poor as firstly illegal residents of the city and then delegitimized them. The process of globalization has made urban land almost inaccessible to the urban poor and all national level policies are based on market solutions for the poor. Thus the hopes are dim and option fewer for the urban poor.

Basic Services for Urban Poor-Innovative Actions and Interventions

Access to land, shelter and basic services is not only essential for physical well-being but is also vital for their ability to earn a living. One of the most direct influences the city administration has on the scale and nature of poverty is in what it does with regard to provision of basic services and shelter construction and improvement. In order to provide water supply services of required standards in slums, it is suggested to provide individual pipe connections to each slum household, promote rain water harvesting, replace damage pipes and improve delivery pressures at public stand posts and remove illegal connections.

Similarly, to improve sanitation standards, it is suggested to construct community toilets where individual toilets are not possible, to extend sewerage networks to slum areas and connect toilet outlets with that, and community management of toilets in common places.

A demand led approach for improvement of access to public transport should be adopted. Appropriate technology should be used for developing road network depending on the geographical conditions and climate etc. and people's participation needs to be promoted in operation and maintenance of public transport.

Solar, bio-gas and non-conventional energy needs to be promoted for street lights as well as in household energy use wherever possible and feasible. Complete coverage of slum households through electric connections should be ensured. In order to ensure proper drainage systems, flood prone habitats should be shifted to higher elevation, canal banks should be raised and protected and retaining walls constructed wherever required.

Among other initiatives, it is suggested to have people's participation in design and implementation of the basic services in slums. The responsibility of O&M should be that of the stockholders and spatial analysis and GIS based databases with decision support system should be established for all the slums in a city along with computerised land records for providing an integrated plan for basic services in the slums.

Access of Urban Poor to Education and Health Services

To understand intra-urban variations in health service access, urban districts were studied on three indicators i.e. proportion of children who received the first dose of oral polio vaccine, proportion of children who were fully immunized and visit by women to health service for antenatal check-up.

The analysis shows that wealthiest 20% of the population received about 25% of the actual government health spending while the poorest 20% received only 15%. The poverty of health is exacerbated not only by wealth but also by other socioeconomic measures, such as sex, race, ethnic group, language, educational level, occupation and residence. Lack of access to formal land market forcing Poor people to inhabit unhealthy environment which creates serious implications on their health and they have to spent higher percentage of their income on health care.

Physical inability, social discrimination by education, caste, sex and economic stratification increases the gap between demand and inadequate supply of services. Besides the physical and social factors, lack of access to money poor are unable to use health services and have less access to the facilities in the public or private sector. They hardly seek heath care when they are ill. The poor have to depend on loans and sale of assets to pay for hospitalisation. Cost is a greater barrier than the Physical access to health providers. There is no provision in the government programme for the unorganised sector to get access to medical benefits while the organised sector employees have provisions for medical benefits.

Author has given a few examples of the attempts made in the country for insurance cover to poor both from both government and NGO sector. As in the case of health services, there are evidence of discrimination between the rich and the poor/disadvantaged children in their access to quality education. The access problem is further compounded along the gender, caste, and physical and mental disability lines.

There is a big difference between the proportion of children accessing education in million plus cities compared to smaller cities. The two critical problems pointing out by the author in this field are access and the quality of education. Quality defines in terms of poor teaching standard and facilities, teacher absenteeism, insensitive curriculum and content, poor motivation of teachers.

This is compounded with lack of physical access and infrastructure. The analysis also shows that smaller million-plus cities have more schools per capita population when compared to four mega polis. Contrary to health services, education infrastructure is poorer in cities with larger population and there is a huge gap in achieving universal access to education in all cities, impacting the disadvantaged children the most and million plus cities, which are hub of economic activities, need to improve access of girl children to education. The proportion of children from marginalised communities in mega cities is very low compared to smaller towns. The draws the following inferences and way forward:

- Health access is poorer in cities from central and northern regions of the country, indicating poor health infrastructure, services and quality of providers.
- Health need for women (especially among SCs/STs and other marginalised groups) and adolescents are not prioritized, and services to these groups are almost non-existent. Delhi needs to improve on access of its services to women.
- Larger a city is, the better is health environment and the lesser prone is it to communicable diseases likes pneumonia and diarrhoea. Similarly, cities from southern states of India have healthier population, while the least healthy are from cities in central India.
- Health access is poorer in cities from central and northern regions of the country, indicating poor health infrastructure, systems and quality of providers.
- Health need for women (especially among SCs/STs and other marginalised groups) and adolescents are not prioritized, and services to these groups are almost non-existent. Delhi needs to improve on access of its services to women.
- Costs of health services (direct cost, indirect cost and opportunity cost) continue as the single largest barrier to access for urban poor. The urban poor are out of coverage of any social security net.
- Education infrastructure is poorer in cities with larger population base and higher urbanization, thus increasing the possibility of marginalizing children of urban poor from education.
- There is still a huge gap in achieving universal access to education in all cities, impacting the disadvantaged children the most.

- Million plus cities, which are hub of economic activities, need to improve access of girl children to education.
- A holistic and integrated approach in response to the specific needs of each area need to be adopted along with adequate resource back-up
- Urban health should be taken up in mission mode, much on lines of the NRHM, to facilitate programmatic focus, resource commitment and accountability for effectively addressing the health needs of the urban population.
- The states should incorporate initiatives for urban health needs in their Programme Implementation Plan.
- Systematic strengthening of the health department of the Municipal Corporation/Municipality
- Increasing role of the corporate, private sectors and NGOs for health services to the poor.
- Development of a social security system that is pro-poor and is inclusive of groups like migrant population, socially marginalised groups and also adolescents.
- Effective monitoring and surveillance system for improving the student-to-classroom and student-to-teacher ratio in the cities.
- Vigorous community mobilization campaigns need to be initiated in urban slums urging the poor households to send their children to schools.
- Innovative approaches to increase school enrolment at primary level and retention rate in schools, particularly for girls.
- Convergence of health and education with other basic services for achieving synergy.

Alleviating Urban Poverty: Income Growth, Distribution, or Decentralization?

The Constitution (seventy-fourth) Amendment, 1992 followed by the Jawaharlal Nehru National Urban Renewal Mission – the two landmark Central government initiatives – looks at and conceptualise policies for urban poverty in a different light altogether. These two initiative rest on the postulate that decentralization and governance are central to urban poverty reduction, a postulate that signals perhaps the most extraordinary shift that has occurred in India in designing policies for poverty reduction.

What then is the new decentralized framework for poverty reduction? This framework centres around four questions:

(i) Which tier of government is most appropriate to handle urban poverty issues? The decentralized framework assumes that urban local bodies are in better position to deal with urban poverty issues. Note should be made that fiscal federalism theory allocates redistribution functions to higher tiers of government: by assigning urban poverty function to the ULBs, the classical local finance system has been shaken up under which local governments were appropriate for providing only the "local public goods".

(ii) What should be the fiscal relations between the state government and the ULBs? What kind of a change does this new functional alignment trigger in the long-established fiscal relations between the states and the ULBs? The Constitutional amendment prefers it to be dealt with by the State Finance Commissions (SFCs), by focusing on an appropriate intergovernmental fiscal system that would meet the need of the urban poor.

(iii) What kind of a governance structure should be in place for reaching out to civil society and other ground level organisations? Decentralization as implied in the Constitutional amendment and the JNNURM assumes that for effective poverty alleviation strategies, it is essential to reach out to the local, civil society groups, and involve them in designing and implementing poverty-related strategies.

(iv) What should be done to make the system accountable to the urban poor? Urban poverty alleviation is this no longer an income growth issue or of transfers. The new thinking is that unless income growth strategy is supplemented by effective decentralization, it may not be possible to make sustainable impact on urban poverty.

The Jnnurm has completed just about two years, and it is too early to evaluate it for its impact on poverty. However, the experience of implementing the Jnnurm shows that decentralization as envisaged has not reached out to the ULBs; urban poverty alleviation activities continue to be in the domain of the higher tiers of government. The SFCs too have not used the leverage of its mandate to incentivise a *defacto* transfer of urban poverty functions to the ULBs. Nor is the intergovernmental fiscal system designed to factor in the extent and depth of urban poverty.

Most ULBs function without any autonomy in terms of designing urban poverty alleviation programmes and activities or in term of determining their tax policies. 'Elite Capture and Marginalisation of the Poor on Participatory Urban Governance: A Case of Resident Welfare Associations in Metro Cities'

'Elite Capture and Marginalisation of the Poor in Participatory Urban Governance: A Case of Resident Welfare Associations in Metro Cities'

The economic liberalization initiated in the country followed by decentralization measures adopted by the government has resulted in gradual withdrawal of the state and increasing private sector participation in capital investment and operation and maintenance of urban services. The institutional vacuum thus created has been filled up by non-governmental organizations (NGOs) and community based organizations (CBOs).

Further, the limited success of the wards committees institutionalized through the 74th constitutional amendment (1992) to usher in decentralized governance has led to the growth of middle class activism through resident welfare associations (RWAs) as partners in the development process of cities. The functioning of these societies, which are concentrated mainly in the middle income & posh colonies, has serious consequences in terms of access of the poor to basic amenities and infrastructural facilities and accentuation of intra-city inequalities. In the participatory model of local governance, the state and local governments, private agencies, parastatal bodies and other civil societies provide support to the RWAs in their efficient functioning.

The involvement of the RWAs has been in areas like management of civic amenities, capital investment in infrastructural projects, planning and participatory budgeting, and maintenance of neighbourhood security. All these have resulted in 'sanitisation of the cities' and policing of public space within their jurisdiction.

Of late, some of these societies have received unprecedented importance in cities, where they have been empowered by the Master Plan to determine the land use of colonies. One may, however, be cautioned that the very mechanism of the functioning of these civil societies, is likely to institutionalize disparity within the cities as most of the urban poor are not covered by these. This would strengthen the process of segmentation and promote exclusionary growth of cities. NGOs, Private Sector, government departments and parastatal agencies are supporting the participatory governance of the RWAs and the States are sponsoring the RWAs with the local governments supporting maintenance of civic services in large cities as well as the small towns.

As per the findings of city wide survey of Delhi, it is only the more powerful RWAs who are able to voice their concern to the exclusion of the poor and there is no involvement of the slums and unauthorised colonies even in the much acclaimed Bhagidari system. Even though its intentions were noble, the system has not been able to penetrate deep across different sections of population.

The analysis shows that the very mechanism of the functioning of RWAs is likely to accentuate and institutionalise disparity within the cities. Attempts are being made to increase the number of RWAs in the capital and other cities but understandably there are serious bottlenecks coming in the way of success. In the present circumstances of exclusionary nature of growth, an inclusive development strategy is called for at the local level where the urban poor would be partners in the development process.

Living Rough Surviving City Streets: A Study of the Homeless Populations in Delhi, Chennai, Patna and Madurai

As per the 2001 census where the total urban homeless population is 7,78,599 people with Delhi having 3.1% of the national level and Bihar and Tamil Nadu having 1.6% and 7.3% respectively. Extreme poverty topped the list of reasons for why people come to the streets with the highest being 73.75% in Chennai. The researchers also reported strong ties with families back home in the villages. Many people interviewed chose the streets because paying a rent would mean no savings and therefore no money sent back home and hence the street was the only options for them. The author believes that most are not "home"-less as much as "house"-less. Their condition is chiefly linked to their lack of adequate shelter.

In an attempt to explain survival on the streets through the seasons, it is noticed that the most disagreeable season for homeless people were the monsoons followed closely by the winter. In Delhi, for over a 100,000 homeless people the government runs 14 night shelters with a maximum capacity of 2,937 people which constitute only 3% of the homeless people in the city.

There are no centres exclusively for women or migrant families. Outside the walled city in Delhi, private players come into play where *thijawalahs* rent out quilts (winter) and plastic sheets (monsoon) for five rupees a night. Iron cots are rented for 15 rupees a night. The majority of homeless people in the four cities were found to live on pavements and sidewalks often in daily danger to their lives from rash and drunken drivers. The next area favoured was bus stands followed by railway stations and then courtyard of places of worship. The biggest threat faced by the homeless at night (according to the survey) was the police. In Delhi, police brutality figured highest at 32% for disturbing homeless people at night.

The majority of homeless people survive through unprotected, uncertain and hard labour through a range of occupations like daily wage work, construction labour, pulling rickshaws, carrying and pushing loads, domestic work and street vending. A small number also earn as professional blood donors and commercial sex workers. Most children and single women were observed as heading homeless households, while the aged and disabled people lived mainly by begging. Work in itself is not assured on a regular basis; the figures are Delhi for 70%, followed by 61% in Chennai and 59% in Patna. Only in Madurai, where begging is the dominant occupation did 90% homeless report regular earnings.

The urban homeless have little and troubled access to the most elementary public services every visit to the toilet, every bath has to be paid for in cash and immediately. The number of homeless using such facilities is thus low leaving them vulnerable to disease. Drinking water while not portable and erratic in supply is still freely available at roadside taps. The quantities of food may sometimes, though not always, be sufficient, the quality tends to be rather monotonous, very elementary and of poor nutritional value and unhygienic. Except those with families on the streets, they rarely get home cooked food. However, a large portion of their income is spent on food varying from 50-90%.

The relationship between the urban homeless and the state was one of mutual acrimony and distrust. This was especially seen in Delhi where police and civil officials believe that squatters *give the city a bad name*. Most homeless in cities, are widely seen by the authorities as people with no rights, as the undeserving poor who choose to live on the streets even though jobs are widely available. In addition, they are widely perceived to be criminals. The laws that criminalize the urban homeless include laws against vagrancy and begging. The record of public services received by the homeless is dismal.

In its attempt to examine the psychology of the street by looking at the coping strategies used by the homeless to deal with loneliness and social isolation, the author points out that the majority of people in all cities investigated, and across all ages and gender, find solace in drugs or intoxication. The most common being thinners freely available from stationery shops followed by smack. At an emotional level, the homeless try a variety of coping strategies. If they are with their families on the street then these families form a mutual protective bond of support. Where families are not immediately available, close ties are maintained with families in the village.

In case neither is available, and this is true especially in the case of teenagers or the aged, a number of interesting social bonds are developed. Many *adopt* relatives where the aged on the street are looked after by younger people as in another case an old woman was taken care of by a young widow and a pseudo-mother daughter bond was formed. More often in the case of teenagers, especially street boys, gangs are formed sharing everything – food, clothes, intoxicants, sleeping under the same sheets and even teaching each other trades.

Urban Informal Sector: The Need for a Bottom-up Agenda of Economic Reforms – Case Studies of Cycle Rickshaws and Street Vendors in Delhi

The case of Cycle Rickshaws: They are a popular mode of transport in most towns and cities of India. There is a growing demand for them as they are versatile and multipurpose and they are seen plying virtually in all colonies across the city. They are most eco-friendly and its removal from the roads would lead to dramatic increase in demand for fuel for an alternate transport system. They as a means of transport are being introduced in Paris and Oxford which are very pollution conscious cities. Instant means of livelihoods and earning potential: For many rural poor migrants it acts as a means of livelihood.

These rickshaws have been banned where they are needed most mainly the arterial roads of Delhi by a High Court Order in the case of Hemraj vs. CP Delhi on the ground that rickshaws as they ply slow lead to traffic to slow down thus leading to congestion.

There are a host of other restrictions as imposed by the license quota raid raj (quotas on number of licenses) and there are many other absurd restrictions. For instance no person can ply a rickshaw unless he is the owner. Meaning a person cannot own more than one rickshaw. This has become a tool of exploitation for the police and MCD officials.

The case of Street Vendors: Street vendors provide a vital link between the producer and the consumer. As per the National Policy for Street Vendors 2.5% of urban population is involved in street vending and hawking, meaning it provides livelihood to almost a crore urban people.

Restrictions and absurd quotas have been imposed on hawking activities by the Municipal Corporations in various cities. The challan system introduced by the municipal authorities has become a tool for corruption through bogus challans which are available for a price.

Total mismatch with ground reality: Though the Supreme Court has declared that street vending is covered under right to livelihood clause of the Constitution municipal agencies all over

India have managed to keep the vast majority of vendors illegal and insecure. The entire process of clearance outlined is a farce.

Though the government is planning to introduce model legislation for street vendors, without the implementing agency in place the new law will suffer the same fate as the National policy for Street Vendors.

Urban Planning

Urban, city, and town planning integrates land use planning and transport planning to improve the built, economic and social environments of communities. Regional planning deals with a still larger environment, at a less detailed level.

Urban planning can include urban renewal, by adapting urban planning methods to existing cities suffering from decay and lack of investment.

History

As an organized profession, urban planning has only existed for the last 60 years. However, most settlements and cities show forethought and conscious design in their layout and functioning.

Agriculture and other techniques facilitated larger populations than the very small communities of the Paleolithic. It may have caused stronger, more coercive governments at the same time. The pre-Classical and Classical ages saw a number of cities laid out according to fixed plans, though many tended to develop organically.

Designed cities were characteristic of the totalitarian Mesopotamian, Harrapan, and Egyptian civilizations of the third millennium BCE.

Distinct characteristics of urban planning from remains of the cities of Harappa, Lothal and Mohenjo-daro in the Indus Valley Civilization (in modern-day northwestern India and Pakistan) lead archeologists to conclude that they are the earliest examples of deliberately planned and managed cities. The streets of these early cities were often paved and laid out at right angles in a grid pattern, with a hierarchy of streets from major boulevards to residential alleys. Archaeological evidence suggests that many Harrapan houses were laid out to protect from noise and enhance residential privacy; also, they often had their own water wells for probably both sanitary and ritual purposes. These ancient cities were unique in that they often had drainage systems, seemingly tied to a well-developed ideal of urban sanitation.

Ur, located near the Euphrates and Tigris rivers in modern day Iraq also had urban planning in later periods. The Greek Hippodamus (c. 407 BC) is widely considered the father of city planning in the West, for his design of Miletus; Alexander commissioned him to lay out his new city of Alexandria, the grandest example of idealized urban planning of the Mediterranean world, where regularity was aided in large part by its level site near a mouth of the Nile.

The ancient Romans used a consolidated scheme for city planning, developed for military defence and civil convenience. The basic plan is a central forum with city services, surrounded by a compact rectilinear grid of streets and wrapped in a wall for defence. To reduce travel times, two diagonal streets cross the square grid corner-to-corner, passing through the central square. A river usually flowed through the city, to provide water, transport, and sewage disposal. Many European towns, such as Turin, still preserve the remains of these schemes.

The Romans had a very logical way of designing their cities. They laid out the streets at right angles, in the form of a square grid. All the roads were equal in width and length, except for two. These two roads formed the centre of the grid and intersected in the middle. One went East/West, the other North/South. They were slightly wider than the others. All roads were made of carefully fitted stones and smaller hard packed stones. Bridges were also constructed where needed. Each square marked by four roads was called an *insula*, the Roman equivalent of modern city blocks.

Each insula was 80 yards (73 m) square, with the land within each insula divided. As the city developed, each insula would eventually be filled with buildings of various shapes and sizes and would be crisscrossed with back roads and alleys. Most insulae were given to the first settlers of a budding new Roman city, but each person had to pay to construct their own house. The city was surrounded by a wall to protect the city from invaders and other enemies, and to mark the city limits. Areas outside of the city limits were left open as farmland. At the end of each main road, there would be a large gateway with watchtowers. A portcullis covered the opening when the city was under siege, and additional watchtowers were constructed around the rest of the city's wall. A water aqueduct was built outside of the city's walls.

The collapse of Roman civilization saw the end of their urban planning, among many other arts. Urban development in the Middle Ages, characteristically focused on a fortress, a fortified abbey, or a (sometimes abandoned) Roman nucleus, occurred "like the annular rings of a tree" whether in an extended village or the centre of a larger city. Since the new centre was often on high, defensible ground, the city plan took on an organic character, following the irregularities of elevation contours like the shapes that result from agricultural terracing.

The ideal of wide streets and orderly cities was not lost, however. A few medieval cities were admired for their wide thoroughfares and other orderly arrangements, but the juridical chaos of medieval cities (where the administration of streets was sometimes hereditary with various noble families), and the characteristic tenacity of medieval Europeans in legal matters, prevented frequent or large-scale urban planning until the Renaissance and the enormous strengthening of all central governments, from city-states to the kings of France, characteristic of that epoch.

Florence was an early model of the new urban planning, which rearranged itself into a star-shaped layout adapted from the new star fort, designed to resist cannon fire. This model was widely imitated, reflecting the enormous cultural power of Florence in this age; "the Renaissance was hypnotized by one city type which for a century and a half— from Filarete to Scamozzi— was impressed upon utopian schemes: this is the star-shaped city". Radial streets extend outward from a defined centre of military, communal or spiritual power.

Only in ideal cities did a centrally-planned structure stand at the heart, as in Raphael's *Sposalizio* of 1504 (*illustration*); as built, the unique example of a rationally-planned *quattrocento* new city centre, that of Vigevano, 1493-95, resembles a closed space instead, surrounded by arcading. Filarete's ideal city, building on hints in Leone Battista Alberti's *De re aedificatoria,* was named "Sforzinda" in compliment to his patron; its twelve-pointed shape, circumscribable by a "perfect" Pythagorean figure, the circle, takes no heed of its undulating terrain in Filarete's manuscript. And, all this occurred in the cities, but ordinarily not in the industrial suburbs characteristic of this era, which remained disorderly and characterized by crowded conditions and organic growth.

Following the 1695 bombardment of Brussels by French troops of King Louis XIV, in which a large part of the city centre was destroyed, Governor Max Emanuel proposed using the reconstruction to completely change the layout and architectural style of the city. His plan was to transform the medieval city into a city of the new baroque style, especially modelled on Turin, with a logical street layout, with straight avenues offering long, uninterrupted views flanked by buildings of a uniform size.

This plan was opposed by the residents and municipal authorities, who wanted a rapid reconstruction, had no resources for grandiose proposals, and resented what they considered the imposition of a new, foreign, architectural style. In the actual reconstruction, the general layout of the city was conserved, but it was not completely identical to that before the cataclysm. Despite the necessity of rapid reconstruction and the lack of financial means, authorities did take several measures to improve traffic flow, sanitation and the general aesthetics of the city. Many streets were made as wide as possible to improve traffic flow.

In the 1990s, the University of Kentucky voted the Italian town of Todi as ideal city and "most livable town in the world", the place where man and nature, history and tradition come together to create a site of excellence. In Italy, other examples of ideal cities planned according to scientific methods, are: Urbino, Pienza, Ferrara, San Giovanni Valdarno, San Lorenzo Nuovo.

Many cities in Central American civilizations also planned their cities, including sewage systems and running water. In Mexico, Tenochtitlan, was the capital of the Aztec empire, built on an island in Lake Texcoco in what is now the Federal District in central Mexico. At its height, Tenochtitlan was one of the largest cities in the world, with close to 250,000 inhabitants.

Shibam in Yemen features over 500 tower houses, each one rising 5 to 11 storeys high, with each floor being an apartment occupied by a single family. The city has some of the tallest mudbrick houses in the world, with some of them being over 100 feet high (over 30 meters).

In developed countries (Western Europe, North America, Japan and Australasia), planning and architecture can be said to have gone through various stages of general consensus in the last 200 years. Firstly, there was the industrialised city of the 19th century, where control of building was largely held by businesses and the wealthy elite. Around 1900, there began to be a movement for providing citizens, especially factory workers, with healthier environments. The concept of garden cities arose and several model towns were built, such as Letchworth and Welwyn Garden City, the world's first garden cities, in Hertfordshire, UK. However, these were principally small scale in size, typically dealing with only a few thousand residents.

It wasn't until the 1920s that modernism began to surface. Based on the ideas of Le Corbusier and utilising new skyscraper building techniques, the modernist city stood for the elimination of disorder, congestion and the small scale, replacing them instead with pre-planned and widely spaced freeways and tower blocks set within gardens. There were plans for large scale rebuilding of cities, such as the *Plan Voisin* (based on Le Corbusier's Ville Contemporaine), which proposed clearing and rebuilding most of central Paris. No large-scale plans were implemented until after World War II however. Throughout the late 1940s and 1950s, housing shortages caused by wartime destruction led many cities to subsidize housing blocks. Planners used the opportunity to implement the modernist ideal of towers surrounded by gardens. The most prominent example of an entire modernist city is Brasilia, constructed between 1956 and 1960 in Brazil.

Reaction

By the late 1960s and early 1970s, many planners realized that modernism's clean lines and lack of human scale also sapped vitality from the community. The symptoms were high crime rates and social problems.

Modernism ended in the 1970s when the construction of the cheap, uniform tower blocks ended in most countries, such as Britain and France. Since then many have been demolished and replaced by more conventional housing. Rather than attempting to eliminate all disorder, planning now concentrates on individualism and diversity in society and the economy. This is the post-modernist era.

Minimally-planned cities still exist. Houston is a large city (with a metropolitan population of 5.5 million) in a developed country, without a comprehensive zoning ordinance. Houston does, however, restrict development densities and mandate parking, even though specific land uses are not regulated. Also, private-sector developers in Houston use subdivision covenants and deed restrictions to effect land use restrictions resembling zoning laws. Houston voters have rejected comprehensive zoning ordinances three times since 1948. Even without traditional zoning, metropolitan Houston displays large-scale land use patterns resembling zoned regions comparable in age and population, such as Dallas. This suggests that non-regulatory factors such as urban infrastructure and financing, may be at least as important as zoning laws.

Sustainable Development and Sustainability

Sustainable development and sustainability influence today's urban planners. Some planners say that modern lifestyles use too many natural resources, polluting or destroying ecosystems, increasing social inequality overheating urban heat islands, and causing climate changes. Many urban planners therefore advocate sustainable cities.

However, sustainable development is a recent, controversial concept. Wheeler, in his 1998 article, defines sustainable urban development to be "development that improves the long-term social and ecological health of cities and towns." He then sketches a 'sustainable' city's features. These include compact, efficient land use, less automobile use yet with better access, efficient resource use, less pollution and waste, the restoration of natural systems, good housing and living environments, a healthy social ecology, a sustainable economy, community participation and involvement and preservation of local culture and wisdom.

As they always have, urban planners try to implement widely accepted social policies and programs. Sustainability must be widely supported by society before planning can realistically modify actual institutions and regions. Real implementations are often complex compromises.

Collaborative Strategic Goal Oriented Programming

(CoSGOP) is a collaborative and communicative way of strategic programming, decision-making implementation and monitoring oriented towards defined and specific goals. Furthermore it is to be based on sound analysis of available information, shall put emphasis on stake-holder participation, is expected to create awareness among actors, and shall be oriented towards the management of development processes. It was adopted like a theoretical model as a starting point for an analysis of redevelopment processes in large urban distressed areas in European Cities.

Background of CoSGOP

CoSGOP has been derived from goal oriented planning. Goal oriented planning was originally oriented towards the elaboration and implementation of projects based on a logical framework approach which was useful for embedding specific project in a wider development frame and defining its major elements. This approach showed its weakness because its logical rules were strictly applied and the defined expert language did not encourage the actor's participation. Considering this background, CoSGOP introduced a new approach characterised by: communication with the active involvement of the stockholders and those who are to be affected by the programme; strategic planning based on the identification of strengths and weakness, opportunities and threats, as well as on scenario building and visioning; the definition of goals as the basis for action regarding the improvement process; long-term flexible programming of interventions by the different stockholders.

Element of CoSGOP

CoSGOP is not a planning method but a process model. It provides a framework for communication and joint decision-making in a structured process characterised by feed-back loops and it facilitates a learning process of all the stockholders involved. The essential elements of CoSGOP are: Analysis of stockholders (This is oriented towards identifying stockholders' perception of problems and their interest and expectations); Analysis of problems and potentials (This analysis does not only include an overview over objective problems but also of problems and potentials as perceived by stockholders); Development of goals, improvement priorities and alternatives (The definition of goals, objectives for development requires intensive communication and an active participation of the concerned stockholders); Specification of an improvement programme and main activities (This programme is based on clear priorities defined with the stockholders); Assessment of possible impacts of the improvement programme; Definition and detailed specification of key project and their implementation; Continuous monitoring of improvement activities, feed-back and adjustment of the programme (Monitoring and feed-back are key elements of learning process and for monitoring success and failure is relevant not only the technical and economic information but also the perception of the stockholders).

Application

CoSGOP has been applied in European cross-border policy programming, as well in local and regional development programming. Recently (2004), CoSGOP model has been applied in the LUDA Project and it was improved starting from analysis of European experience about urban regeneration projects.

Collaborative Planning in the United States

Collaborative Planning in the US arose in response to the inadequacy of traditional public participation techniques to provide real opportunity for the public to make the decisions affecting their communities. Collaborative planning is a method designed to empower stockholders by elevating them to the level of decision-makers through a process of direct engagement and dialogue between stockholders and public agencies designed to solicit ideas, active involvement and participation in the community planning process. Active public involvement helps Planners create better outcomes by informing them of the public's needs and preferences and by using the public's local knowledge to inform projects. When properly administered collaboration can result in more meaningful participation and better, more creative outcomes to persistent problems than traditional participation methods can achieve. It enables planners to make decisions that reflect community needs and values; it fosters faith in the wisdom and utility of the resulting project, and the community is given a personal stake in its success.

Experiences in Portland and Seattle have demonstrated that successful collaborative planning is dependent upon a number of interrelated factors: the process must be truly inclusive with all stockholders and affected groups invited to the table; the community must have final decision-making authority; full government commitment-of both financial and intellectual resources-must be manifest; participants should be given clear objectives by the Planning staff who facilitate the process by providing guidance, consultancy, expert opinions and research; and facilitators should be trained in conflict resolution and community organization.

Aspects of Planning

Urban Aesthetics

In developed countries, there has been a backlash against excessive human-made clutter in the visual environment, such as signposts, signs, and hoardings. Other issues that generate strong debate among urban designers are tensions between peripheral growth, housing density and new settlements. There are also debates about the mixing tenures and land uses, versus distinguishing geographic zones where different uses dominate. Regardless, all successful urban planning considers urban character, local identity, respects heritage, pedestrians, traffic, utilities and natural hazards.

Planners can help manage the growth of cities, applying tools like zoning and growth management to manage the uses of land. Historically, many of the cities now thought the most beautiful are the result of dense, long lasting systems of prohibitions and guidance about building sizes, uses and features. These allowed substantial freedoms, yet enforce styles, safety, and often materials in practical ways. Many conventional planning techniques are being repackaged using the contemporary term smart growth.

There are some cities that have been planned from conception, and while the results often don't turn out quite as planned, evidence of the initial plan often remains.

Safety

Historically within the Middle East, Europe and the rest of the Old World, settlements were located on higher ground (for defence) and close to fresh water sources. Cities have often grown onto coastal and flood plains at risk of floods and storm surges. Urban planners must consider these threats. If the dangers can be localised then the affected regions can be made into parkland or green belt, often with the added benefit of open space provision.

Extreme weather, flood, or other emergencies can often be greatly mitigated with secure emergency evacuation routes and emergency operations centres. These are relatively inexpensive and unintrusive, and many consider them a reasonable precaution for any urban space. Many cities will also have planned, built safety features, such as levees, retaining walls, and shelters.

In recent years, practitioners have also been expected to maximize the accessibility of an area to people with different abilities, practicing the notion of "inclusive design," to anticipate criminal behaviour and consequently to "design-out crime" and to consider "traffic calming" or "pedestrianisation" as ways of making urban life more pleasant.

Some city planners try to control criminality with structures designed from theories such as socio-architecture or environmental determinism. These theories say that an urban environment can influence individuals' obedience to social rules and level of power. The theories often say that psychological pressure develops in more densely developed, unadorned areas. This stress causes some crimes and some use of illegal drugs. The antidote is usually more individual space and better, more beautiful design in place of functionalism.

Oscar Newman's defensible space theory cites the modernist housing projects of the 1960s as an example of environmental determinism, where large blocks of flats are surrounded by shared and disassociated public areas, which are hard for residents to identify with. As those on lower incomes cannot hire others to maintain public space such as security guards or grounds keepers, and because no individual feels personally responsible, there was a general deterioration of public space leading to a sense of alienation and social disorder.

Jane Jacobs is another notable environmental determinist and is associated with the "eyes on the street" concept. By improving 'natural surveillance' of shared land and facilities of nearby residents by literally increasing the number of people who can see it, and increasing the familiarity of residents, as a collective, residents can more easily detect undesirable or criminal behaviour. However, this is not a new concept. This was prevalent throughout the middle eastern world during the time of Mohamad. It was not only reflected in the general structure of the outside of the home but also the inside. The "broken-windows" theory argues that small indicators of neglect, such as broken windows and unkempt lawns, promote a feeling that an area is in a state of decay. Anticipating decay, people likewise fail to maintain their own properties. The theory suggests that abandonment causes crime, rather than crime causing abandonment.

Some planning methods might help an elite group to control ordinary citizens. Haussmann's renovation of Paris created a system of wide boulevards which prevented the construction of barricades in the streets and eased the movement of military troops. In Rome, the Fascists in the 1930s created *ex novo* many new suburbs in order to concentrate criminals and poorer classes away from the elegant town.

Other social theories point out that in Britain and most countries since the 18th century, the transformation of societies from rural agriculture to industry caused a difficult adaptation to urban living. These theories emphasize that many planning policies ignore personal tensions, forcing individuals to live in a condition of perpetual extraneity to their cities. Many people therefore lack the comfort of feeling "at home" when at home. Often these theorists seek a reconsideration of commonly used "standards" that rationalize the outcomes of a free (relatively unregulated) market.

Slums

The rapid urbanization of the last century caused more slums in the major cities of the world, particularly in developing countries.

Planning resources and strategies are needed to address the problems of slum development. Many planners are calling for slum improvement, particularly the Commonwealth Association of Planners. When urban planners work on slums, they must cope with racial and cultural differences to ensure that racial steering does not occur.

Slum were often "fixed" by clearance. However, more creative solutions are beginning to emerge such as Nairobi's "Camp of Fire" program, where established slum-dwellers promise to build proper houses, schools, and community centres without government money, in return for land on which they have been illegally squatting on for 30 years. The "Camp of Fire" program is one of many similar projects initiated by Slum Dwellers International, which has programs in Africa, Asia, and South America.

Urban Decay

Urban decay is a process by which a city, or a part of a city, falls into a state of disrepair and neglect. It is characterized by depopulation, economic restructuring, property abandonment, high unemployment, fragmented families, political disenfranchisement, crime, and desolate urban landscapes.

During the 1970s and 1980s, urban decay was often associated with central areas of cities in North America and Europe. During this time, changes in global economies, demographics, transportation, and policies fostered urban decay. Many planners spoke of "white flight" during this time. This pattern was different than the pattern of "outlying slums" and "suburban ghettos" found in many cities outside of North America and Western Europe, where central urban areas actually had higher real estate values.

Starting in the 1990s, many of the central urban areas in North America have been experiencing a reversal of the urban decay, with rising real estate values, smarter development, demolition of obsolete social housing and a wider variety of housing choices.

Reconstruction and Renewal

Areas devastated by war or invasion challenge urban planners. Resources are scarce. The existing population has needs. Buildings, roads, services and basic infrastructure like power, water and sewerage are often damaged, but with salvageable parts. Historic, religious or social centres also need to be preserved and reintegrated into the new city plan. A prime example of this is the capital city of Kabul, Afghanistan, which, after decades of civil war and occupation, has regions of rubble and desolation. Despite this, the indigenous population continues to live in the area, constructing makeshift homes and shops out of salvaged materials. Any reconstruction plan, such as Hisham Ashkouri's City of Light Development, needs to be sensitive to the needs of this community and its existing culture and businesses.

Urban Reconstruction Development plans must also work with government agencies as well as private interests to develop workable designs.

Transport

Transport within urbanized areas presents unique problems. The density of an urban environment increases traffic, which can harm businesses and increase pollution unless properly managed. Parking space for private vehicles requires the construction of large parking garages in high density areas. This space could often be more valuable for other development.

Good planning uses transit oriented development, which attempts to place higher densities of jobs or residents near high-volume transportation. For example, some cities permit commerce and multi-story apartment buildings only within one block of train stations and multilane boulevards, and accept single-family dwellings and parks farther away.

Floor area ratio is often used to measure density. This is the floor area of buildings divided by the land area. Ratios below 1.5 are low density. Ratios above five very high density. Most exurbs are below two, while most city centres are well above five. Walk-up apartments with basement garages can easily achieve a density of three. Skyscrapers easily achieve densities of thirty or more.

City authorities may try to encourage higher densities to reduce per-capita infrastructure costs. In the UK, recent years have seen a concerted effort to increase the density of residential development in order to better achieve sustainable development. Increasing development density has the advantage of making mass transport systems, district heating and other community facilities (schools, health centres, etc.) more viable. However critics of this approach dub the densification of development as 'town cramming' and claim that it lowers quality of life and restricts market-led choice.

Problems can often occur at residential densities between about two and five. These densities can cause traffic jams for automobiles, yet are too low to be commercially served by trains or light rail systems. The conventional solution is to use buses, but these and light rail systems may fail where automobiles and excess road network capacity are both available, achieving less than 2% ridership.

The Lewis-Mogridge Position claims that increasing road space is not an effective way of relieving traffic jams as latent or induced demand invariably emerges to restore a socially-tolerable level of congestion.

Suburbanization

In some countries, declining satisfaction with the urban environment is held to blame for continuing migration to smaller towns and rural areas (so-called urban exodus). Successful urban planning supported Regional planning can bring benefits to a much larger hinterland or city region and help to reduce both congestion along transport routes and the wastage of energy implied by excessive commuting.

Bibliography

A K Malkani : *Social Work for the Poor*, Mohit Pub, Delhi, 2008.

A K Rizwi : *Social Policy and Social Work*, Mohit Pub, Delhi, 2008.

A S Kohli : *Human Rights and Social Work, Issues, Challenges and Response*, Kanishka, Delhi, 2004.

Abha, Vijai and Prakash: *Voluntary Organisations and Social Welfare*, ABD, Delhi, 2000.

Agarwal, L.B.: *The Harijans in Rebellion*, Taraporewala, Bombay, 1934.

Ahir, D.C.: *Dr B.R. Ambedkar: Buddhist Revolution and Counter-Revolution in Ancient India*, B.R. Publishing, Delhi, 1996.

Ahmed, Akbar : *Pakistan : The Social Sciences' Perspective*, Oxford University Press, Karachi, 1990.

Akash Gulalia : *Social Work Practice : With Mobile Population Vulnerable to HIV/AIDS*, Mohit, Delhi 2008.

Anand, J. H. : *Dalit Literature is the Literature of Protest*, Delhi, ISPCK, 1995.

Ankit Prasad: *Social Welfare and Social Action : YMCA at Work*, Mittal, Delhi, 2005.

Atal, Yogesh: *The Changing Frontiers of Caste*, Delhi, National Publishing House, 1968.

B.T. Lawani and I.S. Subhedar : *Social Work Perspectives*, Om Pub, Delhi, 2006.

Bailey, F. G. : *Caste and the Economic Frontier: A Village in Highland Orissa*, Manchester, University of Manchester, 1957.

Bakshi, S. R.: *Gandhi and Hindu-Muslim Unity*, Deep & Deep Publications, New Delhi, 1987.

Baldwin, Peter: *The Politics of Social Solidarity: Class Bases of the European Welfare State, 1875–1975*, Cambridge, Cambridge University Press, 1990.

Barnes, Bob.: *Social Survey Division in the 1990s*, Population Trends, 1991.

Benjamin, Joseph: *Scheduled Castes in Indian Politics and Society*, New Delhi, Ess Ess Publications, 1989.

Berger, P. L. : *The Sacred Canopy, Elements of a Sociological Theory of Religion*, Garden City, Doubleday & Company, 1967.

Beteille, Andre.: *The Backward Classes and the New Social Order*, Oxford University Press, Delhi, 1981.

Bhagwat, Vidyut: *Dalit Women in India: Issues and Perspectives - Some Critical Reflections*, New Delhi, Gyan Publishing House, 1995.

Bhai, P. N.: *Harijan Women in Independent India*, B. R. Publishing, New Delhi, 1986.

Bhatt, Anil: *Caste, Class and Politics: An Emperical Profile of Social Stratification in Modern India*, Delhi, Manhohar Book Service, 1975.

Bose, N. K.: *The Scheduled Castes and Tribes and Their Present Conditions*, Calcutta, University of Calcutta, 1969.

Bose, Pradip Kumar: *Social Mobility and Caste Violence: A Study of the Gujarat Riots*, Delhi, Adjanta Publications, 1985.

Brijesh Mishra: *Glimpses of Social Welfare in India : Problems and Perspectives*, ABD Pub, Delhi, 2006.

Campolo, T. & Fraser, D. A. : *Sociology through the Eyes of Faith*, San Francisco, Harper & Row, Delhi, 1992.

Carsten, F. L. : *The Rise of Fascism*, London, Methuen and Co., 1967.

Chaklader, Snehamoy : *Sociolinguistics: A Guide to Language Problems in India*, New Delhi, Mittal, 1990.

Charles D Garvin; Lorraine M Gutierrez and Maeda J Galinsky: *Handbook of Social Work With Groups*, Rawat, Delhi, 2007.

Chhaya Patel: *Social Work Practice : Religio Philosophical Foundations : Essays in Honour of Professor Indira Patel*, Rawat, Delhi, 1999.

Cravens, Hamilton: *Before Head Start: The Iowa Station and America's Children*, Chapel Hill, University of North Carolina Press, 1993.

D K Lal Das and Vanila Bhaskaran : *Research Methods for Social Work* : Rawat, Delhi 2008.

D.K. Lal Das : *Practice of Social Research : Social Work* Perspective, Rawat, 2000.

David Lewis and N Ravichandran: *NGOs and Social Welfare : New Research Approaches,* Rawat, Delhi, 2008.

Debotosh Sinha : *Aspects of Industry and Occupational Social Work,* Abhijeet Pub, Delhi, 2007.

Dennis Shirley: *Community Organizing for Urban School Reform,* Austin, University of Texas Press, 1997.

Dietrich, Gabriele: *Dalit Movements and Women's Movement,* Horizons India Books, New Delhi, 1992.

Donaldson, Gordon A. : *Cultivating Leadership in Schools,* New York, College Press, 2001.

Dumont, Louis: *The Caste System and Its Implications,* London, Granada Pub. Ltd., 1970.

Edward Chambers: *Roots for Radicals,* New York, Continuum, 2003.

Elisabeth Relchert: *Social Work and Human Rights : A Foundation for Policy and Practice,* Rawat, Delhi, 2003.

Ellul, J. : *The Technological Society,* Grand Rapids, Eerdmans, 1990.

Fisher, Michael : *A Clash of Cultures: Awadh the British, and the Mughals,* New Delhi, Manohar, 1987.

Frederic G. Reamer : *Social Work Values and Ethics,* Rawat, Delhi, 2005.

Freeman, James M.: *Untouchable : An Indian Life History,* CA, Stanford University Press, 1979.

G.R. Madan : *An Eminent Scholar, Saint and Social Worker,* Radha Pub, Delhi, 2008.

Ghurye, G. S. : *Caste and Class in India,* Bombay, Popular Books, 1950.

Gibson, R. : *Critical Theory and Education,* London, Hodder & Stoughton, 1986.

Glass, Joseph W.: *The Pennsylvania Culture Region: A View From the Barn,* Ann Arbor, UMI Research Press, 1986.

Gorhe, Neelam: *Social Development and Dalit Women,* Gyan Pub. House, New Delhi, 1995.

Gorringe, H.: *Untouchable Citizens : Dalit Movements and Democratization in Tamil Nadu*, Delhi, Sage Publications, 2005.

Grunlan, Stephen A. and Milton Reimer : *Christian Perspectives on Sociology*, Grand Rapids, Mich., Zondervan, 1982.

Gurukal, Rajan: *The Formation of Caste Society in Kerala*, Rawat Publications, New Delhi, 1994.

Hajira Kumar : *Social Work, Social Development and Sustainable Development*, Regency, Delhi, 1997.

Hana Nagpaul : *Social Work in Urban India*, Rawat, Delhi, 1996.

Harry C. Boyte : *Commonwealth, A Return to Citizen Politics*, New York, The Free Press, 1989.

Heinsath, Charles : *Indian Nationalism and Hindu Social Reform*, Princeton, Princeton University Press, 1964.

Hopkins, Thomas J. .: *The Hindu Religious Tradition*, Encino, California, Dickenson, 1971.

I. Sundar: *Social Work Practices in Health and Medical Profession*, Sarup Book Pub, Delhi, 2009.

I.S. Subheda : *Fieldwork Training in Social Work*, Rawat, Delhi, 2001.

Jaffrelot, Christopher: *Dr. Ambedkar and Untouchability: Fighting the Indian Caste System*, New York, Columbia University Press, 2005.

Jainendra Kumar Jha : *Social Welfare and Social Work*, Anmol, Delhi, 2002

Jogdand, P. G.: *Dalit Women in India: Issues and Perspectives*, New Delhi, Gyan Publishing House, 1995.

K. Chakraworthy: *Untouchable Social Work in India*, Sumit, Delhi, 2006.

K.D. Gangrade : *Gandhian Perspective on Global Interdepen-dence, Peace and Role of Professional Social Work*, Authorspress, Delhi, 2008.

K.K. Jacob: *Social Work Education in India*, Himanshu, Delhi, 1994.

Kamble, N. D.: *Deprived Castes and their Struggle for Equality*, Ashish Publishing House, New Delhi, 1983.

Lakshmanna, C.: *Caste Dynamics in Village India*, Nachiketa Publications, Bombay, 1973.

Lal, Shyam: *Caste and Political Mobilisation: The Bhangis*, Jaipur, Panchsheel Prakashan, 1981.

Lindburg, Donald: *Social Organization of the Kutenai.* Chicago: University of Chicago Press, 1962.

M A Khan : *Social Work and Social Policy, Concepts and Methods,* Book Enclave, Delhi, 2007.

M R Kamble : *Social Work With Children,* Aavishkar, Delhi, 2007.

M.N. Parmar and Jagdish Solanki : *Social Work Perspective on Depressed Class Population,* Anmol, Delhi, 2006.

M.S. Bedi : *Social Development and Social Work* , Himanshu, Delhi, 1994.

Mallik, Suneila: *Social Integration of the Scheduled Castes,* New Delhi, Abhinav, 1979.

Manju Gupta : *Child Abuse, A Social Work Perspective* , Mangal Deep Publications, Delhi, 2001.

Margaret Alston and Wendy Bowles : *Research for Social Workers : An Introduction to Methods,* Rawat, Delhi, 2003.

Marshall, P. & VanderVennen, R. : *Social Science in Christian Perspective,* Lanham, MD: University Press of America, 1988.

McGivney, V. : *Informal Learning in the Community, A Trigger for Change and Development,* Leicester, NIACE, 1999.

Moberg, D. : *Wholistic Christianity, An Appeal for a Dynamic Balanced Faith,* Brethren Press, 1985.

Moddie, A.D.: *The Brahmanical Culture and Modernity,* London, Asia, 1968.

Mohammad Naqi : *Social Work for Weaker Sections,* Anmol, Delhi, 2005.

Murli Desai : *Methodology of Progressive Social Work Education,* Rawat, Delhi, 2004.

Murli Desai and Siva Raju: *Gerontological Social Work in India : Some Issues and Perspectives,* B.R., Delhi, 2000.

N.C. Dobriyal : *Social Work for Older and Sick People,* Sumit Enterprises, Delhi, 2008.

Narain, A.K. & Ahir, D.C.: *Dr. Ambedkar, Buddhism and Social Change,* BR Publishing, Delhi, 1993.

Omvedt, Gail : *Reinventing Revolution: New Social Movements and the Socialist Tradition in India,* New York, Sharpe, 1993.

P Murugesan: *Social Welfare Programmes and Fertility Decline,* Abhijeet Publication, Delhi, 2009.

P.K. Bajpai : *Social Work Perspectives on Health,* Rawat, Delhi, 1998.

P.M. Parmar : *Social Work and Social Welfare in India,* Sublime, Delhi, 2002.

Pamela Trevithick: *Social Work Skills : A Practice Handbook,* Rawat, Delhi, 2009.

Patnaik, Nitayananda: *Caste and Social Change: An Anthropological Study of Three Orissa Villages,* National Institute of Community Development, Hyderabad, 1969.

Pekka Himanen: *The Information Society and the Welfare State: The Finnish Model,* Oxford UP, Oxford, 2002.

Perkins, S. & Rice, C. : *More than Equals: Racial Healing for the Sake of the Gospel,* Downers Grove, InterVarsity, 1993.

Prakash M Katare : *Social Work and Folk Culture,* Arise Pub, Delhi, 2006.

Prasanta K. Pattanaik: *Essays on Individual Decision-making and Social Welfare,* Oxford University Press, London, 2009.

Pratima Chaturvedi : *Social Work : Theories and Practices,* Book Enclave, Delhi, 2005.

Premanand Choudhary : *Child Survival, Health and Social Work Intervention,* ABD Pub, Delhi, 2008.

Profulla C Sarker : *Issues and Perspectives on Social Work and Social Development,* Serials Pub, Delhi, 2008.

R.B.S. Verma, H.S. Verma and Raj Kumar Singh: *Empowerment of the Weaker Sections in India : Interface of the Civil Society Organizations and Professional Social Work Institutions,* Serials, Delhi, 2006.

R.P. Arya : *Training for Social Work and Rural Development,* Manglam, Delhi, 2007.

Raj Bala Mathur : *Modernisation of Social Work, Planning and Administration,* Book Enclave, Delhi, 2007.

Raj Bhanti : *Field Work in Social Work Perspective,* Himanshu, Delhi, 1996.

Ramesh Chandra, *Government and Politics of India,* New York, St. Martin's Press, 1995.

Rameshwari Devi and Ravi Prakash: *Social Work : Methods, Practices and Perspectives,* Mangal Deep, Delhi, 2004.

Ranjna K. Devi : *Social Work, Philosophy, Concepts and Dimensions*, Omega, Delhi, 2009.

Rao, M. S. A.: *Social Movement and Social Transformation: A Study of Backward Class Movement*, New Delhi, Macmillian Press, 1978.

Ritter, Gerhard A.: *Social Welfare in Germany and Britain: Origins and Development*, Kim Traynor, New York, 1986.

Robert Fisher and Peter Romanofsky: *Community Organizing for Urban Social Change, A Historical Perspective*, Greenwood Press, Delhi, 1981.

Robert Fisher: *Let the People Decide, Neighborhood Organizing in America* 1984, Twayne Publishers, Delhi, 1997.

Roy Burman, B.K.: *Beyond Mandal and After Backward Classes in Perspective*, New Delhi, Mittal, 1992.

S K Sen : *Social Work Practices*, Book Enclave, Delhi, 2007.

S.K. Bhalla : *Social Work With Lawbreakers of Society*, MD Pub, Mumbai, 2008.

S.P. Ramachandran : *Social Work for Minorities*, Sumit Enterprises, Delhi, 2008.

Sandhya Joshi: *Child Survival Health and Social Work Intervention*, Concept, 1996.

Sangwan, Satpal : *Science, Technology, and Colonisation: An Indian Experience, 1757-1857*. New Delhi, Anmika Prakashan, 1991.

Sanjay Bhattacharya: *Social Work : An Integrated Approach*, Deep and Deep, Delhi, 2003.

Sarat C. Joshi : *Gandhian Social Work*, Akansha, Delhi, 2009.

Seerveld, C. : *On being human: Imaging God in the modern world*, Lanham, MD: University Press of America, 1989.

Shaikh Azhar Iqbal : *Principles and Practices of Social Work*, Sublime, Delhi, 2005.

Shaikh Azhar Iqbal: *Problems of Social Welfare and Social Work*, Sublime, Delhi, 2005.

Sherry Joseph : *Social Work Practice and Men Who Have Sex With Men*, Sage, Delhi, 2005

Shilaja Nagendra : *Social Work and Social Welfare in India*, ABD Pub, Delhi, 2005.

Silverberg, James: *Social Mobility in the Caste System in India,* Mouton Publishers, The Hague, 1968.

Simon, Robert Leopold: *Spiritual Aspects of Indian Music,* Delhi, Sundeep, 1984.

Singh, S. N.: *Reservation: Problems and Prospects,* New Delhi, Uppal Publishing House, 1987.

Skillen, James W. : *A Covenant to Keep : Meditations on the Biblical Theme of Justice,* Grand Rapids, MI: CRC Publications, Center for Public Justice, 2000.

Stephens, S. : *Children and the Politics of Culture,* Princeton, Princeton University Press, 1995.

Tejomayananda, Swami : *Hindu Culture: An Introduction,* Chinmaya Publications, Piercy, CA, 1993.

Tripathy, R. B.: *Dalits: A Sub-Human Society,* New Delhi, Ashish Publishing House, 1994.

V.V. Devasia and Ajit Kumar : *Social Work Concerns and Challenges in the 21 Century,* APH, Delhi, 2009.

Vijendra Kumar : *Problems and Perspectives on Social Work and Social Welfare,* ABD Pub, Delhi, 2002.

Whitley, O. R. : *Religious behavior: Where sociology and Religion Meet,* Engelwood Cliffs, Prentice-Hall, Inc, 1964.

Wolterstorff, N. : *Until Justice and Peace Embrace,* Grand Rapids: Eerdmans, 1983.

Wuthnow, R. : *God and Mammon in America,* New York: Free Press, 1994.

Yolton, J. W.: *John Locke: Problems and Perspectives,* Cambridge Uni. Press, 1969.

Zelliot, Eleanor: *From Untouchable to Dalit: Essays on the Ambedkar Movement,* New Delhi, Manohar, 1992.

Zimmer, Heinrich : *The Art of Indian Asia,* New York, Pantheon, 1955.

Index

□□□